INFORMATION SYSTEMS SERIES

DEVELOPMENT OF BUSINESS INFORMATION SYSTEMS

RON ANDERSON FCMA, FMS, MInstAM(Dip)

Blackwell Scientific Publications
OXFORD LONDON EDINBURGH
BOSTON MELBOURNE

© Ron Anderson 1989
Blackwell Scientific Publications
Editorial offices:
Osney Mead, Oxford OX2 0EL
  (*Orders:* Tel: 0865 240201)
8 John Street, London WC1N 2ES
23 Ainslie Place, Edinburgh EH3 6AJ
3 Cambridge Center, Suite 208
  Cambridge, Massachusetts 02142, USA
107 Barry Street, Carlton
  Victoria 3053, Australia

First published 1989

Photoset in Linotron Times with Futura
by Northern Phototypesetting Company, Bolton

Printed and bound in Great Britain

DISTRIBUTORS

Marston Book Services Ltd
PO Box 87
Oxford OX2 0DT
(*Orders:* Tel: 0865 791155
    Fax: 0865 791927
    Telex: 837515)

USA
Publishers' Business Services
PO Box 447
Brookline Village
Massachusetts 02147
(*Orders:* Tel: (617) 524 7678)

Canada
Oxford University Press
70 Wynford Drive
Don Mills
Ontario M3C 1J9
(*Orders:* Tel: (416) 441-2941)

Australia
Blackwell Scientific Publications
(Australia) Pty Ltd
107 Barry Street
Carlton, Victoria 3053
(*Orders:* Tel: (03) 347 0300)

British Library
Cataloguing in Publication Data
Anderson, Ron
  Development of business information systems.
  1. Business firms.   Management.   Information systems
  I. Title   II. Series
  658.4'038

ISBN 0–632–02597–2

Library of Congress
Cataloging-in-Publication Data
Anderson, Ronald Gordon.
  Development of business information systems/R.G. Anderson.
      p.   cm. — (Information systems series)
  Includes index.
  ISBN 0–632–02597–2
  1. Business—Data processing.   2. System design.   3. Management
information systems.   I. Title.   II. Series: Information systems
series (Oxford, England)
HF5548.2.A73123   1989
658.4'038'011—dc20

CONTENTS

PREFACE

The need for systems development is essential both for the initial introduction of systems in a new business and for their modification, when appropriate, in an existing business. Systems provide the means for standardising business routines covering all the activities concerned with business administration and control. The implementation of new technological methods and techniques in the form of computers is not always the answer when a system fails to achieve its objectives so it is necessary to determine the nature of the problem before effecting a remedy. In other instances the introduction of new technological methods and techniques such as on-line information processing, electronic mail, databases and local area networks may be the answer to the problem. It may eliminate the weaknesses of the present system, often due to applying outmoded practices and outworn machines and equipment incompatible with current needs. When such weaknesses are eliminated a business becomes capable of meeting new challenges or is in a better position to increase productivity.

By implementing change to existing practices and methods businesses 'rearm' with the most relevant and suitable systems and related technology to meet the challenge of increasing volumes of business activity or the threat from competitors. Changing from predominantly manual or mechanically oriented systems to sophisticated electronic systems requires fundamental changes to the nature of resources used, as people tend to be replaced by a preponderance of machine power. It is important to appreciate however that the most highly developed hi-tech systems need an element of manual supportive activities.

Systems designed for the current operational environment will become unsuitable when a business expands or contracts, and it will become necessary to retune the systems and refocus them on the real life situation. Changing circumstances such as business expansion may require a business to consider computerising its systems to obtain the benefits of high speed accurate processing. When the volume of business contracts it may be necessary to consider transferring systems from a large computer to a smaller one or from a smaller computer to manual systems. These situations can only be resolved by the application of relevant systems development techniques. The primary purpose of this book is to outline such techniques and accordingly the book should be extremely valuable to practising accountants, administrators and functional managers for ensuring that the systems for which they are responsible are cost effective and produce the required outputs for effective administration and control. The book may be used as a guide by the non-professional, by management services personnel and trainee systems analysts, to provide an understanding of the underlying principles governing the nature and structure of business systems.

The book illustrates many of the basic diagramming and analysis techniques used in the various methodologies, including rich pictures, procedure charts, activity charts, data flow diagrams, functional decomposition diagrams, entity models, entity life history diagrams, transaction history diagrams and data analysis and modelling using the techniques of normalizing and courting. An outline of prototyping and the use of structured English for specifying processes is also included. The book contains comprehensive case studies demonstrating the use of the structured approach to systems development including the preparation of a logical model and a first sketch of the physical system. The case studies relate to stock control and an integrated order processing system, both of which were prepared specially for this publication. It must be appreciated that the use of symbols for the various diagrams vary according to the favoured methodology of proprietory systems and the requirements of specific organisations. The book does not delve into the detailed design of a physical system as this is not its primary purpose but it does provide examples of the structure of such systems and why specific hardware and processing techniques are considered.

R. G. Anderson

INTRODUCTION

Systems can only be developed by the application of logical thought processes, taking into account all the features and characteristics of business information systems, the purpose they serve and the results they must accomplish. These matters are taken into account by analysing systems to determine, amongst other details, the inputs required to produce specific outputs and the transform processes – business activities – which must be applied to the inputs for their transformation. Relevant systems development techniques are used for this purpose.

The technique adopted by O & M analysts is work simplification which ensures that activities are performed in the simplest way, commensurate with the attainment of system objectives and efficient processing of specific volumes of data and documents. A series of alternative methods are presented by the analysts to management with recommendations of the most suitable one for implementation. An alternative may be to maintain the existing manual system but to improve staff productivity by more effective training or recruitment. A recommendation may be made to computerise specified manual systems because they are inadequate for current operational requirements. Further aspects of the O & M approach are discussed in Chapters 4 and 5.

Soft systems methodology is a technique of systems development which adopts a panoramic view of a business, thereby providing a total systems approach to the development of systems. The methodology commences by defining the problem situation by developing what is referred to as a 'rich picture', not of the problem but of the situation in which a problem exists. A root definition describes the fundamental nature of a particular system. It then proceeds to develop a conceptual model for comparison with the real world, as a basis for implementing feasible and desirable changes.

Structured development methodology requires that the physical equipment aspects of a system should not be considered before its logical requirements have been established. The structured approach places emphasis on the solving of business problems without technical constraints. A logical/conceptual model of the system is constructed specifying the structure of the system required to achieve business goals and objectives, which are subsequently matched to physical devices during the physical design stage of system development. A logical model is generally concerned with data flows and the processes applied to the data for its transformation into system outputs.

Computer aided systems engineering (CASE) is a means of developing systems by automated development techniques applying the structured design approach. This approach uses computer-aided design techniques linked to a knowledge base which stores the meaning of each diagram created. This applies to data flow diagrams and entity diagrams for instance. It stores information only once regardless of the number and type of diagrams in which it may appear. Consequently any changes made in a diagram will automatically be reflected in all other representations of the information. The diagrams are merely a display format for entry and retrieval of the information in the knowledge base. An expert system uses hundreds of structured logic rules to check the accuracy of analysis. If an attempt is made to violate the rules of any of the common diagramming methods the analyst is alerted to the error. Direct, on-screen graphics manipulation simplifies the drawing of diagrams; computerised design technology allows the most complex systems to be fully and accurately described and changes are recorded effortlessly. To build a diagram a mouse is used to point to the location where a diagram symbol is to appear. Each diagram is displayed in a 'window'.

The systems life cycle approach may be defined as the traditional approach to the computerisation of business systems. It embraces a number of defined stages including feasibility studies, planning the project, systems analysis and design, discussing proposals with management, programming, implementation and system evaluation and maintenance. The methodology, although very efficient, does have a tendency to place too much initial emphasis on the physical requirements of a system, e.g. its hardware and software requirements, before establishing the logical requirements. This is likely to result in a situation where the hardware and software is incompatible with the real needs of the system, causing processing problems as well as an unjustified drain on valuable time and cash resources. This will have a dysfunctional effect on system performance – if it ever becomes operational.

Other development methodologies looked at in the ensuing chapters include the use of an expert system to diagnose system problems as an aid to defining the approach to be made for their improvement, and the application of structured English which uses imperative verbs to specify functions for the processing and transformation of data from input to output. It may be applied by non-computer specialists to clearly define system logic for communicating system needs to systems analysts. Prototyping may be applied to develop a model of a system, perhaps using 4GL languages. The model provides the means of demonstrating a system's capabilities to users. The development technique also provides the opportunity for system users to obtain hands-on experience of developing a system and assist in its improvement by the application of changes to the prototype as they become apparent. After successive refinements to the model a system emerges suitable for further development and implementation.

ACKNOWLEDGEMENTS

The author wishes to thank the following for their assistance in the provision of information relating to their system development methodology:

KnowledgeWare, Inc. for permission to reproduce details relating to Information Engineering Workbench (IEW).

Learmonth & Burchett Management Systems Limited, for permission to reproduce details of the LBMS Structured Development Method-LSDM and prototyping.

ORACLE Corporation UK Limited, for details of the ORACLE 4th Generation Environment, including Business Patterns and System Development Dictionary (SDD).

Professor Peter Checkland of the Department of Systems, University of Lancaster for the provision of information relating to Soft Systems Methodology (SSM).

Part 1

The Nature of Business Systems

CHAPTER 1
Business Systems in Perspective

LEARNING OBJECTIVES

The objective of this chapter is to provide a background to the nature of business systems before embarking on a study of the techniques for their development. Businesses vary in nature but all have the need for well structured business systems to support their operations. It is important to appreciate that administrative efficiency requires well-designed manual or computer-based systems, or combinations of both, for operational needs. To be efficient business systems must be integrated into the corporate framework.

PHILOSOPHICAL FACTORS

Businesses vary in nature from those which are manufacturing oriented to those concerned with the leisure industry; from banking and insurance to tour operators and all have one factor in common – the need for efficient and well-structured business systems to support their operations. Business activities take place in a highly complex and dynamic technological environment necessitating the implementation of business systems which will increase the performance of a business in its quest for profitability or even survival. Administrative efficiency requires well-designed manual or computer-based systems, or combinations of both, for performing operational procedures and routines. To be efficient business systems must be well-structured and integrated into the corporate framework. They should function smoothly and harmoniously and be self-monitoring, in order to minimise management intervention. Businesses are often influenced by external influences that are beyond their control, e.g. government legislation requiring businesses to comply with a new Act, or regulations relating to the deduction of tax and National Insurance contributions from employees' pay.

DEFINITION OF SYSTEM REQUIREMENTS

The management of a business, e.g. the board of directors, define the requirements of new systems, outlining what they consider to be the shortcomings and disadvantages of the existing system and what they require to be included in the new system to attain a defined level of performance. These are included in the *terms of reference*, an essential requirement prior to systems development; systems staff are provided with these guidelines on which to base the stages of systems analysis and design. A system specification states the characteristics and features of each procedure – its inputs, processing operations and outputs.

Effective systems are a necessity for the smooth functioning of all types of system, including general administrative and accounting systems, e.g. control of cash flows, customer credit, controlling the cost of production and management of stocks, etc. To be effective systems must attain a specified level of performance and provide the right type of information at the right time and at the right cost. The implementation of efficient systems can only be achieved from the application of effective systems development techniques.

Investment in information processing systems, which include most business systems, must be recognised as an investment in resources, with an adequate return, in the same way as any other investment. It is pointless incurring costs for the production of information which serves no useful purpose and which therefore does not benefit the business. Information processing systems utilise resources in the same way as any other business activity, as all activities in a business require human resources, machines, money and materials. The cost of the resources must be compared with the returns, in terms of improved efficiency and the resulting benefits to the business.

Cost savings are often considered essential to ensure the economic viability of computerised systems. It goes without saying that cost savings should be obtained, wherever it is feasible, from any methods changes to systems but this factor needs careful thought. The normal practice is to compare the annual operating costs of the new or proposed system with those of the current system. If the projected costs of the new system exceed those of the current system then the decision may be made to abort the proposed system. This could be a costly mistake unless all the factors have been taken into account. One factor, perhaps not considered, is the efficiency of the current system, its weaknesses and the problems it is creating. The criteria must take into account the rule: 'If the value of the benefits of the proposed system exceed the cost of obtaining them then it is a viable proposition'. It is of no consequence how the costs of the proposed system compare with those of the current system – the current system may not be coping with the current situation as it was designed for operating circumstances which no longer exist. For example, the business may have expanded both in its operations and information processing needs. It may now be a large corporation with overseas branches, and therefore a major restructuring of the managerial, organisational, financial and information processing activities is required.

An increase in operating costs is an acceptable situation in such instances, especially if the cost of the current system is low merely because it is not achieving the desired level of performance, and it is creating operational, administrative or managerial problems as a result. For example, a manual sales accounting system may be so slow in dealing with customers' orders that orders are lost, and invoices and statements of account may be so delayed that critical cash flow problems occur. Excessive errors may occur or the system may fail to produce the payroll on time because the existing methods cannot cope with the increasing number of personnel employed.

Like 'time and tide' systems are dynamic and volatile in the long term, if not the short term, because systems currently in use only serve a useful purpose for as long as current circumstances remain unchanged. Change is often forced upon a business because of competitors developing more efficient systems or as a result of business takeovers. It may be necessary to reappraise the administrative systems in use, either to standardise them or to remove, or replace, those which are outmoded.

COMPETITIVE FACTORS

Businesses operate in a competitive environment with other businesses which supply similar goods, products or services. Such competition provides what may be described as a two-edged sword situation. One edge of the sword ensures that the most competitive business reaps the greater market share and an adequate return on the capital employed. The other edge ensures that the consumer benefits from higher quality products and possibly lower prices. The less efficient business will be unable to withstand or combat such pressure and is likely to go out of business – only the fittest survive in the business arena. The extent to which a business is competitive is somewhat dependent upon the effectiveness and efficiency of the systems in use and the extent to which information technology is applied. Inefficient systems lead to inefficient management and administration, leading to increased levels of administrative costs which are reflected in the price of the products or services, thus reducing the competitive advantage. It is important to appreciate that the nature of the systems implemented are not wholly dependent upon internal administrative needs but must also take into account the strategy being adopted by competitors. Competitors may be installing computerised systems for increasing administrative productivity and businesses failing to apply commensurate technology will find it difficult to survive.

COMPUTERISED BUSINESS SYSTEMS

When a computer is under consideration for the automation of business systems it is necessary to consider not only the current needs of the business but also the foreseeable future requirements. This may be defined in terms of the current and projected data processing commitment which may be expressed in terms of the specific applications to be computerised, their data volumes, frequency of processing and the output requirements. This may avoid the need to change the whole of the hardware and software, especially if the chosen computer has a clearly defined migration path, allowing the initial implementation of a small system suitable for the current data volumes but which is capable of enhancement to facilitate the anticipated increase in data volumes. Business strategic considerations change through time due to changing circumstances, such as business growth, requiring the support of more powerful systems. At one time computer power was, and still is in many cases, provided by a large centralised computer complex, but due to the diversity and geographical dispersion of operations in some businesses distributed processing facilities are often found to be more appropriate. Multinational corporations, in particular, require computers with powerful communication facilities enabling them to transfer data between computers in different parts of the world at high speed. Distance is no object in the modern technological world, especially with the extensive coverage of the globe by satellite communications. Banks, building societies, gas and electricity boards have widespread branches throughout the country which require powerful processors capable of supporting many terminals on multi-access systems.

Supermarkets require an efficient method of capturing data

relating to commodity details selected by the customer and a means of processing these efficiently in order to improve customer service and the management of supermarket operations. A 'point-of-sale' system generally includes retail terminals at each check-out point which can function as free standing sales registers. They are equipped with a laser bar code scanner; a keyboard and VDU which can be used as a back-up system in the event of a malfunction with the bar code scanner; an in-store minicomputer supporting the terminals at the various check-out points in the supermarket; a printer for printing customer receipts and, if the system is linked to an electronic funds transfer system, a data communication link to the various banks' computers for credit check enquiries and the transfer of funds.

Objectives of Computer Based Systems
The use of computers as an integral element of business systems is often the only way in which system objectives can be achieved. It follows, therefore that the objectives of business systems must relate to the objectives of the business as a whole.

Systems which control critical business activities do so by real-time systems. This type of system, e.g. airline seat reservation systems, require powerful communication-oriented computers which support a network of terminals. Similarly, dealer systems link many share brokers to stock exchange computers for the purpose of obtaining instant information on share prices and processing administrative procedures to support such activities. The primary objective of a real time system is to provide instant information on demand in order to be constantly aware of the status of the system at all times and avoid, in the case of hotel accommodation and aircraft seats, double booking.

Functional objectives such as those set for the marketing, purchasing, technical and manufacturing activities are often achieved by computer-based systems designed to remove the weaknesses of the previous system while building on its strengths. Functional performance is often improved by systems with in-built automatic error checking facilities and by taking advantage of the attributes of computers, including their high computational power, the speed with which they print out information, speedier responses to on-line enquiries and a greater degree of control of operations. So that objectives are meaningful and unambiguous they should be specified in quantitative terms such as 'increase production by 10%'; 'decrease production costs by 5%'; 'decrease scrapped production by 1%'; 'increase holiday package turnover by 10% to achieve an increase in profit of 2%' and so on. It is easy enough to state 'pie-in-the-sky' objectives – it is another matter to ensure they are a practical proposition and capable of achievement. It is yet another matter to stipulate the manner of their achievement. How does one 'improve customer relations' for instance? It is not as simple as improving telephone manner, even though this is an essential requirement of normal business etiquette. It must be established why customer relations are currently unsatisfactory, and then the appropriate course of action must be decided upon and implemented.

Of significance to the financial standing of a business is the need to improve cash flows. How may this be accomplished? It is often difficult to get customers to pay their accounts on time as they, too, may have a similar problem. One way of attempting to improve the flow of cash into the business is to improve the credit control procedure, for instance, its integration with an on-line order processing system. It may help if the preparation of statements of account is speeded up by producing them more quickly after the month end, say two days, instead of the present six days. How may this be done? A computerised integrated accounting system is the most likely remedy to this problem for both large and small businesses. The level of cash can be increased by decreasing the level of the inventory which has the effect of reducing interest charges on funds used for the procurement of stocks and also creates a reduction in the level of funds required for the financing of stocks. This can be achieved only by an effective stock control system. A factory with production problems which manifest themselves by the mix of products being out of gear with sales requirements, because of inadequate planning and control systems, may benefit from implementing a proprietory planning and control package. When overheads are shooting through the roof a remedy may be to install a computerised or manual budgetary control system, or make an existing system more efficient. Very often a business needs to improve its information flows in order to improve control of critical operations and aid problem solving and decision making. What are the remedies in this situation? One must be precise on the nature of the problem. Information storage and retrieval can be improved by on-line information files providing the files are kept up-to-date. Information may also be improved by a centralised or distributed database or by the provision of exception reports. The control of critical operations can be improved by implementing real-time systems as previously stated. Systems performance can be improved upon by on-line banking, building society or tour operator systems. Problem solving may be improved by the use of problem solving software such as modelling packages, spreadsheets and simulation techniques. Decision making can be improved by decision support systems, particularly Executive Information Systems (EIS), which guide management in the choice of actions to take.

SUMMARY OF KEY POINTS

- Businesses vary in nature but all have the need for well structured business systems to support their operations.
- To be efficient business systems must be integrated into the corporate framework.
- Systems should be self-monitoring to minimise management intervention.
- Business activities are often affected by influences from the outside environment which are beyond their control.
- To be effective, systems must attain a specified level of performance.
- Investment in information processing systems must be recognised as an investment in resources which must have an adequate return, the same as other types of investment.
- If the value of the benefits of a proposed system exceed the cost of obtaining them then it is a viable proposition.
- Systems are dymanic and need to change in response to changes in the environment.
- Businesses operate in a competitive environment requiring systems which provide a competitive advantage.
- When developing computerised systems it is necessary to consider not only the current business needs but also the foreseeable future needs.
- The objectives of business systems must be compatible with the objectives of the business as a whole.
- The primary objective of real-time systems is the provision of up-to-date information on demand, relating to the status of the system which changes dynamically as events occur.

SELF-TEST QUESTIONS

1 Businesses differ widely but all function on the basis of a specific requirement. What is this specific requirement?

2 Define and state the purpose of *terms of reference*.
3 Effective systems are required for controlling cash flows, the cost of production and the management of stocks, etc. What must systems achieve to be effective?
4 What factors must be considered when viewing business systems as an investment in resources?
5 When is an increase in operating costs acceptable?
6 Business systems are dynamic and volatile. Discuss.
7 For what reasons may change be enforced upon a business?
8 What competitive factors are encountered in business?
9 What factors must be under review when considering the use of a computer?
10 The use of computers as an integral element of business systems is often the only way in which system objectives can be achieved. Discuss.

FURTHER READING

Business systems and information technology, Ron Anderson, Paradigm Publishing, London, 1988.
Chapter 2, relating to business systems and the business environment.
Business systems, R. G. Anderson, M & E Handbook/Pitman, London, 1986.
Provides a broad coverage of business systems.
Organisation and Methods. R. G. Anderson, M & E Handbook/Pitman, London, 1983.
Chapters 4 and 5, outlining the purpose and objectives of systems, environmental factors, systems problems and standards of performance.
Information processing for business studies, A. E. Innes, Pitman, London, 1987.
Chapter 2, Introducing systems, and Chapter 4, The electronic computer and its place in business.

CHAPTER 2
Framework of Business Systems

LEARNING OBJECTIVES

This chapter continues on from Chapter 1 in providing a background to the nature of business systems, and goes further, by indicating the need for the separation of business activities into functions for administrative convenience. Each function, or group of related functions, is supported by a specific business system, e.g. one for controlling stocks of material in a factory, etc. It is important here to distinguish between the terms data and information. Data represents the details of business transactions. Information is the result of processing data by information processing systems. Typical processing operations are also identified as are the constituent elements of business systems.

BUSINESS FUNCTIONS

In all but the smaller business it is necessary to structure major activities into 'functions' primarily for administrative convenience because no one person can effectively control diverse activities on a large scale (*see* Fig. 2.1). Each function is supported by relevant business systems, including the control of raw materials by a stock control system; control of supplies by a purchasing system; payment of wages and salaries by a payroll system and handling customers' orders by an order processing system (*see* Fig 2.2.). Some systems do not recognise abitrary functional boundaries however and, particularly when computerised, take the form of integrated systems. A case in point is an order processing system which integrates with stock control, credit control, invoicing, sales accounting system, sales statistics and reports. Responsibility for controlling each function and the relevant business systems is delegated to a functional manager. Each function is staffed with specialist personnel possessing the necessary skill, experience and knowledge to perform their duties effectively.

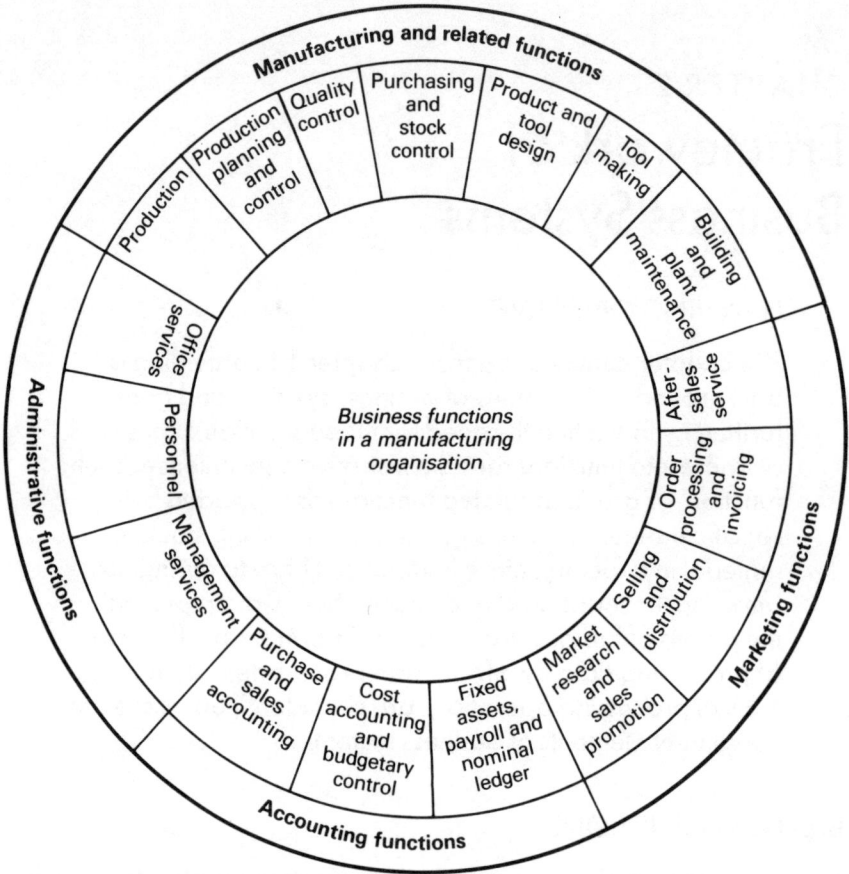

FIG. 2.1 *Business functions in a manufacturing organisation*

A large business will usually have a large volume of administrative paper work to deal with, including a large number of orders from customers requiring the preparation of a large number of manufacturing orders, despatch notes and invoices, as well as updating records with stock transactions and sales accounting activities. The larger business is also likely to employ a greater number of employees, and therefore require additional payroll processing. It is these factors which need to be considered when organising the various functions. Functions may be separately structured for accounting, manufacturing, personnel, purchasing, production planning and control and stock control, etc. A smaller business may combine several functions and related systems when the level of activity of specific tasks does not warrant them being performed by

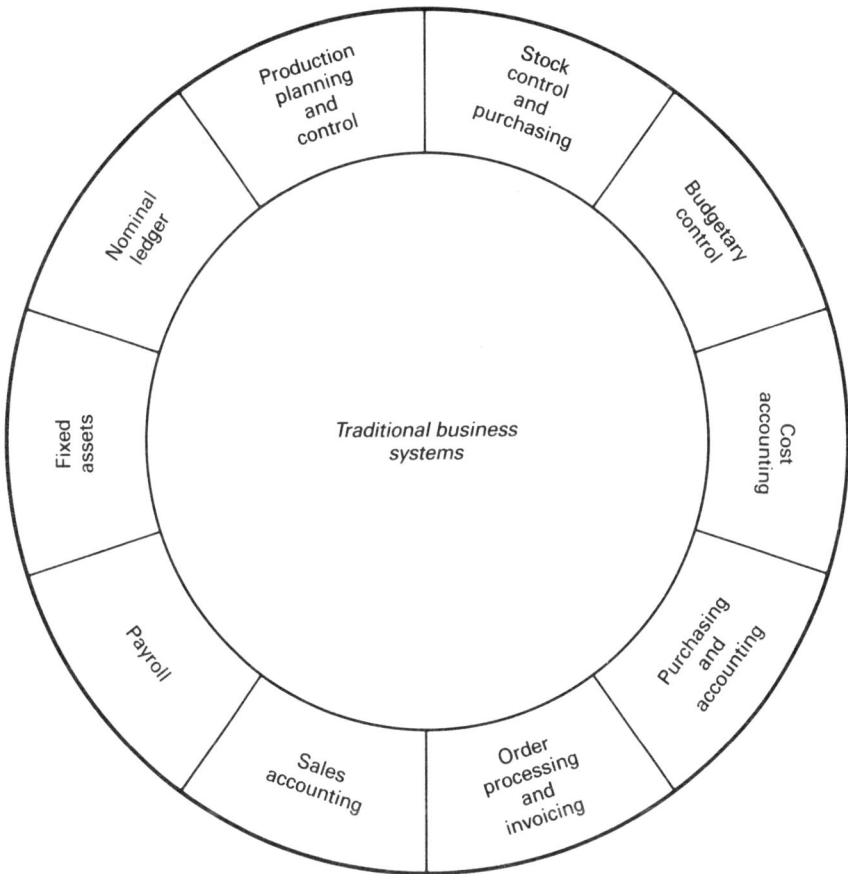

FIG. 2.2   *Traditional business systems*

individual specialists. The small business often has a general office administering a number of systems relating to such matters as personnel management, payroll, typing, telephone, post and reprographics, all under the control of an office manager. A further combination may consist of the procurement and planning and control systems, including those for purchasing all business supplies and those for planning and controlling production and the control of stocks.

DATA AND INFORMATION

The term *data* relates to the details of business transactions which are input to a data processing or information processing system for their transformation into meaningful information. Transaction data emanates from the various functions and is usually recorded on a prime document known as a *source* document. Transactions are recorded as they occur and they are classified by type, a stock transaction for example, and then categorised as an issue, receipt, return to store or return to supplier. A computer program is designed to test for transaction types to enable the software to branch to the relevant instructions to deal with them. The smallest unit of definable data is referred to as a data element, data item, field or attribute. A data element is technically the logical definition of data whereas a field refers to the physical data within the element. For example, the data element 'account balance' is the name of the element which stores the actual account balance of a customer or supplier. When designing business systems data elements need to be precisely defined including the name of the element, the size of the data in terms of the number of characters it consists of, the type of character, whether alphabetic or numeric, and the possible range of values the data may have. These factors are important for developing computer programs with in-built validation routines for the automatic detection of errors – an extremely important requirement to ensure that data is correct before being processed.

After being subjected to validation and processing activities the data is output as information for administrative and control requirements. Information may be presented in printed form, graphically displayed on a video screen or produced graphically on a graph plotter. Printed output may consist of documents, exception reports and complete listings of file contents – essential for accounting and audit purposes. This applies to a stock file, customer file, insurance file, holiday bookings file or work in process file, etc. The information produced is clearly a valuable business asset. A stock list is used as a basis for stock management to avoid excessive stocks or shortages. It must be appreciated that when applications are computerised the data, instead of being entered into a ledger by hand or printed by an older type mechanical accounting machine, can be input to a computer by a terminal located in a branch office or warehouse, or via the keyboard of a work station or microcomputer.

When systems are being developed they must consider external environmental data, e.g. social, political and economic factors. Competitive data will include details relating to the past performance of main competitors, their present activities and future plans and internal environment data relating to the quality of production; levels of performance achieved in the factory, data processing and administrative departments; the level of direct costs, indirect costs and overheads generally; the level of profits achieved and the amount of the losses incurred. It is also important to know financial strengths and weaknesses relating to cash flows and lines of credit. Organisational data is also important, e.g. staffing levels, structure of departments and the span of control. All of this is necessary to provide a framework on which to base systems which, as an integrated whole, provide the administrative machinery for conducting and controlling business operations. Even if systems are initially developed piecemeal, i.e. functionally rather than the 'total systems' approach, management should take into account the possibility of their future integration and ensure that current systems are developed on the basis of this philosophy so that they may be subsequently combined or interfaced with a minimum of disruption – the modular approach is necessary in such instances. Systems development staff should be fully aware of how and where systems fit into overall corporate activities and strategies.

Data flows
Although business activities are functionalised for administrative convenience, data does not recognise these arbitrary boundaries and flows to wherever it serves a useful purpose in the organisation. This requires a detailed analysis of system relationships when systems and procedures are being designed, otherwise systems will not function smoothly – if at all. It must be appreciated that the business as a whole is a complete entity comprising a number of related functions so structured to suit the operational needs of the business in pursuit of corporate goals. It is a well-known fact that data produced by one function is often used by another as a basis for taking some specific action. As an example, the details of items despatched to customers are priced and valued for the purpose of producing invoices. In a non-integrated system a copy of the invoice provides the details to be input to the sales ledger system for updating customers' accounts. In this instance, data relating to despatches provides the input to the invoicing system which produces invoices which may be classed as information relating to the value of sales to a customer. The details on the invoice copy provides the input to the sales ledger system. The output from the sales system also provides valuable credit control, information e.g. the amount owing by each customer and which customers have exceeded the stipulated credit period and credit limit.

Data capture
Business systems must capture data economically and, whenever

possible, avoid having to convert it from human sensible form – readable data in the form of alphabetic and numeric characters – to machine sensible form – binary code, the language of the computer. A data collection system is sometimes used for recording and transmitting data from distant locations such as bank branches or the offices of building societies, insurance companies and tour operators. This is accomplished by means of on-line terminals. The modern method of capturing data in factories is by means of devices known as *factory data recorders* which are strategically located throughout the factory. The recorder consists of a micro-processor which allows data to be input via a keyboard, punched card or badge reader which transmits data directly to a computer. Point-of-sale operations in supermarkets, as mentioned in Chapter 1, use a laser scanning technique for capturing data by scanning an EAN (European Article Number) bar coded label attached to commodities such as tins of beans and bars of chocolate. Data is then transmitted to an in-store computer for pricing and stock management purposes. Banks use auto-teller terminals for collecting details of cash dispensed automatically. The data capture technique adopted in this instance is by means of a keyboard to enable customers to key in their personal identification number (PIN) which is also used for entering the amount of money required. Customers are also provided with a plastic card for validating the personal number. Other methods of data capture include the use of portable computers for collecting stock control data in stores; handprint data entry terminals which enable handprinted data to be captured which is converted into ASCII code and transmitted to a host computer.

Entities

An entity is any object, person, customer, account, supplier, order, job, department or event for which data needs to be stored, referred to or retrieved for processing in accordance with system requirements. An entity is described by its *attributes*, which is another name for data fields, which store specific data such as customer account number, name, address, credit limit, account balance and area code. Entity relationships must be identified as this is an essential requirement for establishing file structures and databases. Such relationships are identified by means of an entity diagram (*see* Chapter 9).

INFORMATION PROCESSING ACTIVITIES AND COMPUTERS

Information systems are often extensions to routine data processing systems which are enhanced to produce analyses and reports for managerial control and decision making. Information systems normally incorporate the management by exception principle of production reports restricted to significant facts. Such reports have the advantage of optimising management's time by only notifying them of matters which command their attention in order to maintain the stability of system performance.

A computerised system is ideal for supporting an information system because of its ability to respond speedily to enquiries in on-line or real-time systems. The objectives of such systems include the provision of information to all levels of management at the most relevant time, at an acceptable level of accuracy and at an economical cost. An essential element of an information system is its ability to incorporate feedback, i.e. the ability to communicate a system's measured outputs to the control system for the purpose of modifying the input by an effector (manager) taking effective corrective action to attain a state of homeostasis. This is essential because in some types of system, such as budgetary control, the level of overhead expenses for a particular function often exceeds the budgeted allowance which is known as the *reference input*, i.e. the desired state.

Information processing includes all those activities concerned with the conversion of a set of related but uncorrelated facts into a meaningful correlated whole which involves subjecting the data to a number of processing operations, outlined below. Although many small businesses process information by clerks, e.g. by manual systems, many businesses, even small ones, process information by small but powerful computers. Computerised systems incorporate rules, conditions and actions into a set of instructions known as a *program*. This is the equivalent to the clerk's instructions in a procedure manual. Computer programs are stored inside the computer in a magnetic memory and are executed automatically, one instruction at a time, under the control of the operating system. Computers, particularly those in batch processing environments, can process large volumes of data at extremely high speeds enabling payrolls and ledgers to be updated faster than is possible by any other means. This attribute often achieves staff savings and should lead to improved administrative systems and the earlier availability of information for problem solving, business control and decision making. Many businesses have similar applications such as payroll and stock control, which can be processed by standard routines very often in the form of package programs for the various applications.

TYPICAL PROCESSING OPERATIONS

Although the following details are written in the computer vernacular it is assumed that the reader appreciates that many of the operations are also relevant to manual clerical operations even though they may be carried out by different techniques and methods. The process of verification is of course only relevant to a computer system when data is encoded from a transaction document to magnetic disc for input requirements.

Verification

Verification is an activity generally applicable to batch processing applications when it is necessary to convert details recorded on primary documents, known as source documents, to a magnetic media. The activity is concerned with verifying the accuracy with which data has been encoded on the magnetic media. Computers cannot recognise handwritten details except in special cases such as when documents are encoded in optical characters, or in magnetic ink characters as used on bank cheques.

Validation

Validation is a process for the detection of errors in the initial recording of data, rather than in encoding the data, as above. Validation is an extremely important requirement for business information processing applications as it prevents the processing of erroneous data. It goes without saying that it is pointless and even dangerous to process incorrect (invalid) data which can often be compounded during computational activities, for example if 1000 units are ordered, instead of 100 units, at £50 each, then the magnitude of the error is a factor of ten and the cost of the units actually delivered would be £50 000 instead of £5000. Apart from anything else this situation could create a cash crisis and the additional 900 units would probably create storage problems and may incur additional storage costs.

Sorting

Sorting is the process of assembling data into a defined sequence, usually the sequence of records in a ledger which, in computer terminology, is known as the *master file*. This enables files to be processed more effectively as it is only necessary to access a record once to deal with all transactions affecting it. Otherwise it would be necessary to refer back to each record each time a transaction affecting it occured.

Calculating

Calculating or computing is concerned with the various computations for converting related items of data into specific information, examples of which are: quantity sold × price for invoicing purposes; hours worked × hourly rate for payroll requirements.

Comparing

Comparing is a very important operation in information processing as the outcome of comparing different items of data affects the course of action which should be taken to control an activity, e.g. when the difference between budgeted expenses compared with actual expenditure is an unfavourable variance, indicating that managerial action is required to remove the cause of the variance.

Updating

Updating records is an activity that posts all current transactions to relevant records on a file so that they represent the current situation of that specific entity, e.g. the amount owed by each customer, the amount owing to each supplier and the quantity of each item in stock. In respect of a stock file it is updated with transaction data, including issues from the stores to production which reduces the quantity in stock, and receipts from suppliers or returns to store which increase the quantity in stock.

Control totals

The generation of control totals by the computer during processing is a means of controlling the throughput of data. The control totals are compared with precalculated totals and any difference indicates either missing transactions or an error in the control total. Investigation will indicate the cause of the difference and appropriate action may then be taken.

BUSINESS DOCUMENTS

Business transactions are generally recorded on source documents, e.g. clock cards for recording attendance time of employees; issue notes for recording items issued from the stores; sales orders from customers indicating their requirements and insurance renewal notices, etc. Many documents of the traditional type are recorded by hand using a ball-point pen or pencil; others are prepared using a typewriter. It is often necessary to design what are known as 'turna-round' documents which are so called because after being printed in optical characters by the computer they are subsequently returned to the system as input for processing. An example of this is the meter reading sheet produced by electricity boards. Initially it is printed in optical characters specifying the consumer reference number and the previous reading. The meter reader records the units consumed by marks in pre-designated columns. The marks are sensed by an optical mark and character reader which are then encoded to magnetic tape in readiness for processing. Similarly, banks issue specially printed cheque forms to customers, with account details printed in magnetic ink characters. The cheques are read into the computer by a magnetic ink character reader/sorter which senses the details magnetically. Some computerised systems display a form outline on a monitor screen for entering details by keyboard, which is similar in effect to entering details on a form by means of a typewriter.

Records
Records are used either for reference or for the purpose of maintaining a transaction history relating to a specific entity. This may be an item of stock, an employee, a client, a customer or supplier, etc. The details in a record are referred to as fields including a reference field for identification purposes such as product, catalogue or employee number, customer or supplier account number.

Records in a computer system are stored on some form of magnetic medium such as tape or disc. In a clerical system records usually consist of ledger cards for recording details of various types of accounts. The ledger cards are often stored in filing cabinets of various types. Records need to be updated periodically so that the latest status of an entity is available, an essential requirement for effective administration. The frequency of updating is largely dependent upon the nature of the activity, the volume of transactions to be posted and the processing technique employed. In respect of a computerised batch processing system records may be updated daily, weekly or monthly depending upon the needs of the particular system. If large volumes of invoices are generated each day then posting may occur with a daily frequency in order to avoid a build-up. On the other hand the posting of transactions may take place immediately events occur during real-time or on-line operations so that they show the latest status of the system. If it is necessary to have up-to-the minute stock information in a wholesale warehouse or supermarket, for instance, then either a real-time control system will be required for updating as stock movements occur, or files will need to be updated frequently on a batch basis.

Files

The nature of files in computerised systems remains the same in principle but differs in the storage medium. In a large installation with a high incidence of on-line processing from branch works and dispersed offices the computer files would be fixed discs, whereas batch processing environments tend to use exchangeable discs or large reels of magnetic tape; small microcomputer installations use a type of floppy disc, or a hard disc known as a Winchester disc. Files in a clerical system are referred to as ledgers, e.g. the purchase, sales, cost, stock or general ledger. Computerised files are referred to as master files. Files are identified physically by means of a file label attached to the file media and identified electronically by the computer by means of a file name, e.g. CUST, for CUSTomer master file. Several file organisation techniques exist and the choice is dependent upon the specific needs of the system and the devices used in the computer configuration. The available techniques include: serial, sequential, indexed sequential, direct addressing or inverted. If information is stored in a database then it may be structured on a hierarchical, relational or network basis (*see* Chapter 10).

SYSTEM PRIORITIES

All parts of a system do not need to be processed with the same priority rating because one part of the system may be controlling a real-time operation known as a 'foreground activity' and another part may be updating ledgers and printing payrolls as a 'background activity'. Priorities enable parts of the system with a low priority to be interrupted in order to deal with real-time requirements. In some circumstances multiprocessing may be adopted using two processors in tandem (incurring high hardware costs) whereby batch processing and real-time processing proceed side-by-side. The batch processor is arranged to switch immediately to the real-time operation in the event of a malfunction occuring on the real-time processor. This is a fail-safe routine to protect the integrity of the data and to avoid 'system downtime' which could be catastrophic.

SUMMARY OF KEY POINTS

- A business is structured on the basis of functions.
- Each function is responsible for carrying out specialised tasks.
- Functional activities are supported by relevant business systems.
- Data represents details of business transactions.
- Information is the result of processing data.
- Information is produced by information processing systems.
- Data flows do not recognise arbitrary functional boundaries.
- Data produced by one function is often used by another.
- Business systems must capture business data economically, avoiding the need to convert it from human sensible form into machine sensible form for processing by computer.
- An entity is a data group which needs to be stored for use in business activities.
- Information systems normally incorporate the principle of management by exception.
- Business systems comprise entities, data, information, data flows, documents, records and files.
- System priorities must be defined.

SELF-TEST QUESTIONS

1 Why is it necessary to functionalise business activities?
2 Distinguish between data and information.
3 What is the purpose of an information processing system?
4 When designing business systems data elements need to be precisely defined. What does this entail?
5 Information may be presented in a number of different ways. List details of three different ways.
6 What categories of printed output may be produced by a business computer?
7 Why is it necessary to analyse and define system relationships?
8 What is data capture?
9 What are entities?
10 List typical processing operations which are essential for processing business data.

11 Define and state the purpose of the following: business documents, records, files.
12 Why do system priorities need to be defined?

FURTHER READING

Business systems and information technology, Ron Anderson, Paradigm Publishing, London, 1988.
Chapters 7 and 8, relating to files and file processing.
Chapters 9, relating to information processing techniques.
Business systems, R. G. Anderson, M & E Handbook/Pitman, London, 1986.
Chapters 3, 4 and 5, relating to the nature of non-financial systems, the nature of financial systems and the nature of management accounting systems.
Information processing for business studies, A. E. Innes, Pitman, London, 1987.
Chapter 3, relating to information systems.
Data Processing Volume 1, 6th edition, R. G. Anderson, M & E handbook/ Pitman, London, 1987.
Chapter 1, data processing concepts and the data processing model.
Chapter 4, computer input and data capture methods and techniques.

Part 2

General System Development Techniques

Aids to System Development

LEARNING OBJECTIVES

The objective of this chapter is to indicate that many different approaches may be adopted for developing business systems. A further objective is to indicate the use of structured English for defining the logic of a system and the way in which an expert system may be applied for diagnosing system problems. Prototyping is also introduced to indicate how a prototype model may be used for developing systems initially.

INITIAL APPRAISAL OF SYSTEMS

The clarity to which the features and characteristics of systems can be observed is inversely proportional to the distance of the observer from the system. The universe may be described as a total system embracing all systems in creation in which case an astronaut descending to earth from orbit would progressively observe increasingly greater degrees of detail of the world. The nearer to earth the space module becomes the greater the amount of detail which will become apparent. The shape of continents and oceans will become clearer until eventually the shape of individual countries becomes defined depending upon the specific hemisphere in view. A pilot of an aircraft flying much lower than a space module observes features of the terrain being flown over which may sometimes be a blurred image due to haze preventing a clear observation. It also depends upon the extent of cloud in the vicinity and the height being flown. Business systems may also become hazy and blurred, for example, when they outgrow their original purpose or when they have not been modified in accord with changing conditions. Therefore the closer the observation the greater the detail observed.

The BBC Domesday system provides varying degrees of detail of specific topics and subjects. Varying levels of details can be obtained progressively from satellite photographs of the UK and countries and island groups; satellite and aerial photographs, text and maps of regions; community photographs; street maps and special feature photographs right down to floor plans of special sites and special feature photographs. Similarly a systems analyst obtains an initial view of a business which appears as a conglomerate of many merging images, consisting of offices, factory departments, machines, equipment and people. A closer look is imperative in order to conduct detailed studies of organisation structures, and the various functions forming the framework of the business, i.e. the corporate system. Each function must then be analysed to identify the systems which supports its operations. A conceptual model is then constructed, identifying the various entities and their relationships; primary functions and the sequence in which they are executed; sub-system interfaces and the boundary of the system under development.

A 'context' diagram can also be prepared as a preliminary to analysing data flows in more detail prior to the preparation of a data flow diagram; each function can also be identified as a series of tasks and activities performed in the transformation of data from input to output. These aspects are dealt with in Chapter 9.

SPECIFYING THE CORRECT APPROACH TO DESIGN

Many different approaches may be adopted for designing business systems, a number of which are to be discussed in this chapter. It is important to appreciate that the design approach should reflect the nature of the problem under consideration and may require a combination of different approaches. Many business systems are data-driven and require a top-down, data-driven approach. There are instances however when the functions, events or devices to be used in a system are more predominant. It is a matter of choosing the relevant approach to suit the circumstances and to achieve an acceptable level of performance at a reasonable cost.

Module-oriented design

A complex system may be analysed into a series of related sub-systems, each sub-system being a 'module' of the overall system. The approach considers logical relationships and it achieves flexibility as a number of modules can be developed concurrently. The approach separates the system into non-overlapping areas with a clear definition of system interfaces. Subsequently the data which is exchanged between the modules is defined. Program debugging, testing and maintenance are facilitated by this approach.

Data-structure oriented design

The philosophy of this approach is that design should be related to the structure of the data to be processed rather than the processes to be performed. Data may be organised on the basis of a hierarchical structure which takes the form of an inverted tree. Access to data starts at the top, proceeding downwards through the structure. This type of data structure often forms the basis of a database. A network is another method of structuring data which is based on the concept of a *sets* which is the relationship between record types, e.g. a customer's order and an order item. This type of structure is also used in the construction of databases and it simulates the logical data relationships existing in the real world of business, such as those which exist between customers, orders, products and order items. Relational data structures also form the basis of sophisticated databases whereby each record type is stored in a table, an array of rows and columns, the rows being the entities (records) and the columns the fields.

Data flow oriented design

The data flow approach portrays the elemental structure of a system including entities, processes, data flows and data stores (files). The approach can show high level data flows outlining the system in very broad terms which may then be subjected to partitioning or levelling to portray data flows in increasing levels of detail down to the ultimate level of what is known as a functional primitive. The Yourdon approach commences with the physical inputs and works through successive transforms to the physical outputs.

Function-oriented design

This approach initially defines the functions, i.e. the tasks which need to be done and the sequence in which they are to be performed. The system is designed to achieve the functional requirements, which also take into account the data flows and the structure of data. A function, in general organisational terms, is a major business activity such as stock control or purchasing and as such forms part of the corporate organisation structure. Each main function is supported by systems which themselves consist of sub-systems or system modules. It is the activities, tasks or processes on which the systems are based which is the subject of the function-oriented approach.

Most modelling and structured design techniques use a form of hierarchical construction, known as functional decomposition, for breaking down (refining) a high level definition of a task, process or function into successively more detail.

Typical business functions or processes include the recording of transactions; computing the value of transactions; updating files and printing documents and reports.

Event-oriented design

Some systems are specifically event-driven as they need fast responses to events occuring in the environment, such as on-line systems which are triggered off by a request for a seat reservation in airline or theatre booking systems, or package holiday enquiries in a travel agency. The relevant tasks to be executed are determined followed by an appraisal of the information which must flow in the system in response to events.

Device-oriented design

This approach recognises that the machines and equipment to be implemented are of major significance. Although it is usual to consider the logical requirements of a system before considering the physical devices to be used for their attainment there are instances when the situation calls for a different approach, for example, where management philosophy is to convert the existing system to an on-line event driven system. If the business has a geographical dispersion of operating sections such as branch offices, factories or warehouses then it will be clear that a high-powered communications oriented computer system is required. The various functions and tasks are then assigned to the devices and the nature of the information to flow between them is then taken into account.

DEFINING LOGICAL PROCESSES IN STRUCTURED ENGLISH

Structured English consists of a combination of English words and program-type instructions and is used to define the logical processes of a system. It is a sub-set of the English language with a limited vocabulary consisting of:

- imperative verbs to express functions
- data dictionary terms including nouns for the name of data items, documents or reports
- reserved words for logic formulation

Its syntax is also limited and omits most punctuation, all adjectives and adverbs. Structured English enables system logic to be easily understood by the user department staff which facilitates productive discussions with systems analysts during the various stages of system development. It incorporates three structures – sequence, selection and repetition (or iteration) which are outlined below:

1 *Sequence*
   Each action follows the next as specified in a computer program.
2 *Selection*
   A control structure allowing tests to be made for conditions using the IF THEN ELSE construct.
3 *Repetition (iteration)*
   Repetition or Iteration continues as long as a condition remains true. It utilises loop statements such as WHILE DO or WHILE WEND, REPEAT UNTIL.

Example of structured English
The following example relates to updating stock records and printing a stock report.

```
PRINT (report header)
READ (stock master record)
   WHILE (not end of file) DO
      REPEAT
         READ (stock transaction)
            IF  (Purchase order) THEN
               Add (purchase quantity to quantity on order)
               Add (purchase quantity to free stock quantity)
   ELSE
            IF  (Issue) THEN
               Subtract (issue quantity from quantity in stock)
               Subtract (issue quantity from quantity in stock)
   ELSE
            IF  (Receipt) THEN
               Add (receipt quantity to quantity in stock)
               Subtract (receipt quantity from quantity on order)
      UNTIL (not this stock record)
      REPEAT (stock master record)
   END WHILE
   PRINT (control totals)
```

The sequence control structure shows the flow of actions one after the other as follows:

- print report header
- read stock master record

- read stock transaction
- update stock record
- repeat processing of transactions until completed
- print control totals

The selection control structure applies the IF-THEN-ELSE conventions together with indentation of actions.

The iteration control structure provides for the repeating of events using the WHILE-DO and REPEAT-UNTIL conventions.

Example
This example relates to customer discounts which are based on quantities ordered.

```
READ (customer order)
WHILE (not end of file) DO
REPEAT
    IF (order quantity is less than 100) THEN
        Compute (discount at 5% of order value) ELSE
    IF (order quantity is between 100 and 200) THEN
        Compute (discount at 7% of order value) ELSE
        Compute (discount at 9% of order value)
ENDWHILE
```

Example
This example relates to customer discounts as before but the discount is based on two factors, order value and the account balance.

```
READ customer order
WHILE (not end of transactions) DO
REPEAT
    IF (order value is less than £100 AND account balance
        is less than £500) THEN
        Compute discount at 2% ELSE
    IF (order value is greater than £100 AND account balance is
        less than £500) THEN
        Compute discount at 3% ELSE
    IF (order value is greater than £100 AND account balance is
        greater than £500) THEN
        Compute discount at 1% ELSE
    IF (order value is less than £100 AND account balance
        is greater than £500) THEN
```

      No discount is provided
      UNTIL (not this customer order)
      READ customer order
  ENDDO

A number of conventions need to be considered when applying structured English. These include:

- Selection control structures using IF-THEN can dispense with ELSE when a condition can only have one possible action to deal with it.
- An iteration can repeat an activity a specified number of times or until a file or transactions are completely processed.
- The completion of an iteration structure should be terminated with an ENDDO or other similar convention.
- Parentheses should be used abounding conditions when using IF or WHILE statements.
- Subordinate sentences should be indented for purposes of clarity.

DIAGNOSING SYSTEM PROBLEMS BY KNOWLEDGE BASED SYSTEMS

Introduction to expert systems
Expert systems are a sub-set of knowledge based systems which form an integral part of artificial intelligence systems. See Fig. 3.1.

An expert system may be defined as a computerised problem solving aid which simulates human knowledge by making deductions from given facts using the rules of logical inference. An expert system can work in one or two ways:

1 Working back through supporting evidence to establish the truth of a previously selected conclusion; the *backward chaining* technique.
2 Appraising the status of evidence in order to select a goal; forward chaining technique.

Expert knowledge
Knowledge about a specific subject is collected from an expert and transferred into a knowledge-based computer system. The knowledge consists of facts, concepts and relationships between facts which may be defined as information which has been collected, analysed and organised so that it is meaningful, understandable and may be used for problem solving or decision making. The provision of a solution to a problem often commences by asking questions, and

the answers are typed in. This triggers off the search process.

Elements of a knowledge based system
A knowledge based system consists of three primary elements – an inference engine which acts as a rule interpreter and functions in combination with a knowledge base. The knowledge base contains rules and facts about a specific subject and a database consisting of facts relating to a particular domain (subject area). The inference engine questions the user and interprets the rules of relationship (*see* Fig. 3.1).

Inferencing
Inferencing is the process of reaching a solution or decision by reasoning, using given evidence. In effect it simulates the human thinking process, and in this way an expert system differs from traditional computer programs which have built-in logic, often derived from the details contained in decision tables prepared for the purpose. By this means the system provides for every condition that could occur in a system together with the relevant action in accordance with specified rules. A computer program does not therefore have an inference facility.

Rules
Rules define relationships between facts and may be defined as

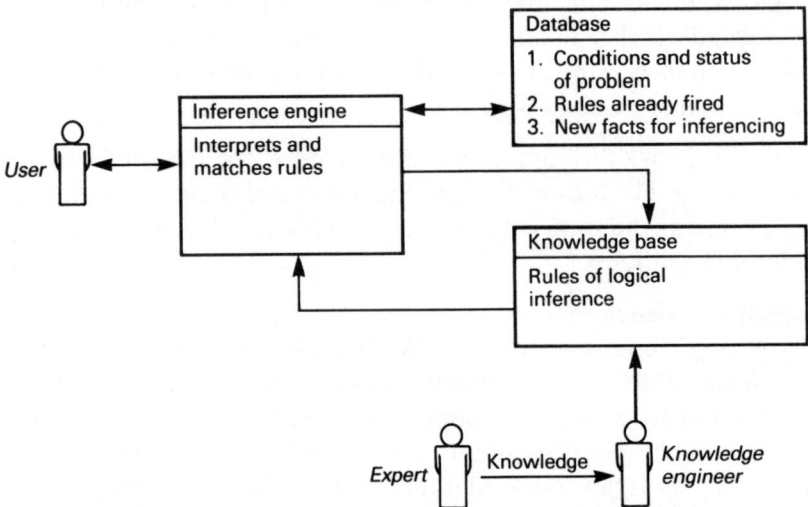

FIG. 3.1.   *Elements of a knowledge based (expert) system*

representations of human reasoning which in combination with an antecedent specify an inference on which to base a specified action. Details are input to the knowledge base in the form of 'production rules' each representing an individual item of knowledge. Rules combine to form a line of reasoning. The conclusion of one rule may become the premise of another and it is this collection of rules that combine to form the knowledge base. Each production rule consists of two parts. The left-hand side contains an IF clause consisting of a premise or condition, the right-hand side contains a THEN clause consisting of a conclusion, action or consequence. If the premises in a rule are true or the condition is met, the right-hand part is also true. The rule is then 'triggered'. When the right-hand side of the rule is implemented it is said to be 'fired'. This process consists of taking a specified action when specific situations are true on the basis of – IF A is true AND B is true THEN do a stated action. Production rules are useful for representing all types of knowledge for attaining goals. Every rule has one IF clause and one THEN clause. A clause is similar to a sentence with a subject, a verb and an object that states some fact.

Most commercial systems apply the IF-THEN format when solving logical problems by the application of structured English, as demonstrated below.

Examples
1 Rule contains an IF and THEN clause
    IF the quantity in stock is equal to the reorder level THEN
    Place an order to replenish supplies.
2 Rule contains an IF, THEN, ELSE clause.
    IF the order quantity is greater than 1000 THEN
    Provide a discount of 5% ELSE
    Provide a discount of 2%
3 Rule contains an IF, AND, THEN clause
    If the volume of production is less than 50000 units AND the
    production cost per unit is greater than £5 THEN
    Do not pay bonus.
4 Rule contains an IF, OR, THEN clause
    IF the volume of production is greater than 50000 units
    OR the production cost per unit is less than £5 THEN
    Pay a bonus of 6%

Goals
A goal is a conclusion that the system developer requires the expert

system to reach during a consultation. It is made up of one or more rules that determine the required conditions to attain the stipulated goal.

Help, why and how facilities
An expert system provides a help facility to provide the user with assistance on questions, goals and rules to establish an understanding of the nature of the system. The 'why' facility explains why a question is being asked. The 'how' facility explains how a particular conclusion was arrived at. A user may not understand or even agree with an answer provided by an expert system and, in such instances, will want to know how the system arrived at its conclusion. The system may do this by displaying the rules which formed the basis of the conclusion and the sequence in which they were dealt with from details stored in the database. In this way the user can assess the line of reasoning by going through the rules sequentially assessing the logic inferences at each stage of assessment. Some systems incorporate explanatory statements in the rule which may be studied by the user. This is an important facility because it provides confidence in the system which is essential for making important decisions, based on the conclusions provided.

Example: Defining the nature of the problem
It is possible to build a simple expert system for diagnosing system problems thereby providing a computerised logical approach for indicating the actions required to solve them. A systems analyst provides answers to questions asked by the expert system which, by means of expert system software, applies the rules of logical inference to provide a remedy to solve a specific problem. Boolean algebra is used for defining the logic of a problem which is based on two possible truth values, true and false. The system for diagnosing system problems can be run on a microcomputer using a menu-driven approach. The expert system for this knowledge requirement incorporates details in the knowledge base. This contains rules that deal with specific system problems as in the following menu, which is built into the expert system demonstrated below:

MAIN MENU

DIAGNOSING SYSTEM PROBLEMS

1. Data flows
2. Processing method

3. Personnel
4. Quality of output

The expert system software displays questions on the screen in respect of option 1, relating to data flows as shown:

A = Do data flows produce the required information?
B = Is the information produced on time?

Conclusion, action or consequence

C = Modify data flows
D = Improve processing method
E = No change required to system

Inferred conclusions are derived from the process of forward chaining performed by the inference engine after interpreting and matching rules in the knowledge base with information stored in the database. Option 1 contains four rules as follows:

Rule 1 – IF A AND B THEN E ELSE
Rule 2 – IF NOT A AND B THEN C ELSE
Rule 3 – IF A AND NOT B THEN D ELSE
Rule 4 – IF NOT A AND NOT B THEN C AND D

Rule 1 may be interpreted as:

If data flows produce the required information AND the information is produced on time THEN no change is required to the system.

Rule 2 may be interpreted as:

IF data flows do NOT produce the required information AND the information is produced on time THEN modify data flows.

Rules 3 and 4 may be similarly interpreted.

There now follows an outline of the operation of the expert system for diagnosing system problems demonstrated in structured English.

NAME: PROBLEM SOLVER: DATA FLOWS
GOAL: OPTIMISATION OF SYSTEM PERFORMANCE
HELP:
PRINT (The rules contained in this knowledge base drive the inference engine when answers are provided to the questions displayed on the screen, relating to the state of the system under investigation. Such answers provide solutions by inferencing.)
END HELP

PRINT (SELECT option from menu)

PRINT   MAIN MENU
PRINT   DIAGNOSING SYSTEM PROBLEMS
PRINT
PRINT   1. Data flows
PRINT   2. Processing method
PRINT   3. Personnel
PRINT   4. Quality of output
PRINT

PRINT   Depress key 1—4 to obtain desired option

WHILE (not end) DO
IF KEY ENTRY = 1 THEN
    PRINT (Do data flows produce the required
           information?)
    PRINT (Enter Y or N)
    INPUT A (Response Y or N)
    PRINT (Is the information produced on time?)
    PRINT (Enter Y or N)
    INPUT B (Response Y or N)

Rule 1
IF A AND B THEN
    PRINT (No change required to system)
    PRINT (Do you wish to know how the conclusion is reached?)
    PRINT (Enter Y or N)
IF response is Y THEN
    PRINT (Because you entered Y to the first question and Y to
           the second question the conclusion is that data flows
           produce the required information and the information
           is received on time. This situation infers that the system
           does not have data flow problems and no changes are
           required.)
           ELSE

Rule 2
IF NOT A AND B THEN
    PRINT (Modify data flows)
    PRINT (Do you wish to know how the conclusion is reached?)
    PRINT (Enter Y or N)

IF response is Y THEN
    PRINT   (Because you entered Y to the first question and N to the second question the conclusion is that data flows do not produce the required information but it is received on time. This infers that data flows need to be modified.) ELSE

Rule 3
IF A AND NOT B THEN
    PRINT (Improve processing method)
    PRINT   (Do you wish to know how the conclusion is reached?)
    PRINT (Enter Y or N)
IF response is Y THEN
    PRINT   (As data flows produce the required information but it is not received on time the conclusion that it is necessary to improve the processing method by the most suitable means.)
ELSE

Rule 4
IF NOT A AND NOT B THEN
    PRINT   (Modify data flows and improve processing method)
    PRINT   (Do you wish to know how the conclusion is reached?)
IF response is Y THEN
    PRINT   (As data flows do not produce the required information and it is not received on time then it is inferred that it is necessary to modify the data flows to ensure they accord with information needs and to speed up the flow of information by the most suitable means.
RETURN TO MENU

The expert system would provide solutions to the remaining three menu options in a similar manner.

PROTOTYPING

Characteristics and purpose
A prototype is a model of a system which is developed to demonstrate to users how their information needs can be achieved by the new system. The technique may be used at various stages of the

development cycle. Prior to developing a system the prototype strategy must be determined as it is possible to expend resources on this activity without achieving commensurate benefits. Projects which are likely to benefit from the application of prototyping include the development of new systems or projects in dynamic application areas of the business. A number of factors need to be considered when determining strategy, including the complexity of the system under review, the clarity of user requirements and the urgency of getting a system up and running. Logical Structured Design Methodology recognises three approaches to prototyping.

Approach 1
This approach uses screen development aids to build a series of menus and screens and may be used where processing is straight forward and user requirements well defined. Users process transactions as they would in a live system but this approach does not incorporate system logic or database. If the design is accepted by the user then they can participate in further development of the model. If the user finds the prototype unacceptable due to inconsistencies, omissions or other weaknesses then these matters are further considered. Once the prototype model has been approved it can be developed further.

Approach 2
This approach requires the building of a 'throw-away' sub-set of the system for user trials. In addition to the availability of menus and screens a database and some system logic is also incorporated into the prototype. This approach may be used for larger more complex projects when user requirements are not well defined. The prototype may be refined to be compatible with user requirements. The prototyping software is unlikely to have the performance and facilities for implementation as part of the physical system. It would, however, be used to identify user requirements and to specify the most relevant dialogue design.

Approach 3
This approach is similar to the second approach but the software is not meant to be disposed of, but should form part of the final system. The prototype may be extended into a working part of the system that will be implemented. This would often become the pilot for a project with a phased implementation plan. The prototyping software must

incorporate facilities to accomplish performance objectives.

SUMMARY OF KEY POINTS

- The clarity to which a systems features can be observed is inversely proportional to the distance of the observer from the system.
- Many different approaches may be adopted to the development of systems reflecting the nature of the problem.
- The logical processes of a system can be clearly defined by structured English.
- Expert systems are rule-based systems for imparting the knowledge of experts to non-experts.
- Expert systems are used for problem solving and may be applied to diagnosing system problems.
- Prototyping can be used for the development of new systems.

SELF-TEST QUESTIONS

1 Define the features of the following approaches to the development of business systems:
  module-oriented.
  data-structure oriented
  data flow oriented
  function oriented
2 What is structured English and how may it be applied in system development?
3 What is an expert system and how is it structured?
4 For what purposes may an expert system be applied in system development?
5 What is prototyping?

FURTHER READING

Crash Course in Artificial Intelligence and Expert Systems, Louis E. Frenzel, Jr, Howard W. Sams & Co. 1986.
Chapter 4, Introduction to Expert Systems, Chapter 5, Developing an Expert System.
Business Information Systems, Chris Clare and Peri Loucopoulos, Paradigm Publishing Ltd, 1987.
Chapter 8, Prototyping.

The O & M Approach to Systems Development – 1

LEARNING OBJECTIVES

The objective of this chapter is to introduce the 'organisation and methods' (O & M) approach to the development of business systems. It emphasises the importance of collecting facts relating to the existing method or procedure in order to become familiar with its operational features, which is an essential prerequisite to implementing improvements. Important facts required for this purpose relate to organisational aspects of business systems, operational data, an analysis of the existing communications, company policy matters, and so on. The essentiality of verifying facts is also intimated.

THE NATURE OF O & M

Organisation and methods (O & M) studies may be defined as the process of collecting and analysing facts about existing systems to obtain an appreciation of their nature, characteristics, problems and weaknesses as a basis for developing more effective systems. The term O & M analysis is used to distinguish the activity from systems analysis. O & M analysis is concerned with improving or simplifying systems, procedures, methods and working practices by the most suitable means. This may require the implementation of computerised systems, in which case the O & M analyst will recommend this course of action and either continue with the development of a computerised system as part of a systems development team, or hand over the project to the systems analysts concerned with computer applications. It should be appreciated that highly automated systems require supportive clerical activities for the routine recording of data relating to business transactions prior to its conversion to a form suitable for input to a computer, and data control activities to ensure that all data received for processing is input to the computer and that the required output is produced and distributed to the originating departments. It must also be appreciated that all systems do not warrant the use of a computer due to a number of factors, such as low volumes of data for processing, infrequent processing of business routines, activities with low priority output requirements and so on. In such cases O & M analysts improve systems and methods according to the nature of the current system's weaknesses and operational problems.

The stages of O & M analysis include the provision of terms of reference by management, indicating the area and boundaries of the assignment, and the carrying out of a preliminary survey to identify the type of problem to be dealt with and to obtain facts relating to the nature of the procedure, method or system under consideration. This is followed by planning the project, collecting, verifying, recording and examining the facts. These stages are then followed by systems design.

O & M analysts are responsible for analysing systems as a preliminary to developing new or improved versions of existing systems. The analyst must therefore be a good communicator, have imagination, the ability to get on with people and to be a good listener as well as having an understanding of the underlying principles for the development of effective organisation structures; the principles of good forms design; effective staffing and staff training techniques; requirements for effective communications in the office and matters conducive to effective office layout.

The analyst must advise user department staff of the benefits they may expect from the use of new methods and techniques and how they may be used effectively to enhance the level of productivity. A system should never be 'imposed' on operating departments as they are likely to resist this action and refuse to operate the system or method. Analysts must work harmoniously with user-department staff on a co-ordinated basis to ensure that the system/method ultimately accepted for implementation functions effectively. O & M analysts analyse various aspects of the current system including data, document and file analysis, discussed later in this chapter, and consider what checks and controls should be included in the new system (these are established during discussions with the internal audit staff), define actions to be taken in respect of specified conditions; develop screen layouts for on-line entry of data; establish file security procedures; ensure the privacy and confidentiality of data by the most suitable means; prepare operating and procedural instructions for the various activities to be performed; document the system to provide a means of reference to facilitate training and to accomplish continuity of system development; monitor the performance of the system to ensure it is attaining its defined purpose and objectives and is cost effective.

Many of the activities listed above are concerned with system design and implementation. This is because the O & M analyst performs all related activities concerned with system development.

COLLECTING THE FACTS

Collecting facts is extremely important because it enables the O & M analyst to collect details of the existing method, procedure or system in order to become familiar with its characteristics and features – an essential prerequisite to implementing improvements. The specific facts depend upon the nature of the system and the terms of reference, but generally they will include details relating to the following factors:

Operational data
This includes details relating to the number and grades of personnel engaged in the various activities; the number and type of machines in use for specific operations; the different types of forms and stationery in use and other operating supplies; the nature and volume of the various activities, the time taken to perform them and their volume and frequency. It also includes details of bottlenecks and delays in the system as well as any other strengths and weaknesses. Operational data also includes the costs of operating the current system or method with regard to the use of resources. Operating costs include staff and managerial salaries; electricity for heating and the supply of power to machines; machine and building maintenance and insurance costs; the cost of operating supplies; inter-department service costs and computer bureau charges, depreciation of machines and buildings, etc.

Organisational data
This type of data relates to the number of personnel engaged on each activity, their job titles, superior/subordinate relationships and the span of control of the various supervisors (the number of staff under their direct control).

This type of data relates to the O in O & M which indicates that the analysts must not only consider work simplification and methods changes but must also look to the nature of the organisation structure in the search for improvements. Organisations often become unbalanced through the passing of time due to the many changes to procedures and methods causing under or over staffing and spans of control which are either too great or too small for the current circumstances.

Communication analysis
Identifying the communication pattern within a business is of extreme importance, as efficient lines of communication and communication techniques are essential for the effective functioning of business operations. It is often necessary, therefore, to analyse the lines of communication within a system and between related systems, in order to be aware of the pattern of communications between personnel in the same department or system and between other departments and systems. The facts obtained from the analysis may indicate the need for on-line computer terminals, electronic mail, access to a database, distributed processing for inter-communication between computers and random enquiry facilities, etc.

Company policy matters
When developing systems it is essential to be aware of the different policies which exist and the manner in which they may relate to the systems. Personnel policy, for example, embraces matters relating to long-service increments and annual salary increases which relate to the payroll system; a sales system includes details relating to the policy of applying discounts in relation to sales values; the credit limit and credit period allowed to customers which varies according to customer classification – whether wholesale or retail, etc; and the policy regarding the conditions for determining delivery charges which is often based on the value of sales.

Data analysis
This is establishing the nature of the data used in the business, the users and its purpose.

METHODS OF COLLECTING FACTS

The collection of facts, whether for work simplification or with a view to computerising a system, must be done methodically to avoid overlooking those of importance. This may be facilitated by using a pre-prepared check list enabling details to be obtained relating to factors of extreme importance to the study being undertaken. The check list is based on a framework of fundamental questions, the first of which is *what* is done? This requires a definition of the activities performed which may be, for instance, the calculation of sales values for goods despatched to customers which are recorded on invoices, the values of which are posted to the customer's account in the sales ledger.

This is then followed by the question *why* is it done? If the answer to the question 'why is it done?' does not imply a positive purpose then this is a case for discontinuance. If the response indicates that it serves a useful purpose then additional questions may be asked as follows:

- *how* is it done?
- *who* does it?
- *where* is it done?
- *when* is it done?

The method
How is it done? Details are required of the methods used to perform the activities including the forms and machines and equipment used. This may include details of word processors, reprographic processes; electronic typewriters; microcomputers; use of computer software; desktop calculators, pocket calculators; filing and collating equipment, etc.

Personnel
Who does it? Details of the personnel performing the activities are required, including job grades; job descriptions; the number of personnel engaged on the various activities – both full-time and part-time; whether male or female and the skills required to perform the activities.

Location
Where is it done? Details relating to where activities are performed including which branch works, office or warehouse, and whether at the head office, with a centralised computer installation, or performed locally at each operating unit by means of distributed processing using a local or wide area network.

Time/sequence
When is it done? This question can relate either to the time period – e.g. daily, weekly, monthly, annually or bi-annually or the sequence in which the activity is performed, e.g. before or after an event or activity. Sequence is of particular importance as it provides the basis

of preparing procedure charts depicting the logical order in which activities are performed.

It has already been intimated that a check-list aids the collection of facts. In addition a number of recognised techniques are used for the purpose, including interviewing, observation, questionnaires and inspection.

Interviewing
Interviewing is a method of collecting facts from the personnel concerned with the system under discussion. Interviewing may be aided by means of a check-list as previously discussed. An interviewer should apply a number of important principles during the course of conducting interviews: i.e. the need to arrange interviews well in advance, allowing the interviewee sufficient time to make arrangements to cover work commitments; clearly stating the objectives and purpose of the interview to avoid any misconceptions; encouraging the interviewee to volunteer facts rather than having to ask leading questions; listening carefully to the interviewee as facts are more readily obtained in this way than by direct questioning. Finally, technical terms should be avoided unless they have been previously explained or they are already understood by the interviewee.

Observation
Facts may be obtained by observing the processing of forms; the operation and utilisation of machines and equipment; the communications occuring between individual personnel and working groups; the frequency of referring to files; the state of the files and the frequency and distance of movement of forms and personnel between work stations; the time spent on the various activities and the extent of delays and interruptions. This may be supplemented by the technique of activity sampling. Observing various aspects of a systems operation and use of resources may also be used to verify the facts collected during interviews.

Questionnaires
A questionnaire is a type of check list except that it may be given to an interviewee for completion without an interviewer being present – however, some questionnaires, e.g. for market research, are compiled by asking interviewees questions and the researchers completing the forms. Questions should be asked in a simple way to avoid any misunderstanding and should be asked in a logical

sequence to enable their significance to be more easily understood. Questions which suggest an answer, i.e. leading questions, should never be used as this can cause facts to be hypothetical rather than factual.

Inspection

Facts may be collected by inspecting various elements of a system, such as inspecting documents to assess the type of characters they contain such as alphabetic or numeric, and the size of fields as a basis for the possible redesign of input documents and output reports. The structure of any coding system in use should be scrutinised as they often need restructuring when developing new or amended systems, particularly if they are to be computerised. In this instance it may be necessary to incorporate self-checking code numbers such as that provided by the technique of check-digits.

Verify the facts

It is essential to verify that the facts obtained by the various techniques outlined above are factual and representative of the real situation. For this reason it is necessary to appraise the facts. Facts collected from an interview may be verified by asking the same questions of another person in the same operating area. The responses obtained may then be compared and any substantial differences subjected to further verification by the application of alternative methods such as observation or inspection or by restructuring questions asked of the original interviewee. Major differences can be subjected to further discussion.

DATA ANALYSIS

Information processing systems are concerned with converting transaction data into meaningful information. It is therefore imperative to investigate and analyse the data that exists, or that which will be required to exist, in an organisation. The analysis may be carried out in the normal investigatory manner on the basis of the following check list.

- *what* is the nature of the data?
- *what* purpose does it serve?
- *what* benefits does it provide?
- *what* would be the effect of not using the data?
- *what* is the structure of the data?

- *what* other data is it related to?
- *which* system uses the data?
- *when* is the data used?
- *how* is the data originated?
- *where* is the data originated?

This analysis will highlight data that does not serve any useful purpose and identify duplicated data. It is important to be aware of data of an inter-functional nature, i.e. data which flows between related systems, to ensure it is not eliminated even though it is not used specifically in the particular system under consideration. Data is a primary business resource which, after processing, produces an output of information which may be printed on routine business documents such as invoices or payslips or management operating reports – all for the purpose of effective administration and management control, ensuring a business runs smoothly and attains the planned level of profitability and other defined objectives. The analysis of data facilitates the construction of a data dictionary as a preliminary to the implementation of a computerised database. The dictionary is, in effect, a catalogue which specifies each data element and indicates which files and systems it applies to.

DOCUMENT ANALYSIS

'X' chart
This type of chart is also known as a 'grid' chart as it takes the form of a grid construction or matrix. It is used to define the relationship of the various documents in a procedure or system. The chart clearly displays the documents containing similar data elements which aids the redesign of forms to eliminate duplication, either by combining documents or eliminating those which can be incorporated into others.

The chart is called an 'X' chart as the letter 'X' is entered into specific columns of the matrix or grid to record specific entities as outlined in the specimen shown in Fig. 4.1.

Document analysis form-input
This type of form allows the contents of source documents to be analysed in a logical manner to provide the details required for the subsequent design of inputs to be processed by the system. Typical details contained in the analysis form are:

1 Identification of the document including the form number and

Data elements \ *Document*	*Holiday booking form*	*Accommodation file*	*Customer file*	*Confirmation of booking*
Booking reference	✖	✖	✖	✖
Customer name and address	✖	✖	✖	✖
Telephone number	✖		✖	
Date of booking	✖		✖	
Holiday reference	✖			
Departure date	✖	✖	✖	✖
Departure airport	✖		✖	✖
Arrival airport	✖			✖
Number of nights	✖	✖	✖	
Hotel name or tour name	✖	✖	✖	
Meal plan	✖	✖		
Number of people	✖	✖	✖	
Room grade	✖	✖	✖	
Unit price	✖	✖	✖	✖
Total price	✖		✖	✖
Deposit paid	✖		✖	✖
Balance outstanding			✖	
Single supplement	✖	✖		
Date booking confirmed		✖	✖	✖
Date booking cancelled		✖	✖	
Travel insurance	✖		✖	
Date hotel vouchers and airline tickets issued			✖	
Details of itinerary				✖
Name and address of tour operator				✖
Name and address of travel agent				✖
Invoice number			✖	✖

FIG. 4.1 *X chart: tour operator documentation and records*

title.

2 Purpose of the document.

3 Point of origination.

4 The elements of data contained in the document.

5 Analysis of each data element:

a description of each field

b sequence of fields

c pre-printed fields
d computed fields
e fields which may be required but are not currently in existence
f type of character, alpha, numeric or alphameric (mixture of both types)
g size of fields, i.e. number of characters, maximum, average and minimum size
h classification of field, i.e. fixed or variable length
6 Volume details:
  a maximum and average number of source documents
  b seasonal variations in volume
  c projected increase/decrease in volume
7 Frequency of compilation.
8 Files affected by the document.

The form should be prepared for every document in the existing system.

Document analysis form-output
This type of analysis form aids the collection of details relating to the information produced by the current system as a guide to designing the requirements of the proposed system.
    Typical details contained in the analysis form are:

1 Identification of the document including the form number and title.
2 Distribution of the document (persons, sections, departments).
3 The use made of the document by each recipient.
4 Frequency of compilation.
5 Elements of data including:
  a control key,
  b elements of data which are computed as opposed to being input from the source document or from a file
  c source of each element of data
  d maximum, average and minimum size of each element
6 Volume of documents:
  a maximum and average number
  b maximum and average number of lines on each document
  c future trends of volume anticipated
7 Format:
  a layout of the document
  b data which is preprinted
  c data produced by the system.

It will be necessary to determine which data elements can be eliminated and which new elements need to be incorporated to suit the current information needs of the business.

Output analysis chart
This chart is used for recording the source of data contained in reports. Output documents are listed down the left-hand side of the chart. Information fields contained in reports are listed along the top of the chart. The type of character contained in files is classified as follows:

N   = Numeric
A   = Alphabetic
A/N Alpha/numeric

Information fields derived from records are indicated by the designation R, and those obtained from source documents by S. Fields which are originated by computation are designated C. Field marked R must be contained in master records and those marked S must be contained in source documents.

FILE ANALYSIS FORM

This analysis form is used for the purpose of defining the construction of files and typically contains the details outlined below:

1 Identification:
  a file name
  b system (application)
2 Purpose
3 Type of record
4 Size of record-maximum, average and minimum size in terms of characters,
5 Size of file:
  a volume of records on the file-maximum, average and minimum number,
  b file activity (hit rate), i.e. maximum and average transaction volumes affecting the file.
  c anticipated future size of file, i.e. number of records,
  d anticipated future volumes of transactions affecting the file,
  e effect of seasonal variations on file processing load.
6 File organisation:
  a control key,

b sequence of records,
c method of accessing records.

The following chapter deals with recording facts including the construction of procedure charts prior to the development of improved systems or methods.

SUMMARY OF KEY POINTS

- The O & M approach to systems development commences with terms of reference specifying the area and boundaries of the assignment.
- A preliminary survey is carried out for the purpose of identifying the nature of the system, method or procedure under review.
- Collecting facts is an important activity performed for the purpose of obtaining a knowledge of the current system prior to making an attempt to improve the existing situation.
- Facts are required relating to the manner in which activities are organised, operational details, details of existing communication facilities and networks and matters relating to company policy.
- A number of methods are used for collecting facts.
- Primary questions to ask for obtaining facts are:
  why is it done?
  how is it done?
  who does it?
  where is it done?
  when is it done?
- Facts must be verified.
- Data analysis is concerned with determining the nature and purpose of data, the benefits derived from its use, its structure, where it is originated and so on.
- Various techniques are used for analysing documents such as an 'x' chart and document analysis forms.

SELF-TEST QUESTIONS

1 O & M analysis is concerned with improving or simplifying systems, procedures, methods and working practices by the most suitable means. How does this differ from the work of systems

analysts?

2 What is the purpose of terms of reference?

3 Why is a preliminary survey carried out?

4 O & M analysts need to possess a number of important attributes. List what you consider to be such attributes.

5 Analysts must never impose a system on operating departments. Why is this?

6 What type of facts are needed when conducting systems investigations?

7 What primary questions may be asked when collecting facts?

8 What methods may be used for collecting facts?

9 How would you verify facts previously collected?

10 During data analysis what type of facts would you obtain?

11 What purpose does data analysis serve?

12 What method would you adopt to define relationships between documents in a system?

13 How would you analyse documents?

14 What information would you collect relating to files?

FURTHER READING

Organisation and Methods, 2nd edition, R. G. Anderson, M & E Handbook/Pitman Publishing, London, 1980.
Provides a broad and detailed coverage of the subject.

CHAPTER 5

The O & M Approach to Systems Development – 2

LEARNING OBJECTIVES

The objective of this chapter is to introduce various techniques used by O & M analysts for the recording of facts. Such techniques include the use of procedure narratives to describe systems or procedures; procedure charts for detailing facts contained in procedure narratives symbolically by means of ASME symbols; and the use of procedure maps. Of extreme importance are the factors to consider for simplifying procedures and methods and the need to develop alternative solutions to problems. The need to present recommendations and their implementation and follow-up is also stated.

RECORDING TECHNIQUES

Having collected facts relevant to the current system it is necessary to marshal them into a logical construction representative of the events and activities occuring in the physical system. A number of recording techniques can be used depending on the type of facts to be recorded. These include:

a procedure narrative
b procedure chart
c procedure map
d activity chart
e organisation chart

PROCEDURE NARRATIVE

A procedure narrative is a written description of a procedure detailing the activities performed and the sequence in which they are executed. It is used to complement a procedure chart. A procedure chart may be constructed from the details contained in the narrative which should be written in simple unambiguous terms using verbs to describe primary activities, e.g. record, sort, check, post, calculate, collate and print, etc. The narrative should be well-structured, providing cross references to procedure charts and other analysis documents. A procedure narrative should typically be based on the framework outlined below, which identifies a number of aspects relating to a payroll system:

a identify the procedure: Payroll
b purpose and objectives of the procedure: To compute employees' wages accurately by 5 pm, Thursday evening
c policy matters relating to the procedure: Long service and merit awards
d legislative aspects: PAYE and NHI deductions
e type and sequence of processing activities
f departments involved with the procedure
g forms used: Payslips
h reports produced: Payroll
i machines and equipment used
j files used: Payroll file

Procedure narrative: payroll procedure
A wages clerk RECEIVES transaction data in the form of employees' clock cards containing details of the hours each employee has been in attendance at his place of work. The clerk places the clock cards in an in-tray. The clock cards are then VALIDATED to ensure the data is accurate and conforms to normal values, e.g. the hours worked are not abnormal. Any hours in excess of 40 could be construed as being abnormal unless supported by an overtime authorisation note. The clerk then RETRIEVES the hourly rate applicable to each employee from a rates file. The clerk then COMPUTES the gross earnings for each employee by the simple process of multiplying the hours worked by the hourly rate. The clerk then RETRIEVES details of each employee from a payroll file. The details include the tax code and National Health insurance contribution rate; other deductions such as savings, tax paid and earnings to date and National Health insurance contributions to date. The clerk then COMPUTES the tax payable to date by adding the current gross wages to the gross wages to date, up to the previous week. The difference between the tax payable to date and the tax previously paid is either a refund or deduction for the current week depending upon the level of gross wages earned or whether the employee was

absent. The clerk then RECORDS the computations onto a payroll and pay advice slip which informs the employee of his earnings, tax and other deductions for the current week. The clerk then SENDS the payroll to the accounting department for recording in the books of account. The payroll is also referred to by internal auditors. The clerk then WRITES bank transfer slips recording the amount of net wages to be credited to each employee's bank account. The transfer slips are then POSTED to the bank and the pay advice slips are SENT to the respective departments for distribution to the employees.

Analysis of payroll procedure
Prior to preparing a procedure chart it is necessary to read through the procedure narrative outlined above in order to summarise the various aspects of the procedure. This includes an analysis of the source document(s) providing input data, the processing activities performed on the data, the files used during processing and the information retrieved from them and the reports and documents produced. The summary is outlined below:

Purpose and objectives: To compute accurately employees' earnings, tax and other deductions.

Type of operation

RECEIVE employee clock cards containing hours worked	operation
PLACE clock cards in in-tray	delay
VALIDATE hours worked	inspection
RETURN invalid clock cards to employee's department	transportation
RETRIEVE hourly rate from rates file	operation
COMPUTE gross wages	operation
RETRIEVE employee details of gross wages and tax deducted, etc. from payroll file	operation
RECORD computations on payroll and pay advice slips	operation
SEND payroll to accounting department	transportation
WRITE bank transfer slips	operation
POST bank transfer slips to the bank	transportation
SEND pay advice slips to respective departments	transportation

Forms used:
Clock card recording attended hours
Input to the procedure

Reports/schedules produced:
Payroll
Output from the procedure

Documents produced:
Pay advice slip
Output from the procedure

Files used:
   a Rates file which contains employee hourly rates of pay
   b Payroll file containing details of employee number, employee
      name, department, tax code, NHI number and rate, taxable
      gross to date, tax to date, taxable gross previous employment,
      tax previous employment, holiday credit to date, total NHI
      contributions to date, fixed deduction, employee bank details.

It is now possible to convert the procedure narrative to a procedure
chart (see Fig. 5.1) based on the above summary using the appropriate symbols for the construction of procedure charts outlined in Fig.
5.2.

PROCEDURE CHARTS

Details of procedures are normally recorded on procedure charts
from facts contained in a procedure narrative, as previously stated.
Activities are recorded by means of symbols indicating the different
types of activity, e.g. an operation, which is a primary processing
operation as distinct from an inspection activity. Charts have the
advantage of providing a visual impact of the characteristics and
features of the procedure as they are presented pictorially. Procedure
charts also enable facts to be assembled into a logical sequence. It is at
this juncture that facts may be further verified by requesting the
operating staff to check the charts for completeness, duplication of
activities, inputs or outputs and any inaccuracies. The verification of
facts is important as it is necessary to establish their reliability before
embarking on system improvements.

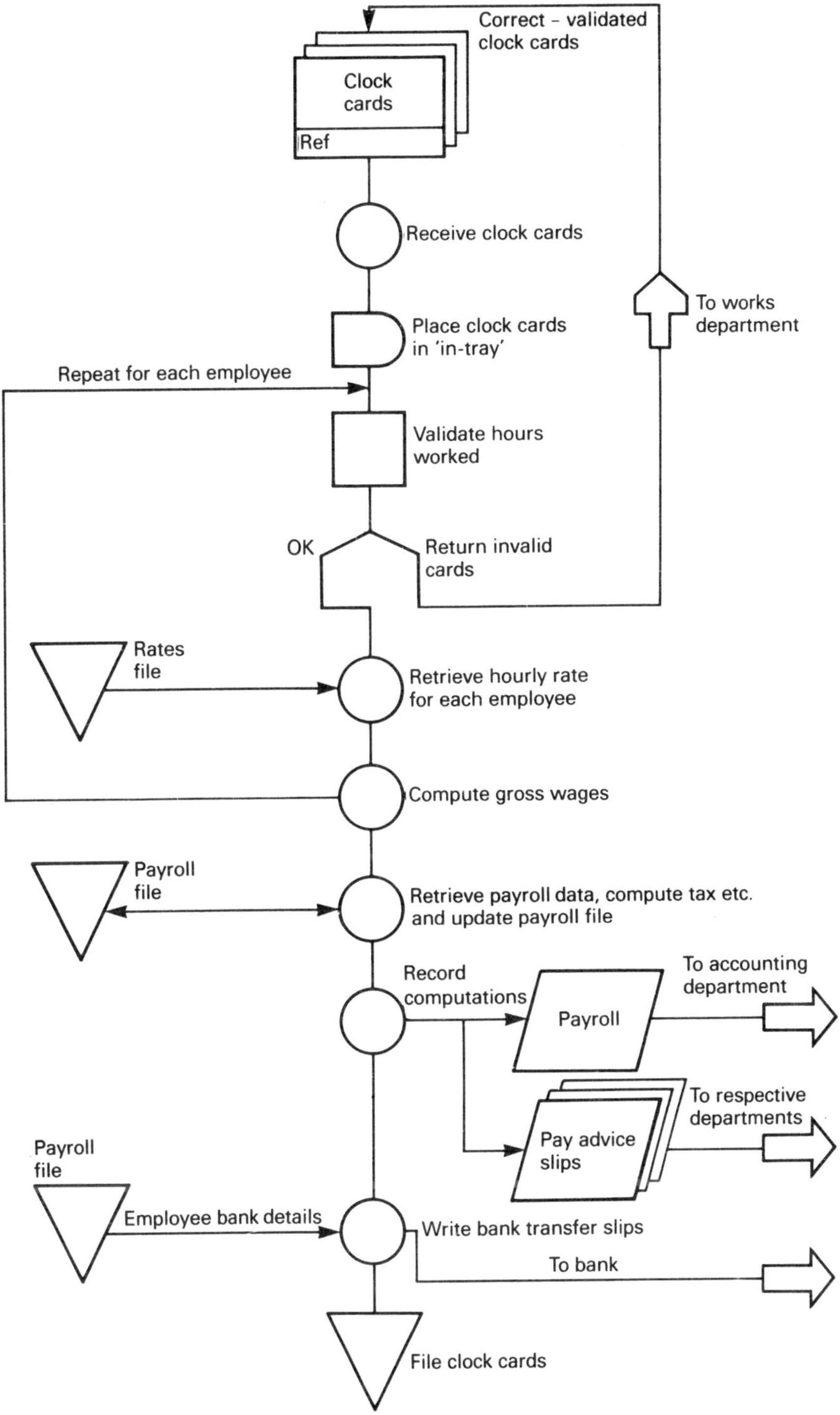

FIG. 5.1   *Procedure chart: payroll procedure*

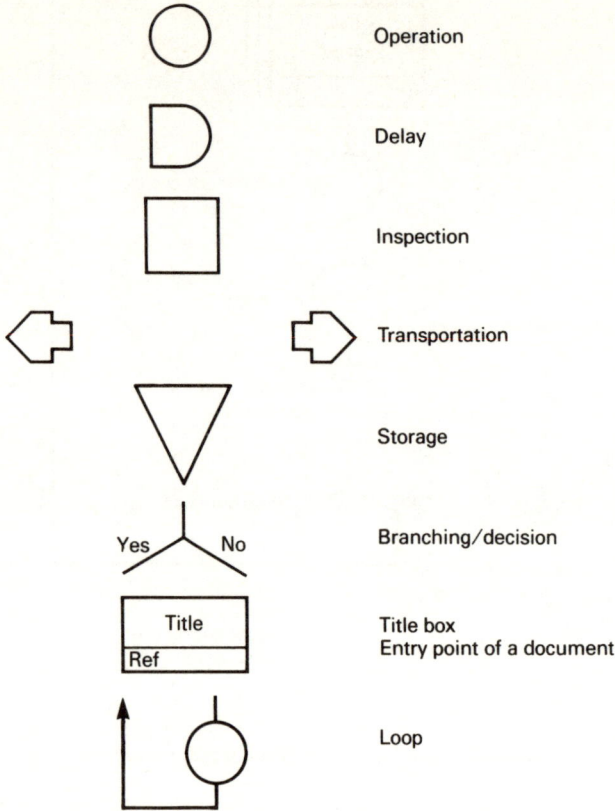

◯	Operation
⌓	Delay
▢	Inspection
⇦ ⇨	Transportation
▽	Storage
Yes ⟋⟍ No	Branching/decision
Title / Ref	Title box / Entry point of a document
↑⟲	Loop

FIG. 5.2   *ASME symbols for the construction of procedure charts*

Symbols for the construction of procedure charts

Procedure charts are constructed from five basic symbols, originated by the American Society of Mechanical Engineers. They are referred to as ASME symbols, *see* Fig. 5.2.

A typical procedure chart, based on these symbols, is illustrated in Fig. 5.1. The primary activities represented by the various symbols are:

Operation
This is a primary processing activity or action, e.g. recording transaction data on an attendance record.

Delay
This is for the purpose of recording a delay in a procedure when immediate action is not possible. This is applicable when a procedure

is halted while waiting for data to be processed, or delays caused by the correction of errors on transaction documents. When documents are not processed immediately they are temporarily placed in an 'in tray', which is a delay situation often caused by haphazard document flows in the system.

Inspection
This is an activity concerned with verifying specific details of transactions such as checking the accuracy of a calculation, or checking that details on related documents are compatible, e.g. ensuring that the quantity of goods recorded on a delivery note is compatible with the quantity invoiced.

Transportation
The transportation symbol is used to illustrate movement in a procedure, e.g. when a document is transferred from one work station to another.

Storage
The storage activity may be referred to as 'filing', as when documents are filed after being dealt with during the procedural activities or when ledger cards are replaced after being referred to for obtaining information or after being updated.

Other types of symbol
Additional symbols are also illustrated in Fig. 5.2. These are:

Branching
This symbol provides for branching to alternative parts of a procedure as a result of various conditions which arise. In a stock control system, for instance, a branch would be necessary to a stock re-ordering sub-routine if an item of stock had reached the re-order level. Otherwise the normal routine is carried out. Branching is executed after testing for a defined condition on the basis of branching if the condition exists and not branching if the condition does not exist.

Title box
Indicates the point at which a document enters a procedure. The symbol normally has the title of the document shown in the upper section and a reference number in the lower section of the title box.

Repeat or loop
Used to indicate a loop in a procedure to repeat a sequence of activities on different transactions of the same type.

Advantages of procedure charts
Procedure charts are valuable for the analysis and design of clerical and computer oriented systems as they represent a procedure or system in an easily understandable manner. They can be constructed very quickly once the facts are available and have a greater impact than written details of a procedure although both are complementary. They clearly illustrate the point where documents are introduced into a procedure and the activities performed on them. In addition, the relationships which exist in a procedure are easily identified by means of relational flow lines. An appreciation is quickly obtained of the features of a system and the whole of a procedure can be observed at once, simplifying the detection of omissions and duplicated activities. Excessive delays are also easily identified.

PROCEDURE MAP

A procedure map, sometimes referred to as a **forms specimen chart**, maps, or displays, the forms used in a procedure. Most procedures are concerned with form processing and a procedure map allows duplicated data or forms to be easily observed as a preliminary to their elimination. The sequence in which data flows from one form to another is also displayed. Specimen forms containing specimen entries are pasted to a backing sheet and joined together by coloured tapes to show relationships between them.

DEVELOPMENT OF ALTERNATIVE METHODS AND PROCEDURES

The O & M analyst must at this juncture draw on his or her skill and experience for the process of evolving more efficient methods of carrying out activities, or developing simplified procedures, capable of achieving the specified purpose and objectives more effectively. The analyst should also develop procedures which eliminate the weaknesses and build on the strengths of the current system. If the circumstances warrant the use of a computer to replace manual operations then the analyst must make sure that the proposed system is not merely an automated version of the current system without improvements. It is essential that the proposed system contains features superior to the current system. It is also essential to make sure the procedure or system under consideration does in fact have a positive and useful part to play in the administration of the business. Some procedures remain in existence long after their useful purpose has disappeared. This occurs due to piecemeal, ad hoc, fire alarm changes to procedures to contend with imminent changes in business circumstances. In such cases one procedure may be changed but a related procedure which is no longer necessary remains in existence because someone failed to give an instruction to dispense with it.

Changes to procedures may require redesigning forms, as existing forms may not contain data required by current administrative activities. Some forms may be eliminated and others may be combined. Work simplification may be the answer in some instances, requiring forms to be simplified when they are too complex for their purpose. In other instances it may be appropriate to simplify operations by separating some tasks into several. This may be the action needed to remove bottlenecks. The resequencing of operations may reduce the time taken to perform them, increasing the level of productivity as a result.

Other improvements may be obtained by modifying the office layout or resiting filing cabinets to make them more accessible. Both instances may have the effect of eliminating unnecessary movement of staff. Many different methods changes can be selected depending upon the needs of the procedure under development. Typing productivity may be improved by replacing old mechanical type-writers by electronic models and where large volumes of standard letters of letter quality are required then word processors may be brought in. In instances when frequent communications occur between staff in dispersed offices then valuable time may be saved by the introduction of electronic mail, eliminating the frustration of making repeated telephone calls when people are out of the office. All that is necessary is to transmit a message which is then stored electronically on the addressees' microcomputer. A response is obtained in a similar way when the person returns to the office. Electronic filing and retrieval systems may also increase productivity by saving valuable time in searching for information in document files. The introduction of databases will allow systems to be integrated and eliminate conflicting information that can occur when separate functional files containing common information are not updated at the same time.

Modern work stations allow staff to perform many different activities simply by switching between different routines for word processing, electronic mail, data processing, accessing a database and the use of spreadsheets with graphics. In other instances systems may be improved by recruiting the right calibre of personnel. This is particularly relevant during this hi-tech era as many clerical activities involving the recording of entries on documents and forms by hand is superseded by the need for keyboard skills for entering data directly into a computer or for encoding data to magnetic media prior to processing by computer.

PRESENTING RECOMMENDATIONS

This stage of system development is very important for the ultimate acceptance of recommendations. The analyst must be well prepared to demonstrate and discuss the merit of his or her recommendations, indicating which course of action would create the greatest benefits and productivity improvements. In most cases the proposals must be seen to be cost effective – as discussed in Chapter 1. A written report may be used for the formal presentation of recommendations, but this should be complemented by the personal touch, as often the personality of the analyst and his or her ability to demonstrate new innovations may be the deciding factor in their acceptance.

IMPLEMENTING RECOMMENDATIONS

When recommendations have been accepted the O & M analyst may suggest to the user department how best to implement the relevant changes. It may be decided that the analyst is the best person to carry out the task due to his or her detailed knowledge of the proposals or he or she may be invited to supervise the operating department staff during implementation.

It is important to plan each stage of implementation and major changes may require the preparation of a time schedule to control the situation. Some projects may require detailed planning as it may be necessary to consider ordering machines and equipment well in advance to ensure they are available for operational requirements by a stated date; the lead time required for the printing of new forms must also be taken into account; the time to commence modifying the office layout and the installation of new furniture and filing equipment should also be assessed. If the changes to be implemented are uncomplicated, such as replacing a manual typewriter with an electronic model or a word processor, or the introduction of a new form then, providing advance training has been carried out, the changeover may be done immediately. If however the proposals are

to affect dispersed offices in an organisation and involve the installation of terminals, for instance, then restricting the implementation
to one operating unit would be advisable in order to test and obtain
operational experience of the modified operations and identify and
resolve problems before implementing the changes on a wider basis.
If the change is to a large computer installation then parallel operation of the current and proposed system is imperative as a fail safe
procedure. It must be certain that the new system is achieving
accurate results free of problems before the previous system is
dispensed with.

FOLLOW-UP

After the new procedure or method has been implemented it is
necessary for the O & M analyst to maintain a watching brief to
ensure the operating performance is in accordance with expectations.
This is the time when problems are resolved and to ensure personnel
are adhering to the procedure outlined in the procedure manual.
Personnel may require further instruction or additional explanations
so that they become more conversant with the new situation and fully
understand operational requirements.

SYSTEM MAINTENANCE

This activity is a means of implementing change dynamically by
recognising when a procedure or method has outlived its useful
purpose in its present form. Of course it may be unnecessary to
analyse the system in such great depth for subsequent changes,
providing the current situation is well understood.

SUMMARY OF KEY POINTS

- Having collected facts as outlined in the previous chapter
  it is necessary to marshal them into a logical order for
  detailed examination.
- Procedure narratives are written descriptions of
  procedures.
- Procedure charts are pictorial representations of
  procedures prepared from procedure narratives.
- Procedure charts are constructed using ASME symbols.
- ASME symbols are used for various classes of activity
  including Operation, Inspection, Delay, Transportation,

and Storage.
- Symbols are used used to represent other system features including branching, title boxes, repeat or loop.
- A procedure map displays forms used in a procedure.
- Simplified procedures are developed for achieving the specified purpose and objectives.
- Procedures should be developed which eliminate the weaknesses and build on the strengths of the current system.
- Changes to procedures may require the redesign of forms, modifications to office layout, reallocation of activities to personnel or changes in the way in which processes are performed – the method.
- Recommendations must be presented to management relating to proposed changes.
- When recommendations have been accepted they must be implemented.
- After implementation it is necessary to monitor the system for the purpose of detecting problems and for ensuring the desired level of performance is attained.
- Systems must be maintained so that they are suitable for current needs.

SELF-TEST QUESTIONS
1 What is the nature and purpose of a procedure narrative?
2 What is a procedure chart, how is it constructed and what is its relationship to a procedure narrative?
3 Define the nature and purpose of ASME symbols.
4 What is the purpose of a procedure map?
5 What should an O & M analyst have in mind when developing alternative methods and procedures?
6 How would you present recommendations to management?
7 What is the purpose of 'follow-up'?
8 Why is it necessary to maintain systems?

FURTHER READING

As for Chapter 4.

Organisation and Methods, Second Edition, R. G. Anderson, M & E Handbook/Pitman, London, 1980. Provides a broad and detailed coverage of the subject.

CHAPTER 6
Soft Systems Methodology (SSM)

This chapter aims to define the meaning of the technique of soft systems methodology – it addresses human activity and differs from conventional and structured systems methodology, which are sometimes classified as 'hard system' techniques. SSM is concerned with problem situations and takes action to improve the problem situation. It is important to make a clear distinction between real world and systems thinking about the real world. The point to be aware of is that 'system' is an intellectual construct, not a real world entity. The technique encourages the system developer to assess a particular system, department, office or other operational location in the context of the business as a whole, providing a 'total' systems approach.

THE HUMAN ACTIVITY SYSTEM

Soft systems addresses human activity which is considered to be at a logically higher level than that of the conduct of physical operations. Soft systems methodology adopts a panoramic view applying the notion of holism which considers that a whole is more than simply a combination of its parts. This differs from conventional and structured systems methodology which are classified, by some writers, as 'hard systems' techniques. SSM in essence finds out about a problem situation and action is taken to improve it. It makes a clear distinction between real world and systems thinking about the real world. So 'system' is an intellectual construct not a real world entity. It encourages the system developer to assess a particular system, department, office or other operational location in the context of the business as a whole. In this way it is made possible to be more purposeful in establishing the needs of the business. It provides a 'total' systems approach rather than a 'piecemeal' approach. Soft systems thinking is attributable to Professor Peter Checkland of the Department of Systems, University of Lancaster and its development and nature are described in his book *Systems Thinking, Systems*

Practice (Wiley, 1981).

The methodology is based on a number of defined stages, which are listed below:

1 The problem situation: unstructured;
2 The problem situation: expressed;
3 Root definitions of relevant systems;
4 Conceptual models;
   a formal system concept
   b Other systems thinking
5 Comparison of 4 with 2
6 Feasible desirable changes
7 Action to improve the problem situation.

Stages 1, 2, 5, 6 and 7 are real-world activities involving people in the problem situation. Stages 3, 4, 4(a) and 4(b) are systems thinking activities which may or may not involve those in the problem situation depending upon circumstances of the study.

STAGE 1 UNSTRUCTURED PROBLEMS

The methodology commences by defining 'unstructured problems'. An unstructured problem may apply, for example, to a situation in which management appreciates that the use of information technology in specific activities and functions would achieve benefits to the business but it is not clear what form this should take – that is the unstructured problem. Such problems arise in the world; we cannot define them as a scientist can define his or her problem in the laboratory.

STAGE 2 STRUCTURING THE PROBLEM – THE RICH PICTURE

The approach to defining the problem situation is to develop what is referred to as a 'rich picture', not of the problem but of the situation in which there is perceived to be a problem. A rich picture may be defined as 'the expression of a problem situation compiled by an investigation, often by examining elements of structure, elements of process and the relation between the two, referred to as the situation climate'.

Before embarking on further details of the nature of a rich picture and before studying a complex rich picture of a manufacturing and marketing organisation, (Fig. 6.3), it is appropriate to introduce the idea of a rich picture by two less complex illustrations. Fig. 6.1

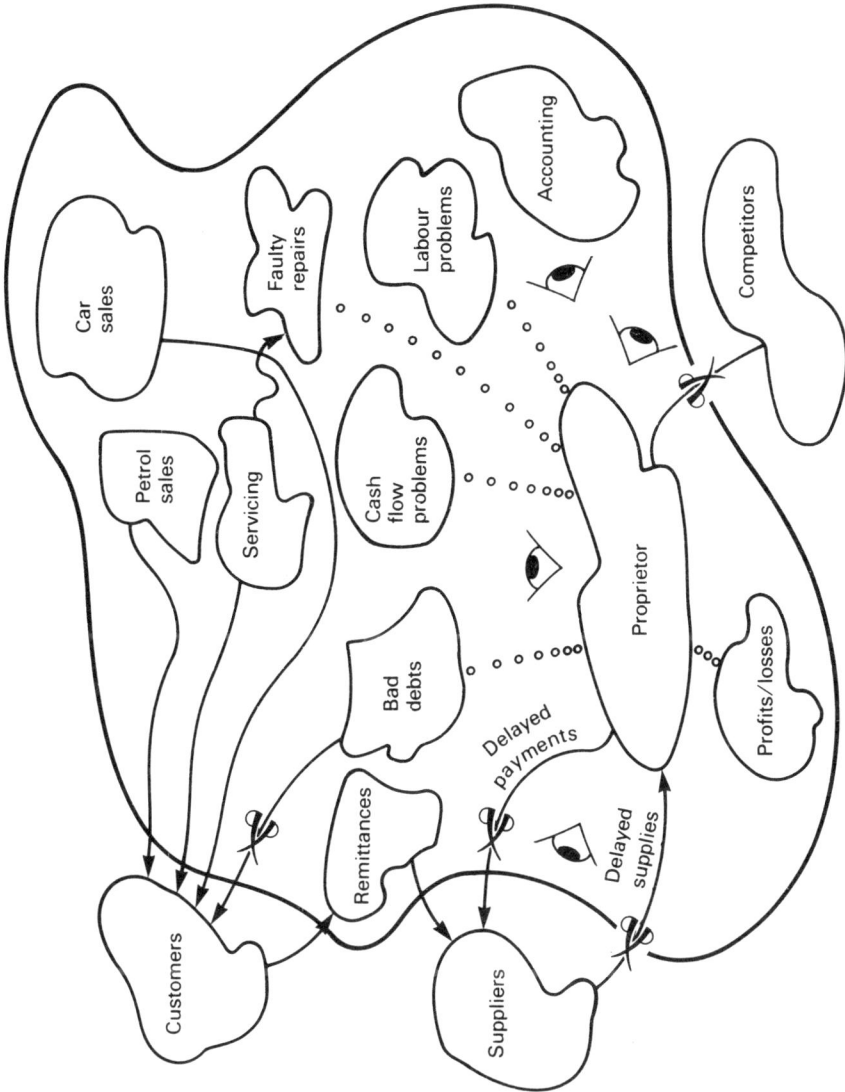

FIG. 6.1   Simple rich picture of a garage business

provides a rich picture of a garage business. The picture provides a situation climate showing elements of process (primary processes), crossed swords to show conflict, matters of concern to the proprietor which are depicted as thought bubbles, an eye indicates matters monitored by the proprietor and relationships are shown by directional arrows. The boundary of the system is shown by a thick line.

Relationships
- customers
- suppliers

Conflict
- competitors
- customer bad debts
- suppliers due to delayed payments from proprietor
- suppliers due to delayed supplies

Monitoring
- suppliers
- garage operations in general
- competitors' actions
- accounting activities

Primary activities
- car sales
- petrol sales
- servicing
- accounting

Matters of concern
- bad debts
- cash flows
- labour problems
- profits/losses

A further illustration of a rich picture is shown in Fig. 6.2 which outlines a tour operator business. The same features are included as shown in the example of the garage business.

Relationships
- customers
- travel agents

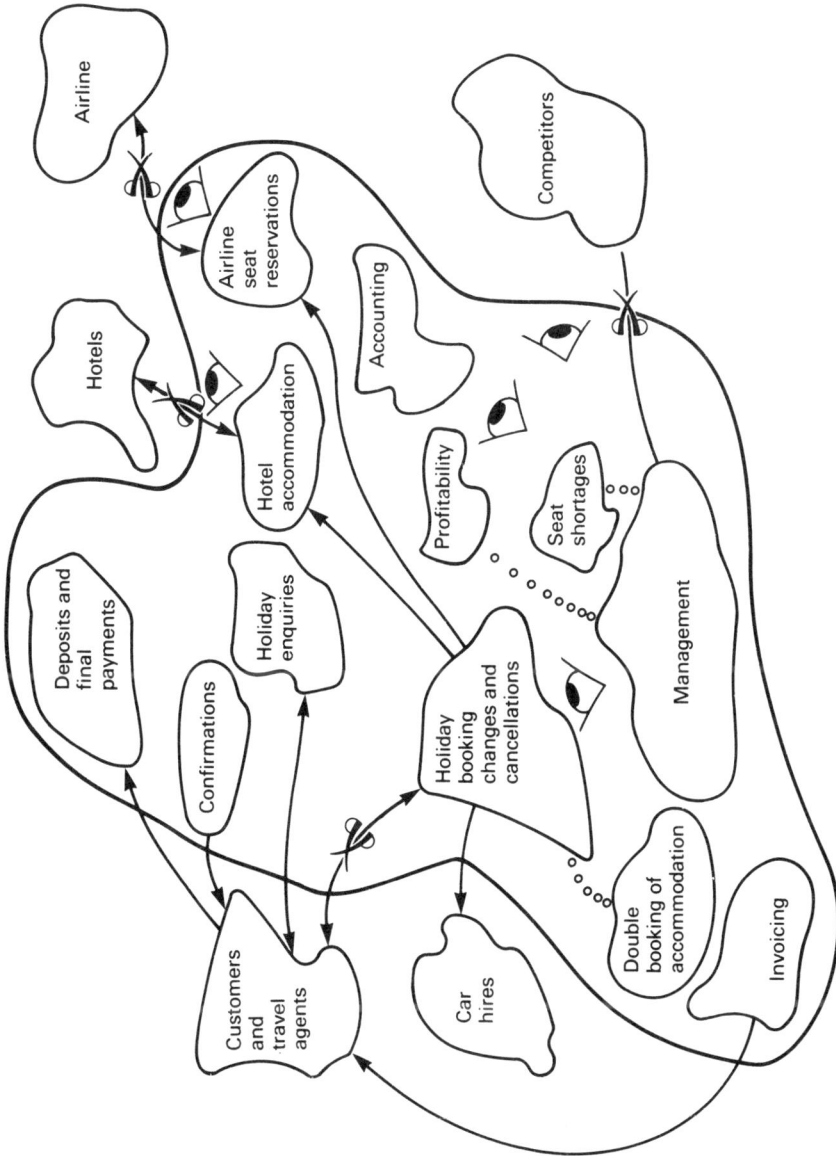

FIG. 6.2.   Rich picture of a tour operator business

- hotels
- airlines
- car hiring companies

Conflict
- competitors causing cut-throat competitive strategies
- hotels due to confused booking accommodation
- airline due to seat shortages/too many reservations
- customers and travel agents due to failure to remit final payment by due date or late changes or cancellations to bookings.

Monitoring
- holiday bookings
- competitors' actions
- hotel accommodation status
- airline seat reservation status
- accounting activities

Primary activities
- holiday enquiries
- holiday bookings, changes and cancellations
- booking hotel accommodation
- aircraft seat reservations
- car hiring
- invoicing
- accounting

Matters of concern
- airline seat shortages
- double booking of accommodation
- profitability

Structure may be analysed from different viewpoints including the pattern of communications, as intimated below; the network of organisational units making up the complete organisation; organisation of records and the structure of personnel. The term 'process' refers to the basic activities within a situation for the transformation of input to output. It includes testing for conditions, processing transactions, monitoring performance and the effects of the output on related parts of the organisation. A rich picture enables a selection to be made of several viewpoints from which to study the problem situation further. It is ideal to obtain a wide range of perceptions of a problem from a wide range of people with roles in the problem situation. In contrast, traditional systems investigations applying 'hard system methodology' tend to give high priority to the goals to be achieved and the preparation of a conceptual model (stage 4 of this methodology) as a preliminary to designing a well-structured system to attain them.

It must be constantly kept in mind that the objective, in this instance, is establishing the information technology requirements of the business. Many administrative departments of a business are structured on the basis of operational sections consisting of groups of specialised activities. Such activities should not, however, be seen as 'closed systems' because they are in fact best viewed as 'open systems', communicating on an inter-departmental or inter-sectional basis. A communication analysis could be usefully applied to establish the existing intercommunication network as a basis for its improvement by the implementation of electronic mail facilities, for instance.

Facts for developing the rich picture are obtained from investigation and other traditional methods of collecting facts such as observation, examination and interviews. A rich picture should illustrate such factors as policy, plans, strategy, management structures, functions, legislative constraints, operational constraints, rules, regulations, competitors, methods, techniques, conditions, customers, stock, areas of conflict, duplicated activities, information flows or whatever facets and features a specific type of business has. The problem situation now begins to take shape. The main purpose of the first two stages is to display the situation so that a range of possible and relevant choices can be revealed including the names of the notional systems of purposeful activity which from the analysis phase seem relevant to the problem.

Rich pictures often display crossed swords to show conflict of interest. An example of this may occur, for instance, when an accountant requires a record to be kept of all transactions so that they may be recorded in the respective accounts. On the other hand storekeepers and factory personnel would prefer to dispense with all paperwork so that they may concentrate on their main physical activities of handling stores items and processing materials to produce the required products for sale. It is obviously necessary in such an instance that a problem exists which must be overcome in the interests of the business as a whole. Matters which concern individuals in a system can be shown by thought bubbles and the monitoring process may be shown graphically by an eye intimating that someone is keeping sight of certain activities. Rich pictures help both the problem owner – e.g. the accountants, and the problem solver, e.g. the systems analyst, to become more acquainted with the problem situation than may otherwise be possible. The point is that such pictures display relationships more easily than can be done in prose.

Figure 6.3 portrays a rich picture of a manufacturing and marketing organisation. It clearly shows the organisational relationships which exist between the various activities and the cause of conflict between them – the crossed sword situation. Conflict exists, for example, between the production function and the employees' participating in its activities. Such conflict is perhaps due to unacceptable working practices in respect of excessive overtime, causing the employees to react by go slow or strike tactics. The production function is also in conflict with the planning and control activity due to production failing to meet scheduled output targets. The production function is also in conflict with the marketing function because of orders creating an unbalanced product mix, which is partly the reason for the conflict which exists with the planning and control activity. The cashier is in conflict with suppliers because of delayed payments to them because of cash flow problems. The cashier also has an eye on customers' accounts assessing those who are bad payers and those who delay payments and are the root cause of the cash flow problems. The management of the business are always thinking of product strategy as a basis for increasing profits and prospective lines of credit to finance operations. They also have their eye on unprofitable orders being accepted by the marketing function. The stock control function thinks about ways to improve the control of stock levels to avoid excessive stocks building up on the one hand and stock shortages on the other. Conflict arises between stock control and the stores personnel who think they handle too many documents, which they consider is not a part of their duties.

STAGE 3 ROOT DEFINITION

Root definitions are intended to indicate the fundamental nature of a selected relevant system (relevant, that is, to bringing about improvement). The definition is a statement of what the system is. A root definition may be described as a concise description of a purposeful 'human activity system' which states the nature of the system and the activities to be performed which are viewed as transformation processes. Root definitions have the status of hypotheses concerning the eventual improvement of the problem situation by means of

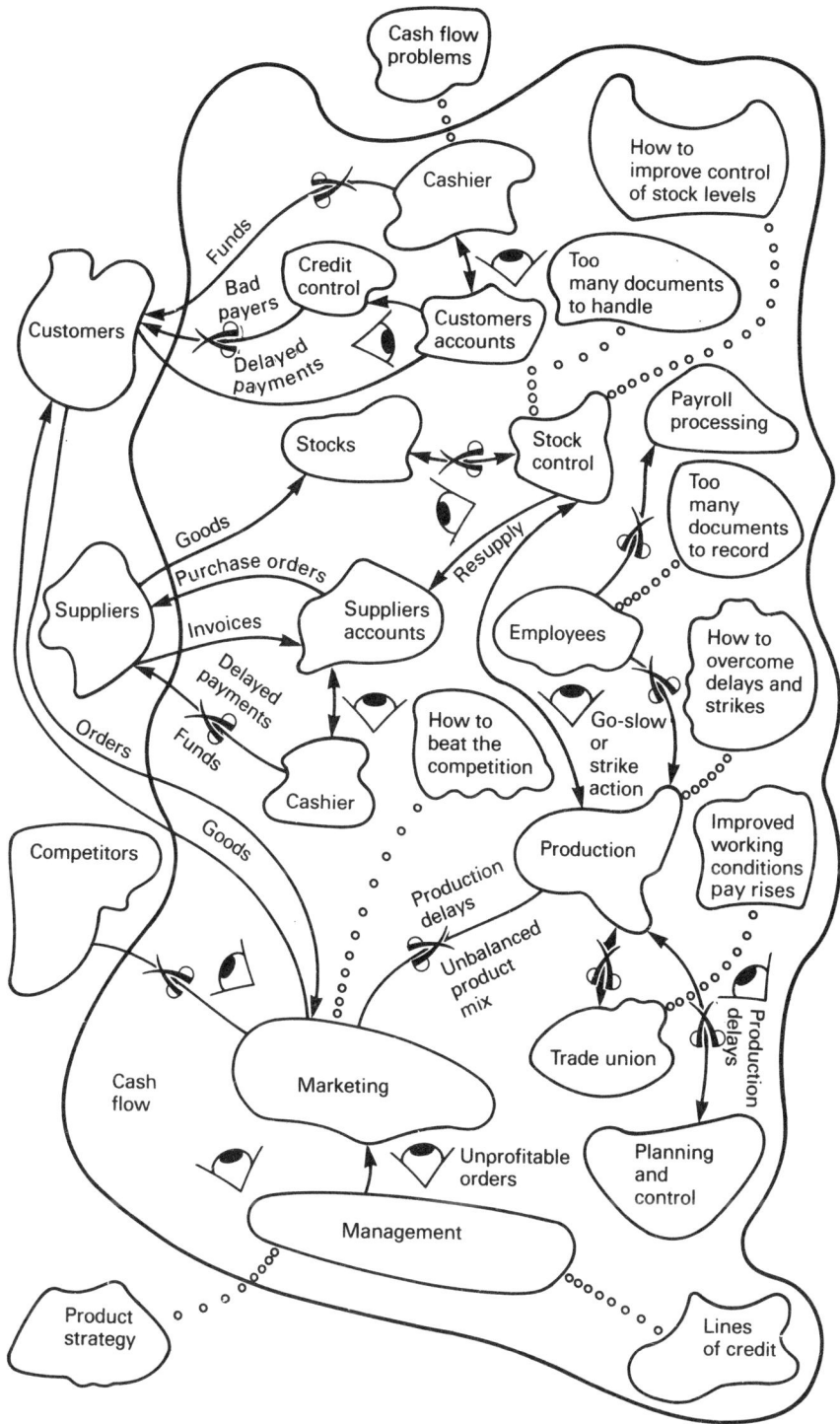

FIG. 6.3 *Rich picture of manufacturing and marketing business*

changes which are both desirable and feasible in the situation in question. How may one define a routine accounting system? It may be defined, for example, as a system for simulating the transactions of the real world – it does so because it represents on paper or magnetic records events which have occurred in the business. A wider definition would be to describe the accounting function in terms of the CATWOE checklist as shown below. CATWOE enables any root definition to be well-formulated.

Customer/client Beneficiary or victim affected by the system's activities.

Actors The agents who carry out or cause to be carried out the main activities of the system, that is its transformations.

Transformation process The means by which defined inputs are transformed into defined outputs. The transformation will include the direct object of the main activity verbs subsequently required to describe the system.

World view/Weltanschauung An outlook, framework or image which makes the root definition meaningful.

Ownership of the system Some agency having a prime concern for the system and the ultimate power to cause the system to cease to exist.

Environmental constraints Features of the system's environment or wider systems which this system takes as given.

The accounting system may be regarded as owned by the accountant (O) and operated by accounting staff (A) for planning, controlling and processing financial accounting transactions (T) relating to customers, suppliers and other entities (C) – and the preparation of final accounts in the form of balance sheets, trading and profit and loss accounts, in the shortest possible time after the end of the accounting period (T). It may be responsible for ensuring that all business transactions are recorded in proper books of account and for safeguarding the assets of the business (E); implementing internal check procedures and the physical control of cash receipts and payments and the maintainence of statutory records relating to wages and salaries and VAT, etc. (W).

STAGE 4 DEVELOPING THE CONCEPTUAL MODEL

This stage requires the construction of a model of the relevant system from the root definition – an accounting system in this instance. The conceptual model is used as a basis for setting out an idealised form of the system in question. It must show the activities which must be performed in order to be identified as the system referred to in the root definition. It can then be used to structure an organised examination of what exists in the real world – differences between model and reality leading to ideas for changes.

The purpose of the conceptual model is thus to condense a rich picture into core activities. It should not reflect who does what, i.e. the individuals performing the various tasks, as the analyst is only concerned with what the human activities fundamentally are – *not* the individuals currently performing them. There may exist square pegs in round holes, of course, which may be one of the problems. Some members of the staff concerned with the operation of a specific system may perform several activities – switching from one to the other, and in such situations it is necessary to pinpoint each activity. It is essential to be aware of what is done rather than who currently does it.

A model may be defined as a structured set of activities which receive a series of inputs and are transformed into specific outputs, a description that fits accounting and data processing human activity systems. The model is an account of the activities which the system must carry out in order to be compatible with the idea stated in the root definition. It is important to realise that the conceptual model does not portray any actual specific system but indicates the activities required in a logical system as stated in the root definition. Its purpose is to generate the debate/comparison as a basis for its improvement. An accounting system is essentially both a transfer system and a transformation system because data is transferred from the various activity locations of the business to the accounting system where the data is transformed into defined outputs. The model must show WHAT activities have to be performed in WHAT sequence. As the model represents a human activity system it will be constructed of verbs structured in logical sequence.

The progression from root definition to conceptual model is of extreme importance. A conceptual model when compared with a so called 'formal system model', a general model of any purposeful activity developed for use in SSM, may reveal inadequacies either in the system itself or in the root definition. It is necessary to ensure that the model specifies levels of performance, related sub-systems, the operating environment and system boundaries.

STAGE 5 COMPARISON OF CONCENPTUAL MODEL WITH THE REAL WORLD

In this stage the problem solver is concerned with advising the problem owner of weaknesses in the real situation as a basis for more detailed study and areas in which change is both advisable or unnecessary. It may be found that an accounting system provides for formal planning and policy making but the system suffers from a lack of continuity as it fails to convert policy statements into action; consequently the system goes out of phase, or out of tune, with requirements. In addition, the real world version of the system may have ineffective feedback causing delay in the reporting of variations in performance to the desired level – this may apply to production or sales volumes achieved – consequently events have become historical before previous situations have become apparent. Delayed feedback causes delayed action to be taken, causing the system to oscillate needlessly. It may even go completely out of control. Such situations may be resolved by more effective control procedures, more timely information flows and more effective management. It is necessary to identify and list the features of the model which are particularly different from the present situation as a basis for implementing changes.

STAGES 6 AND 7 FEASIBLE AND DESIRABLE CHANGES AND THEIR IMPLEMENTATION

The primary purpose of this stage is the definition of changes in the real world which would bring about improvement. Those changes should be arrived at via discussion of possibilities with the personnel in the problem situation. Whatever changes are considered must be feasible, e.g. they must be no more complicated than necessary, they must be acceptable in the culture of the situation and to the problem owner and be cost effective. Changes which may be implemented include such things as changing structures, reorganising activities, creating or modifying information flows, changing span of control and/or functional responsibilities. Other changes may be of a procedural nature relating to the nature of the activities performed involving changes, e.g. to documentation, which may have to be redesigned, or it may be relevant to resequence the flow of work or to add, delete or combine existing activities.

In conclusion, to quote from a paper kindly presented to the author by Professor Peter Checkland, the overall leaving of SSM is outlined below.

After several hundred studies by its originators and by other groups in many countries who have taken it up, the overall leaving from the development of SSM can be briefly summarised in a few propositions, as follows:

1 In SSM 'the system' is not some part of the real world but is the organized process of inquiry itself.
2 The concept 'system' is not a label-word for something in the perceived world, but is an abstract concept which can be used to help make sense of the world.
3 Given its nature as a system of inquiry, the use of SSM has to be participative. The role of the 'expert' in SSM is restricted to helping the people in the situation carry out their own study.
4 Thus users of SSM should not try to create and preserve its status as a body of professional knowledge. They should be trying to give it away to people in problematical situations.

SUMMARY OF KEY POINTS

- SSM addresses human activity.
- SSM is concerned with problem situations and taking action to deal with them.
- A clear distinction should be made between real world and systems thinking about the real world.
- The technique encourages the system developer to assess a system in the context of the business as a whole.
- The methodology is based on a number of defined stages.
- The methodology commences by defining 'unstructured problems', that is, problems which are not clearly defined.
- The approach to defining a problem situation is to develop a 'rich picture' not of the problem but of the situation in which there is perceived to be a problem.
- Root definitions indicate the fundamental nature of a selected relevant system.
- SSM adopts a CATWOE checklist which enables any root definition to be well-formulated.
- The conceptual model is constructed of the relevant system from the root definition.
- A model may be defined as a structured set of activities which receive a series of inputs which are transformed

into outputs.
- The conceptual model is compared with the real world. Feasible and desirable changes are implemented.

SELF-TEST QUESTIONS
1 What is the purpose of SSM methodology?
2 SSM interprets the term 'system' as an intellectual construct not a real world entity. Discuss.
3 What does SSM address?
4 The system developer is encouraged to assess a system in a particular context. What is this context?
5 What is a 'rich picture' and what purpose does it serve?
6 Root definitions are an important aspect of SSM. What is a root definition?
7 What does CATWOE mean?
8 On what basis is a conceptual model constructed?
9 What is a model in the systems context?
10 What is an unstructured problem?
11 What are the stages of SSM?

FURTHER READING

Systems thinking, systems practice, Professor Peter Checkland, Wiley, 1981. A global knowledge of the technique by its founder.

CHAPTER 7

Traditional System Life Cycle Approach to System Development

LEARNING OBJECTIVES

The objective of this chapter is to define the nature of the traditional system life cycle approach to system development, stating its main disadvantage of having a tendency to be technique-oriented too soon. A further objective is to specify the importance of terms of reference and feasibility studies to the effective development of systems. The chapter also indicates aspects to consider if a computer does not already exist in the organisation and the various stages of the system life cycle.

STAGES OF THE SYSTEM LIFE CYCLE

The stages of the traditional system life cycle are very explicit but the approach tends to suffer from an important disadvantage which is that it has a tendency to be technique-oriented too soon. Hardware and software considerations have a tendency to prominence before the logical requirements of a system have been thoroughly analysed. The traditional systems life cycle approach uses the technique of flowcharting, involving the construction of systems flowcharts outlining clerical and computer operations, including computer run charts. Such charts display the logical sequence of processing steps but tend towards thinking in terms of the physical rather than the logical requirements of users. The stages of system life cycle development methodology are discussed below.

TERMS OF REFERENCE

Terms of reference constitute the authority to systems development staff to undertake a feasibility study of a specified system(s). The 'terms' should preferably be in writing to avoid any possible future misinterpretation or ambiguity. Typical contents of the terms of reference include:

Nature of the problem

The nature of the problem must be precisely defined otherwise a good solution to a non-existent problem may be implemented – which, of course, is no solution at all – in fact a different problem to that which existed initially will be generated. The 'grass roots' problem may relate to information flows not serving the current needs of the system or information is available too late for effective decision making and control of business operations.

Boundaries of assignments

It is important that the boundary of an assignment is clearly defined or investigations can needlessly be pursued into the domain of other systems. It is a simple matter to 'stray' into adjoining operational areas because of the close relationships which exist between many sub-systems. If, for instance, the boundary is stipulated as being the 'stock control system' then it should not infiltrate into the purchasing system even though both sub-systems are closely related.

Purpose and objectives

The purpose of a system(s) must be clearly defined otherwise the project would have no defined aims. The purpose of a stock control system, for instance, may be defined as, 'to record details of stock transactions on stock records in order to be aware of the current status of each item in the stores for stock management purposes.'

The objectives of a system must also be clearly defined so that it is clear what the system has to achieve in terms of operational performance. The objectives of a stock control system may be defined as 'to control the level of stocks by means of stock control parameters, including minimum, maximum and reorder levels, as a basis for optimising stock levels – the most suitable quantity of each item to store under existing operational conditions taking into account the time it takes to obtain new supplies (lead time) and the rate of usage of parts in the factory, or the demand for finished goods stored in the warehouse. Also to avoid frequent stock shortages while minimising quantities held in the stores to avoid excessive stock holding costs'.

FEASIBILITY STUDY

A feasibility study may be defined as a preliminary survey of the business environment for establishing if a business would benefit from the implementation of a computer, for general business use, or for computerising specific accounting applications. Management will make a decision on the basis of a feasibility study report. The correct decision is crucial, particularly if a mainframe or minicomputer is under consideration, because of the relatively high cost of such hardware and the cost of the resources employed in developing systems. If management make a decision not to implement a computer when one could be used to advantage, then a 'competitive advantage' will be foregone because operational efficiency will be below that of competitors who have implemented computers into their organisation. On the other hand, the implementation of a large computer when one is not needed is not to be recommended because of the administrative chaos which will ensue. The smooth operation of systems will also be disrupted needlessly due to system development activities; the newly computerised systems may not operate smoothly and fail to achieve objectives because they did not need to be computerised in the first place. This can arise as a result of insufficient analysis of the business environment and the true needs of the systems in question. Some systems may only need a 'facelift' or be 'retuned' to make them suitable for current needs. This may require the redesign of forms, restructuring working groups and the layout of the office, work simplification or the elimination of outmoded systems. The success of any computerised system depends upon the extent to which the inherent problems and weaknesses of current systems are identified. It is therefore essential to discuss problem areas with relevant managers and operations staff; examine the forms and documents processed; the machines and equipment in use; the calibre of staff engaged on the various activities; policy matters relating to such aspects as discount rates in relation to value of sales orders; delivery charges in relation to value of orders and delivery distance; credit policy in relation to specific classes of customer and so on.

FEASIBILITY STUDY REPORT

A feasibility study report may typically consist of four main sections including hardware and software, personnel and organisation structure, operating costs and expected benefits. These matters are discussed below.

Hardware and software

Matters to consider include the need to assess the suitability of the alternative types of computer configuration available for the various applications. Standby facilities are a 'failsafe' requirement to minimise possible disruption to operations in the event of a mal-function or breakdown of the in-house computer. The elimination of unnecessary delays in processing important data is important especially for such applications as real-time control systems and the weekly factory payroll. The suitability of application packages (software) must be established for the various jobs to ensure they will process data and provide reports in the form required. The compatibility of the software with the hardware must also be determined to ensure that the performance of the system as a whole is optimised.

Personnel and organisation structure
When a large computer is to be installed into the framework of a business it cannot be accomplished without some important considerations. One of the questions to be resolved relates to the availability of experienced computer personnel for operating the computer perhaps on a three shift basis. Another important factor is the incidence of redundancy of existing clerical personnel who will be displaced when the work they previously did is computerised. Some displaced personnel may be suitable for training so that they become compatible with the needs of the computerised systems. The extent to which the organisation will need restructuring when systems are transferred to the computer also needs to be considered, to avoid unbalanced working groups. Some working groups will be phased out, others will be depleted in numbers and a new computer department will come into existence while other sections of the organisation will be merged.

Technical feasibility
It is necessary to assess the technical capability of any proposed computer system to ensure it can cope with the demands on the system, e.g. the traffic density of terminal operations dealing with random enquiries or on-line data input workstations. It is also important to know if the proposed system can achieve the speed of response required for real-time control of critical operations – the control of fast moving warehouse stocks, for instance. Matters relating to cost/benefit appraisal are discussed in Chapter 1.

RECOMMENDATIONS, DECISIONS AND PLANNING

After the feasibility report has been compiled the subsequent stages of the systems life cycle include:

- Presentation of report to management with recommendations.

- Management make a decision to abort or continue with project.
- Plan the project including time scales and allocation of personnel to the project.

SYSTEMS ANALYSIS

This subject has been dealt with in considerable detail in Chapters 4 and 5 relating to the O & M approach to system development. Whether a computer will ultimately be implemented, or whether an existing system will be improved by work simplification, the nature of the facts required are identical. The extent to which a system is analysed depends on the findings from the initial feasibility study or preliminary survey. Even if the structured methodology is applied to systems analysis similar facts about a system are essential. Typical facts required are summarised below:

- environment and functional analysis
- data analysis
- document analysis
- data flow analysis
- procedure analysis
- verifying the facts
- recording the facts

SYSTEM DESIGN

At this juncture the systems analyst, being in possession of all the relevant details of the current system, considers a number of possible ways of achieving management requirements in the most economical manner. A study of the procedure charts and details of the data flows in the system will therefore be needed, as well as an assessment of processing techniques and machines and equipment. If a computer is to be considered for the proposed system and it already exists, it is then a matter of assessing whether its configuration is compatible with the needs of the system or whether additional equipment will be required, such as terminals for on-line processing. Large volumes of data to be processed and stock records to be updated in a stock control system, for instance, would tend to imply the use of a small mainframe or minicomputer equipped with fixed hard discs (e.g. Winchesters) of a capacity of 20–40 Mb. A multi-access system would facilitate the input of transaction data whereby data is input by several users simultaneously by a keyboard connected directly to the processor.

Other design activities
Additional design activities include the need to define actions to be taken when specific conditions exist, by means of:

- decision tables
- design input and output documents and reports
- design file structures and layout
- develop the structure of computer runs by means of run charts
- evaluate run times
- design screen layouts for on-line terminal operations
- develop dialogue to be used by terminal/work station operators
- develop fail-safe and restart procedures and procedures for file security
- discuss checks and controls to be incorporated with audit staff
- prepare system specification (system definition) specifying system details including clerical and computer procedures, block diagrams, system flowcharts, decision tables and a narrative providing a general description of the system; input, output and file specification and layouts
- schedule of equipment required by the system including new equipment needs and alternative equipment proposals
- the use and allocation of passwords to authorised personnel for access to databases or specified files.

Discussion and decisions
- present alternative proposals to management
- discuss proposals with management
- management decision – choice of proposals

PROGRAM DEVELOPMENT

Program specification
A statement of program requirements is prepared, including a specification of the parameters to be incorporated and the processes required for the transformation of inputs to specified outputs. Test data and testing procedures are also defined as are the checks and controls to be incorporated and the requirements for exception reporting. Additionally, decision tables are analysed for establishing the conditions and actions to be provided for in the programs.

Programming
Programmers prepare program flowcharts from which program

coding is performed. Test data is determined and testing procedures specified. Validation checks and other controls to be incorporated into the system are established and source programs are converted to object programs by assembling or compiling software. Programs are then debugged.

FILE CONVERSION AND SYSTEM TESTING

File conversion

Existing files of the manual system are typically stored in human sensible form on record cards. The details relating to customers, suppliers and employees stored on the record cards need to be converted into a magnetic disc which is a machine readable storage medium. New coding structures may be required for the computer files in order to provide self-checking facilities for the automatic detection of transposed digits by means of check digit verification.

System testing

Programs are initially tested by the technique of desk checking, known as dry runs, for the purpose of ensuring that the program instructions achieve the desired results. Amendments are made to the program when errors or omissions are detected. Live testing is then performed whereby the results of running test data are compared with precalculated results. Deviations are noted and appropriate action taken to remove bugs in the program. The cause of the errors may be due to an inadequate system specification which is a 'back to the drawing board' situation.

Management are informed of the results obtained from system testing and future action is discussed. Appropriate modifications are made to system or programs which are recompiled.

IMPLEMENTATION

If a computer already exists then it is a matter for implementing the new application and monitoring its performance. If a new computer is being installed, however, then this must be done in advance of system testing. The implementation stages include:

- plan system implementation
- carry out parallel running of old and new system – implement direct changeover or pilot scheme as appropriate
- prepare manuals for supporting department (users) and operation

departments including data input and data control clerks

EVALUATE RESULTS WITH EXPECTATIONS

- monitor system performance in co-ordination with user department;
- report to management to discuss the situation and decide on appropriate action.
- make relevant adjustments to the system.

MAINTAIN SYSTEM

- develop, test and implement improvements
- modify system to accord to changing circumstances
- integrate related systems to improve processing efficiency

It is important for the reader to appreciate that the 'system life cycle' approach to system design and development is the traditional approach but there are now a number of structured analysis and design methodologies currently available, including Michael Jackson Systems Limited, who have expanded their structured programming philosophy into the realms of structured systems design. Others included in this book are LBMS AUTO-MATE from Learmonth, Burchett Management Systems Limited and Information Engineering Workbench from KnowledgeWare Inc.

SUMMARY OF KEY POINTS

- Terms of reference constitute the authority to undertake a feasibility study.
- Typical contents of terms of reference include the nature of the problem, boundaries to the assignment and the purpose and objectives of the system.
- A feasibility study is a preliminary survey of the business environment, either to establish if it is feasible to introduce a computer into the business, or to computerise specific systems on an existing computer.
- A feasibility study report typically consists of four sections including hardware and software; personnel and organisation structure; operating costs and expected benefits.
- Important stages of the system life cycle include: terms of

reference, feasibility study, systems analysis, system design, program development, file conversion and system testing, implementation, evaluate results, maintain system.

SELF-TEST QUESTIONS

1 What are terms of reference and what purpose do they serve?
2 List the contents of typical terms of reference.
3 What is the nature and purpose of a feasibility study?
4 What are the typical contents of a feasibility study report?
5 What is the purpose of systems analysis?
6 List important aspects of systems design.
7 Why is it necessary to convert files when changing to computerised applications?
8 How are newly computerised applications tested?
9 What are the activities concerned with the implementation of a newly computerised system?
10 Why is it necessary to evaluate the results obtained from a new computerised application?
11 What activities are concerned with system maintenance?

FURTHER READING

Practical systems design, Alan Daniels and Don Yeates, Pitman Publishing, London, 1986.
Chapter 3, Managing systems development.
Systems analysis, L. Antill and A. T. Wood-Harper, Made Simple Computerbooks, Heinemann, London 1985.
Chapter 11, Overview of systems analysis.
Structured systems development techniques: strategic planning to system testing. Garfield Collins and Gillian Blay. Pitman Publishing, London 1987.
Chapter 3, Overview of systems development.
Management information systems, conceptual foundations, structure and development, second edition, Gordon B. Davis and Margrethe H. Olson. McGraw-Hill series in Management information systems 1985.
Chapter 18, Life cycle approach to application systems development.

Part 3

Structured Development Techniques

CHAPTER 8

Structured Development Methodology (SDM): An Overview

LEARNING OBJECTIVES

This chapter provides an overview of structured development methodology with the objective of providing an initial introduction to the subject before dealing with it in more detail in later chapters. The importance of structured methodology is stressed for the effective analysis and design of business/information systems. The chapter also indicates the importance of separating, during a system study, *what* is required of a system to meet its objectives and *how* they are to be achieved.

INTRODUCTION

In the past many systems were not developed efficiently and consequently the systems were costly to operate and inflexible in dealing with other than routine predetermined events. Such failures were often identified with inadequate systems definition, which resulted in systems which were unable to deal with current needs. Structured methodology addresses these issues by the development of models and diagrams specifying the logical features of a system. Structured analysis defines in unambiguous terms *what* a system's requirements are. Structured design applies the same techniques specifying *how* a system will be built. The modern system development methodology emphasises the solving of problems without technical constraints. A logical/conceptual model of a system is constructed specifying the requirements to achieve desired information flows and outputs to achieve business objectives. These logical needs are subsequently matched to physical machines and equipment during the physical design stage of system development. Logical models are constructed of data flows, processes and entities to obtain an appreciation of the nature of the elemental structure of a system as it now exists and what changes are required to suit what a system's requirements are before determining how they are to be accomplished.

ADVANTAGES OF AN EFFECTIVE DEVELOPMENT METHODOLOGY

An efficient system development methodology is essential because it reduces the risk of wasting resources on systems development, and increases the productivity of development staff by providing a standard method of developing each project, and provides the right tools and techniques for analysing and designing various elements of the system. The structured systems analysis and design method (SSADM) includes review procedures to enable errors to be identified and eliminated before system implementation. The method is widely used for systems development by the UK government. An effective methodology allows the system developer to accurately identify user information needs and at each stage management have a check list for reviewing project progress for assessing what tasks should be completed and what deliverables are due. Long and complex narratives are replaced with graphical methods and structured English examples, (see Chapter 3).

A data-driven top-down structured approach is often applied, emphasising the use of data flow diagrams (referred to as DFDs) data analysis, data modelling and definition of processes by functional decomposition. The data-driven approach recognises that all applications have a data structure which does not change through time to any great extent, apart from routine amendments to data stored in files or databases, e.g. changes to employee tax codes and wage rates; customer and suppliers' addresses, etc.

Most information systems are concerned with building data structures on conventional files or databases; accessing and extracting data from files and updating. On the other hand processes can vary due to developments in electronic technology – the impact of the microcomputer and local area networks, for instance. Structured methodology allows users to participate through all stages of development enabling them to meet their specific requirements. It provides frequent walkthroughs, i.e. reviews which are designed to detect errors, omissions and ambiguities in any stage of development. The methodology provides for the checking of system logic during the analysis and design phases instead of discovering them during the later stages of writing program specifications, program writing, program testing or during live running. Some proprietary systems of structured methodology, such as LSDM, also cover physical system design including definitions of files or databases, programs and computer runs, resource usage estimation and optimisation.

STAGES OF THE STRUCTURED APPROACH

The stages of structured methodology vary according to circumstances and the nature of business activities but initially the same approach as O & M analysis is adopted. The terms of reference are obtained from management specifying the problems, strengths and weaknesses of the current system and what is required from the proposed system. The current system is then analysed for the purpose of becoming familiarised with its characteristics (see Chapters 4, 5 and 7).

Conceptual model. After the preliminary analysis stage a conceptual model, a high level flowchart, is constructed showing each entity and their relationships; the boundary of the system and its interfaces with other related systems; data flows in and out of the system and the processes for the transform of data. *See* Fig. 8.1.

An entity life history diagram is then prepared specifying for each entity the events which modify or update the entity's data. It is important to know what event (logical transaction) will trigger the creation of an entity, say a new record of an item to be added to a file (insertion); the event that will change the status of the entity (amendment); or which will eliminate it (deletion) (*see* Fig. 8.2). Stock records exist as long as the stock item is not obsolete. Such records need to be updated regularly in order to know how many items are currently in stock, on order and reserved for special orders or jobs; how frequently the maximum stock level is exceeded and so on. Entity life history diagrams ensure that every entity has an event for its creation and deletion.

This is followed by the preparation of a transaction history diagram (*See* Fig. 8.3) showing how an entity changes with time – it represents in chronological sequence transactions affecting an entity within a particular system. In respect of a stock record it will show the nature of the various transactions including items ordered, issues, receipts and returns; details of receipts rejected – either part or full order quantity, stock shortages and reorder levels, etc.

A context diagram (*see* Figs. 8.4 and 8.5) is a high level chart or block diagram which provides an overall view of the system, showing the primary inputs, data flows in and out of files, and outputs. It is used as an initial overview of the data flows and is therefore a means

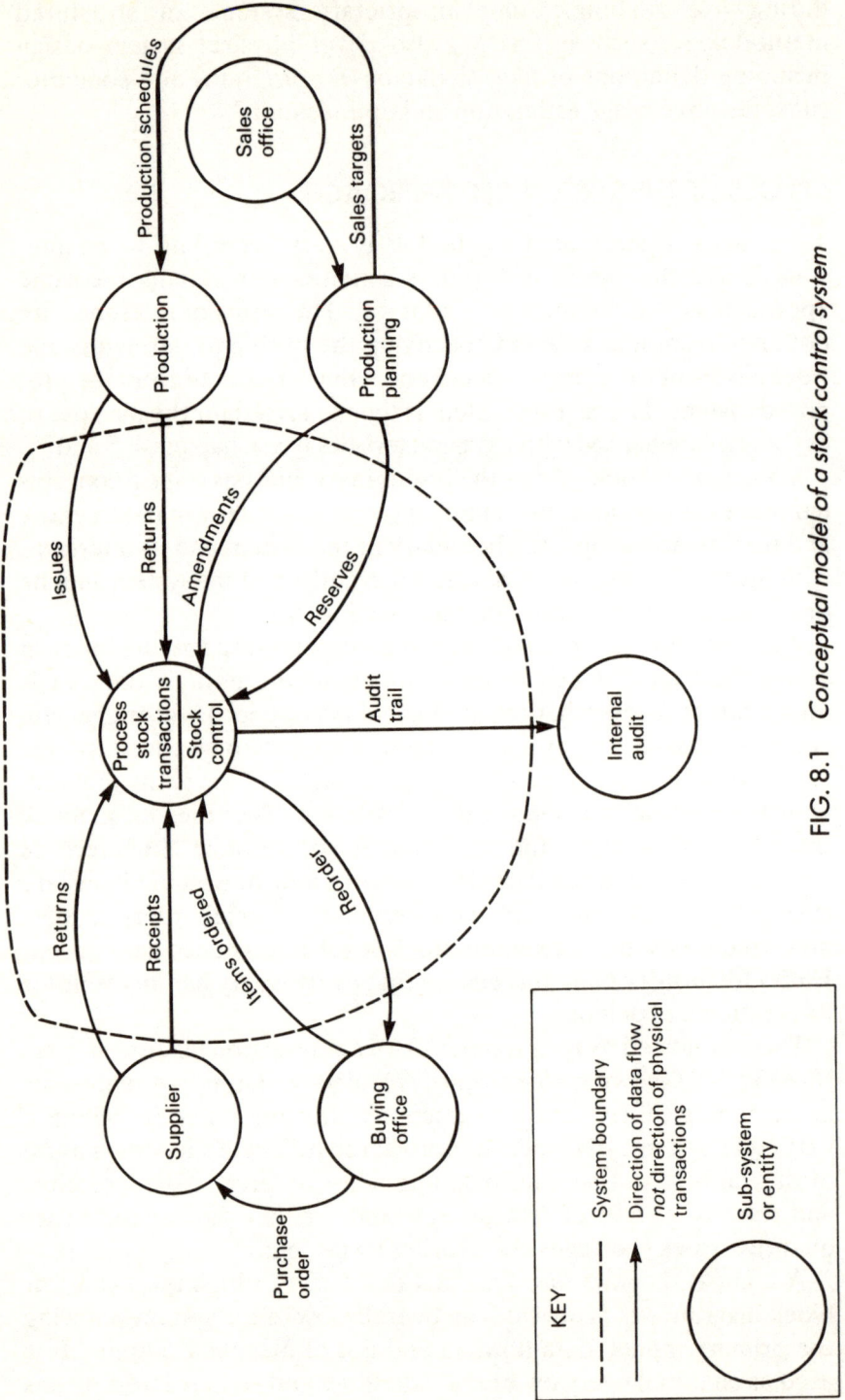

FIG. 8.1   Conceptual model of a stock control system

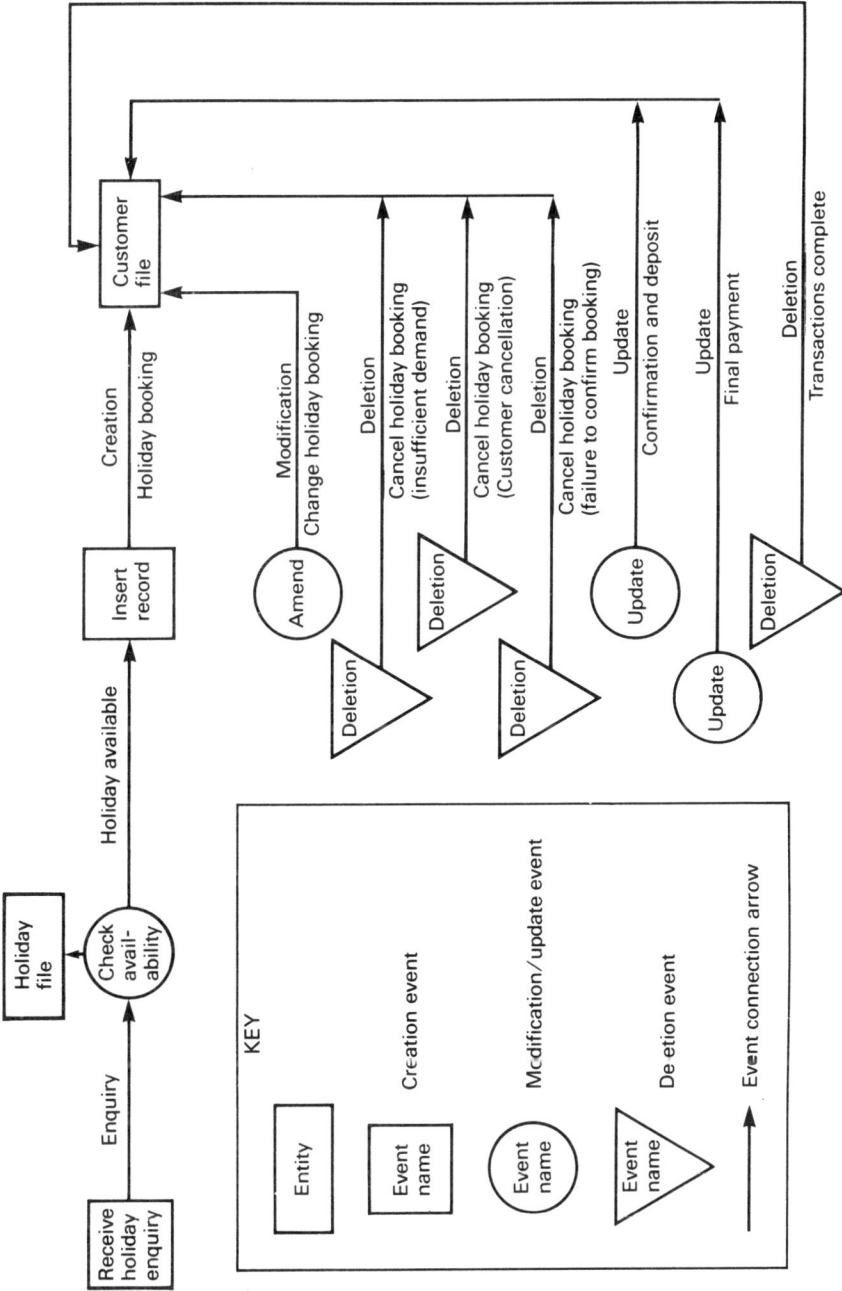

FIG. 8.2 Entity life history for a customer of a tour operator

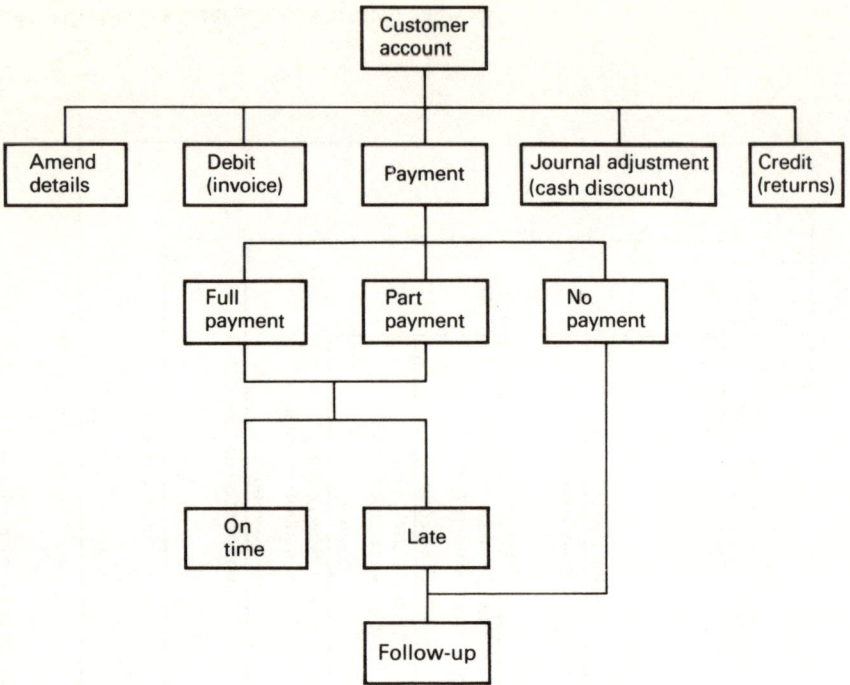

FIG. 8.3   *Transaction history diagram of a customer account*

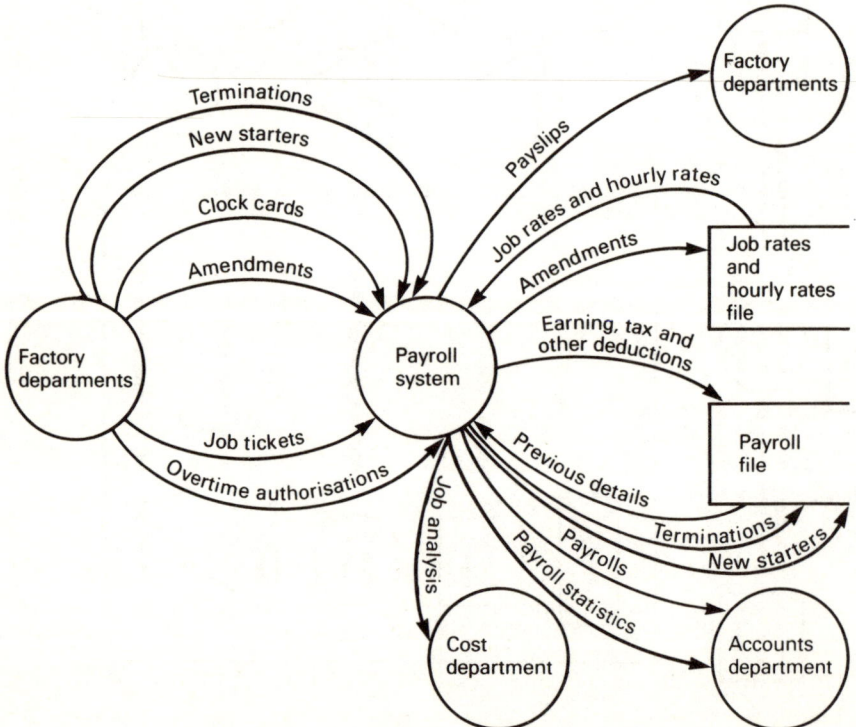

FIG. 8.4   *Context diagram of a payroll system*

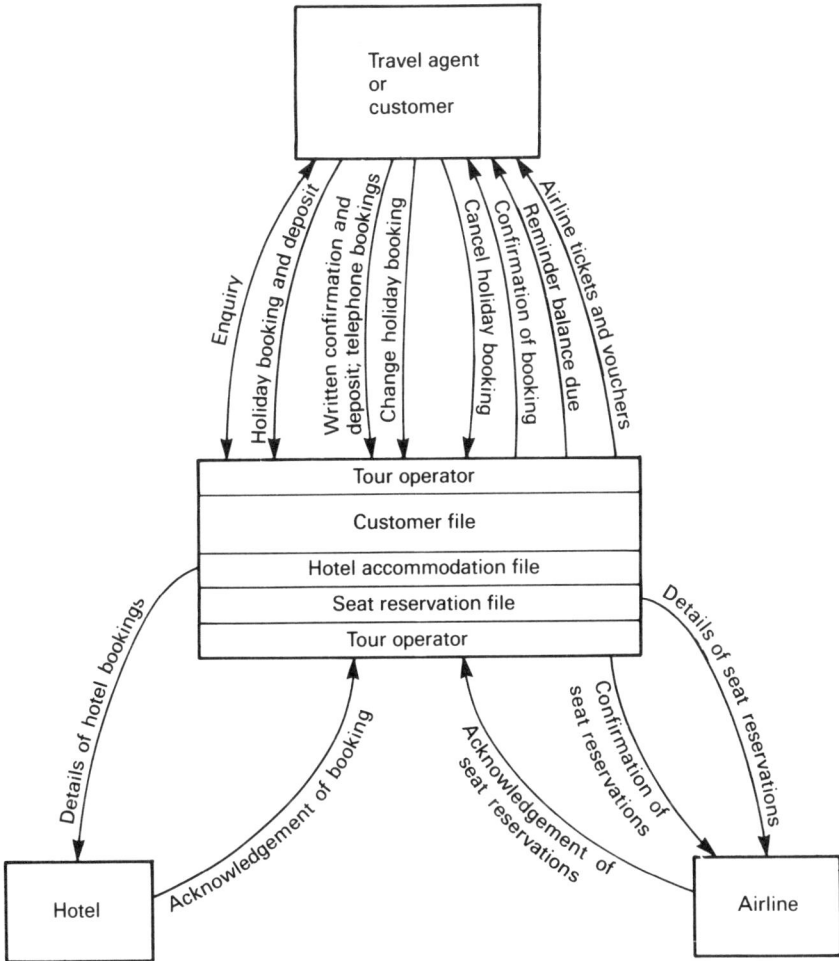

FIG. 8.5   *Context diagram of a tour operator system*

for developing more detailed data flow diagrams.

The data elements (attributes) relating to each input data flow are then specified, which is an essential requirement for the subsequent design of forms and data modelling as a prerequisite to the design of file structures.

Data flow diagram. Data elements (attributes) of output data flows and the origin of each data flow are established supplemented by the preparation of a data flow diagram (*see* Fig. 8.6) outlining processes which are subjected to transform analysis for decomposing each data flow to its lowest level of detail. This is referred to as levelling. Data modelling is then undertaken, using an entity diagram, showing

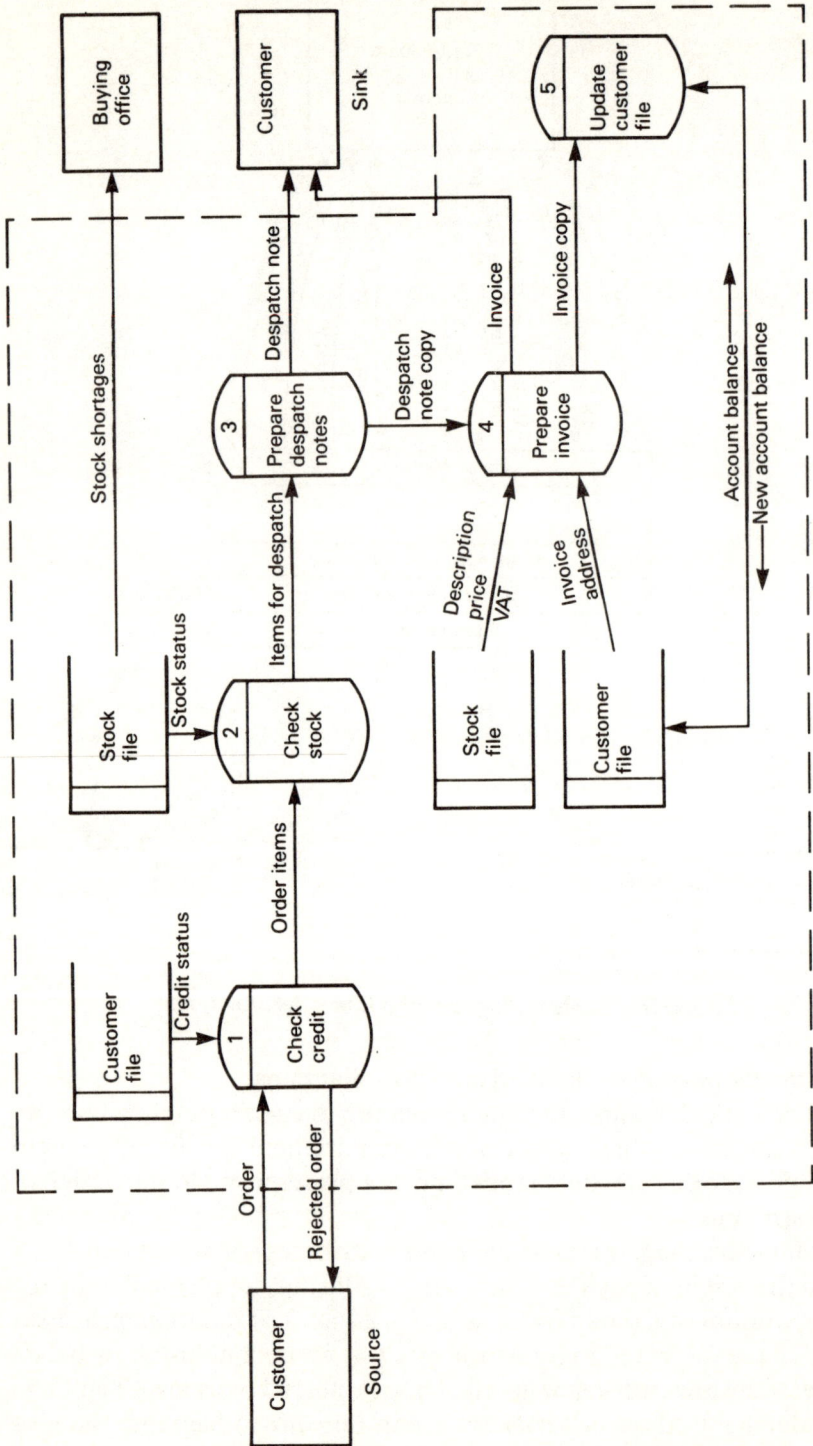

FIG. 8.6   Simplified data flow diagram of order processing system

relationships between data items, their entry points and access paths.

Decomposition diagram. A decomposition diagram is then prepared which analyses high level definitions of a function into more
detailed functions for further analysis. The decomposition diagram of
this refinement process forms an inverted tree structure. A flowchart
is then constructed outlining the logical features of the system which
is used as a basis for assessing the physical design requirements of the
information system. When the machine and technical options have
been considered an initial flowchart of the physical system is prepared, which is referred to as the 1st sketch. This is further illustrated
in the case studies at the end of this book.

SUMMARY OF THE STAGES OF THE STRUCTURED APPROACH

- obtain terms of reference and conduct feasibility study
- analyse current system in respect of:
    operational details
    entities
    data
    events
- construct conceptual model
- construct entity life history diagram
- construct transaction history diagram
- construct context diagram
- specify data elements (attributes) relating to each input data flow
- specify data elements (attributes) of output data flows and the
  origin of each output data flow
- prepare data flow diagram specifying input and output data flows
  and an outline of processing activities
- transform analysis-levelling of data flows
- transform analysis: transactions
- data modelling using an entity diagram to depict the relationship
  between data items, their entry points and access paths
- functional decomposition of processes
- construct flowchart portraying logical model of the system
- initial flowchart of physical system – 1st sketch

AUTOMATED APPROACH TO SYSTEMS DEVELOPMENT – USE OF CASE TOOLS

Business today must take every opportunity to develop efficient and
effective information systems to accomplish a defined level of

performance, quality assurance, speedy access to information and cost effective system operation. In order to achieve these goals and improve the productivity of systems development automated methodology should be implemented using CASE tools, i.e. Computer-Aided Systems Engineering, which replaces the Dickensian method of pencils and plastic flowchart templates. The detailed preparation of diagrams, charts and data dictionaries are delegated to the computer resulting in superior quality computer systems produced much more quickly than with less sophisticated techniques. These factors ensure that the user has quality assurance and acceptable deliverable outputs, and the management and systems developers obtain the benefits of increased productivity.

CASE tools generate increased profitability and a short pay-off period as more projects can be undertaken in a given time with the same number of staff.

General benefits of CASE tools:

- development productivity increased
- development costs have a shorter pay-back period
- quality assurance improved
- deliverable outputs in a shorter time period

Automated development methods provide for consistency and completeness checks searching for inconsistencies such as:

- data flows in a detailed (child) diagram not brought up to the high level diagram (parent)
- unnamed symbols
- unnumbered processes
- undesignated data flows
- dangling symbols or data flow lines (open loop)
- data flows not connected to a process
- input flow lines attached to output flows
- output flow lines attached to input flows

SUMMARY OF KEY POINTS

- In the past many systems failed to be developed efficiently often as a result of inadequate system development methodology and failing to provide an adequate system definition.
- Structured methodology develops models and diagrams specifying the logical features of systems without

considering physical hardware and software requirements.

- An efficient system development methodology increases development staff productivity by the provision of suitable tools and techniques for analysis and design.
- The structured approach to system development requires a number of specific stages.

SELF-TEST QUESTIONS

1 What is the objective of structured analysis?
2 A data-driven top-down structured approach is often adopted which emphasises the use of data flow diagrams. Why is this?
3 By what means are errors detected during system development?
4 List the typical stages adopted for applying the structured approach to systems development.
5 Automated system development uses CASE tools. Define what is meant by CASE.
6 Automated development methods provide for consistency and completeness checks. List a number of inconsistencies which need to be discovered.

FURTHER READING

Refer to Chapter 9.

Structured Development Methodology

LEARNING OBJECTIVES

This chapter indicates the need to conduct a feasibility study to determine if the system under consideration should continue to be subjected to further development or whether the system should be eliminated because it does not serve a useful purpose. The chapter also indicates the important aspect of analysing the current system including the identification of entities and events and the need to construct a conceptual model and data flow diagrams. The importance of sources and sinks is also stated.

FEASIBILITY STUDY

Before system development commences it is often necessary to conduct a feasibility study for the purpose of identifying problems, strengths and weaknesses of the current system and what is required of the proposed system. The feasibility study provides details of the current system on which to base a report to management either to continue further development or to eliminate the system if it does not serve a useful purpose. *See* Chapter 7.

ANALYSIS OF CURRENT SYSTEM

Operational details

The feasibility study establishes if a system serves a useful purpose, and is then followed by a more detailed analysis of the current system to become more familiar with its characteristics, its operational efficiency, the data flows between sub-systems and departments, transformation processes, the nature and type of personnel and equipment used on the various processes and activities, as a basis for its redevelopment into a much improved computerised system. *See* Chapters 4, 5 and 7.

Identify entities: entity diagram
System analysis also establishes the nature and identity of the various entities, their attributes and relationships. Entities include customers, suppliers, orders, products and departments, etc. which represent data groups for which records need to be maintained during the course of business activities. Refer to Fig. 9.1 which portrays an entity diagram of a stock control system.

Data analysis
Data analysis commences with an appraisal of the functional specification indicating the requirements of the user department of the system being reviewed. Data requires very detailed analysis during the course of system development as a basis for subsequently specifying the contents of functional files or databases. Data analysis obtains details which typically include:

- the data originating point
- how the data is used, by whom and for what purpose
- the frequency of preparation and access
- data validation requirements
- the activities or processes using the data
- volume statistics, maximum, average, minimum and growth rates

  Analysis of attributes:

  a key fields
  b size of fields
  c sequence of fields
  d data validation
  e type of characters in fields

- Reports in which the data is used

Events
It is important to appreciate events that occur in an environment to which the system must respond in a specific way to achieve a defined result. For example, in a tour operator system events which trigger off particular actions are:

- holiday enquiry – refer to status of holiday accommodation and aircraft seat availability. Inform customer;
- holiday booking – create record on customer file and enter details on hotel accommodation file, inform hotel, reserve aircraft seats, record entry on seat reservation file and inform airline;

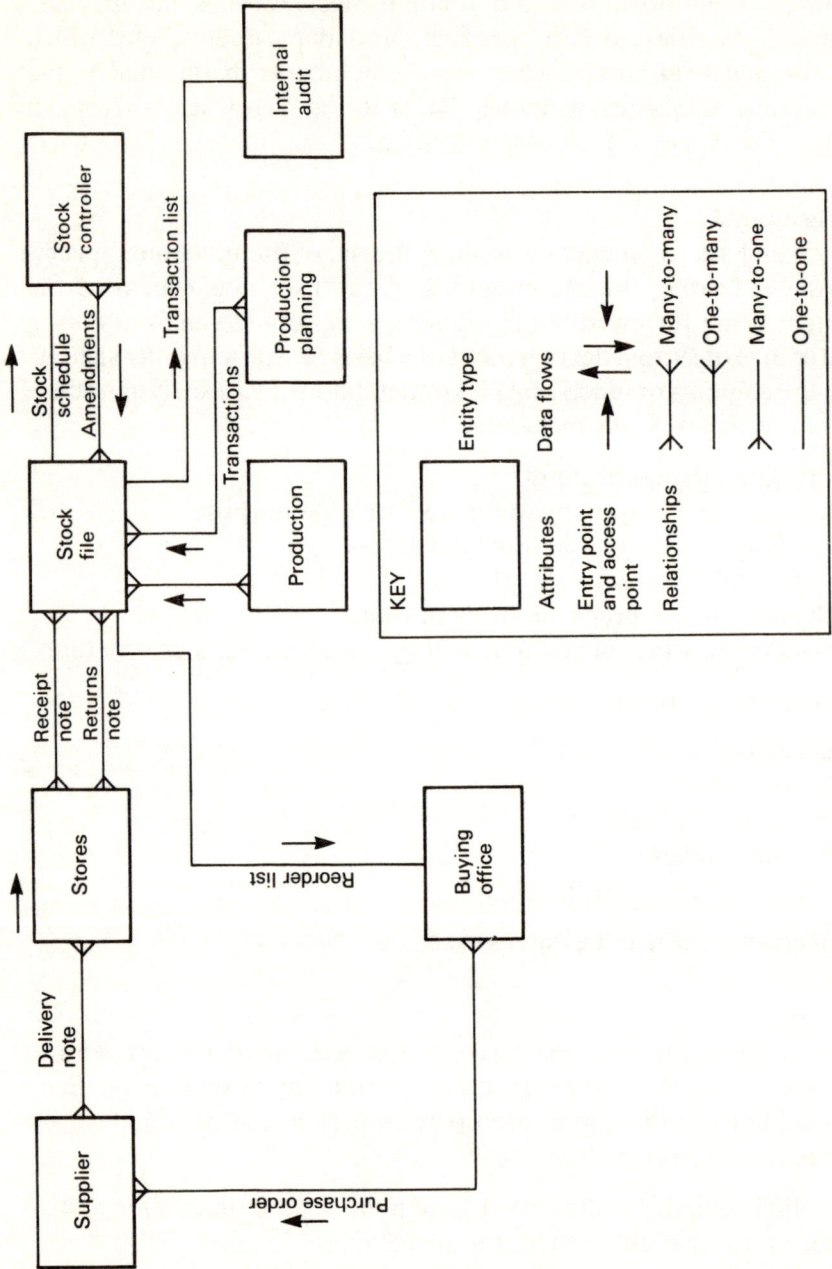

FIG. 9.1   *Entity diagram of a stock control system*

- change of booking – record change on customer file and accommodation file and inform hotel. Amend seat reservations file and inform airline;
- cancel booking – delete customer record, cancel accommodation and inform hotel, cancel seat reservations and inform airline.

An events list is used for this purpose, and provides a valuable means of communication between system developers and users for identifying and agreeing on events which occur or which should occur during system operation.

Conceptual model
After the preliminary analysis stage a conceptual model (a high level flowchart) is constructed showing each entity and their relationships; the boundary of the system and its interfaces with other related systems; data flows in and out of the system and the processes for the transformation of data. Fig. 9.2 outlines a conceptual model of a stock control system.

Entity life history diagram
It is important to know what event (logical transaction) will trigger the creation of an entity, say a new record of an item to be added to a file (insertion); the event that will change the status of the entity (amendment); or which will eliminate it (deletion). Some entity types will exist for only a short time, e.g. details of orders on a daily orders file, which will be replaced the following day by a new set of orders. The previous orders may now be known as 'orders for despatch'. Random enquiries are only of a transitory nature, i.e. they do not remain in existence beyond the point when the required information is communicated. On the other hand customer accounts remain in existence so long as the customer exists – especially if it is essential to maintain an up-to-date account status showing an age analysis of amounts outstanding. Customer records may also be maintained for sales history purposes and may remain in existence even though no current business transactions occur as long as an outstanding balance remains in existence. The writing off of the balance would constitute a closing of the account, triggering its deletion.

Entity life history diagrams portray a logical flow involving sequence, iteration and alternative paths, but no decision-based branching. They ensure that every entity has an event for its creation and deletion and as a means of analysing system logic. Fig. 9.3 shows the entity life history for the customer of a tour operator.

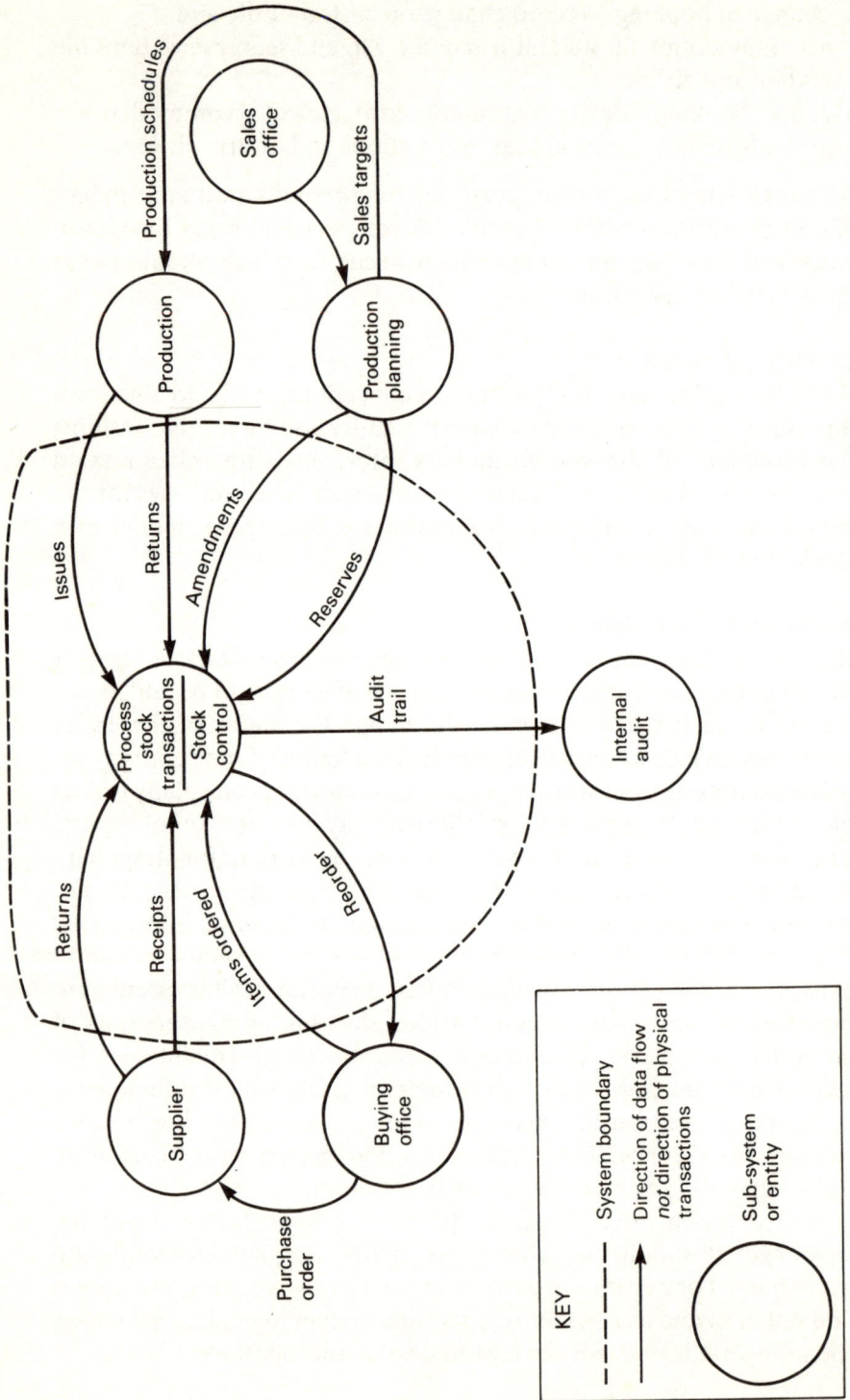

FIG. 9.2   *Conceptual model of a stock control system (same as 8.1.)*

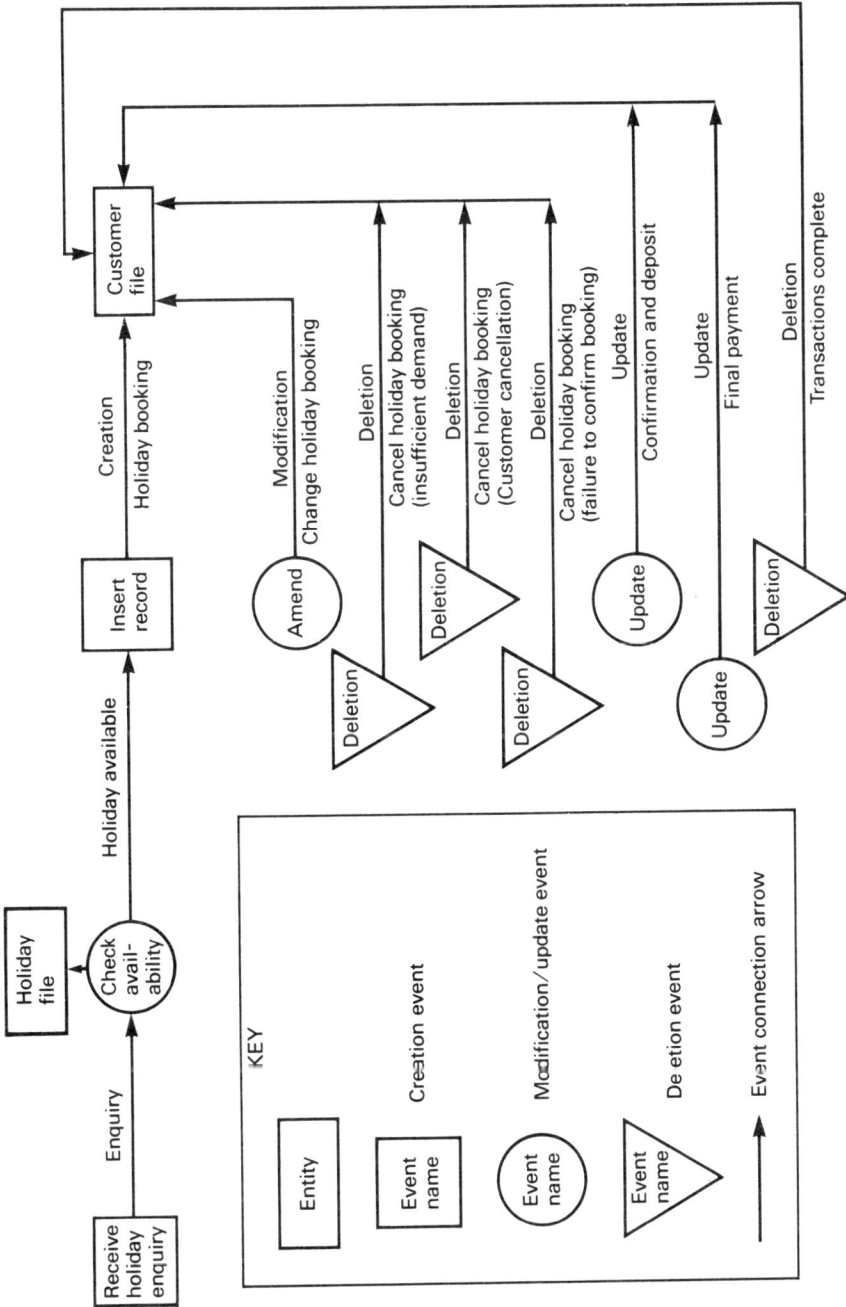

FIG. 9.3   Entity life history for the customer of a tour operator (same as 8.2)

Transaction history diagram: time dependent behaviour

A transaction history diagram may also be called a state transition diagram as it portrays the dynamic, time dependent behaviour of a system. It shows how an entity changes with time and represents in chronological sequence transactions affecting an entity within a particular system. There exists a correspondence between entities depicted in an entity model and the data stores shown on a data flow diagram. As an example in respect of the entity-customer account, a transaction history diagram may show the details in chronological order (see Fig. 9.4). This shows that a customer's account is charged with a debit amount from an invoice representing the value of goods despatched on the basis of a credit sale. The next transaction could be a credit note for goods returned or a payment from the customer. The customer account may also include attributes relating to sales history for sales promotion and administration purposes. Payments by the customer may be made in full or may only be a part payment. A part payment will create arrears, e.g. the account would be overdue. Payments may also be categorised as being on time or late and so on.

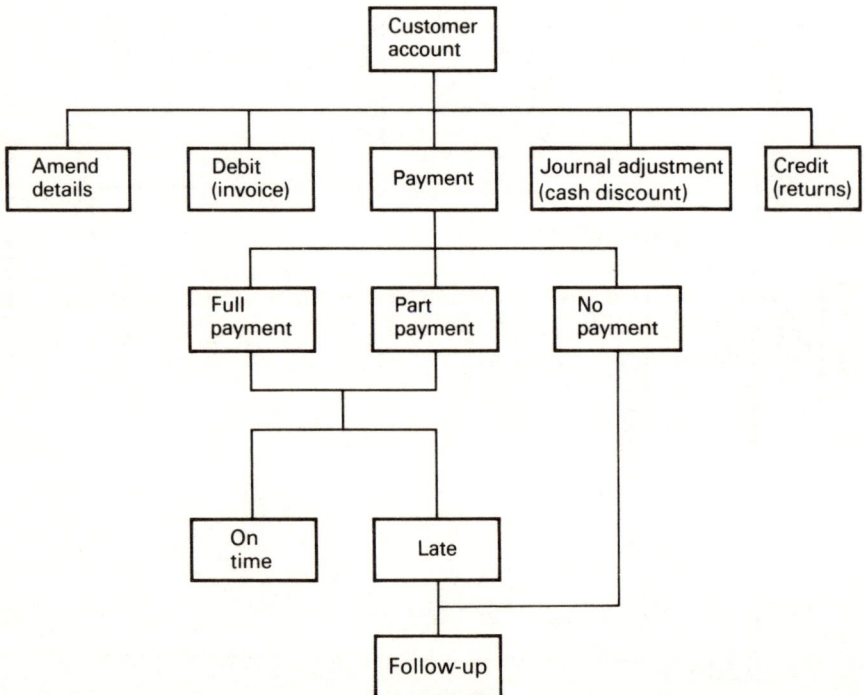

FIG. 9.4   *Transaction history diagram of a customer account (same as 8.3)*

Context diagram

Before preparing a detailed data flow diagram it is a good idea to construct a 'context' diagram portraying the sources of data flows in and out of the system. This aspect is shown in Fig. 9.5 which outlines a tour operator system. The context diagram provides an overall view, one may say a panoramic view, of the system before zooming in for a closer look at detailed data flows. This also provides a valuable start point for discussion, communication and comprehension between users and systems staff. From little acorns great oaks grow.

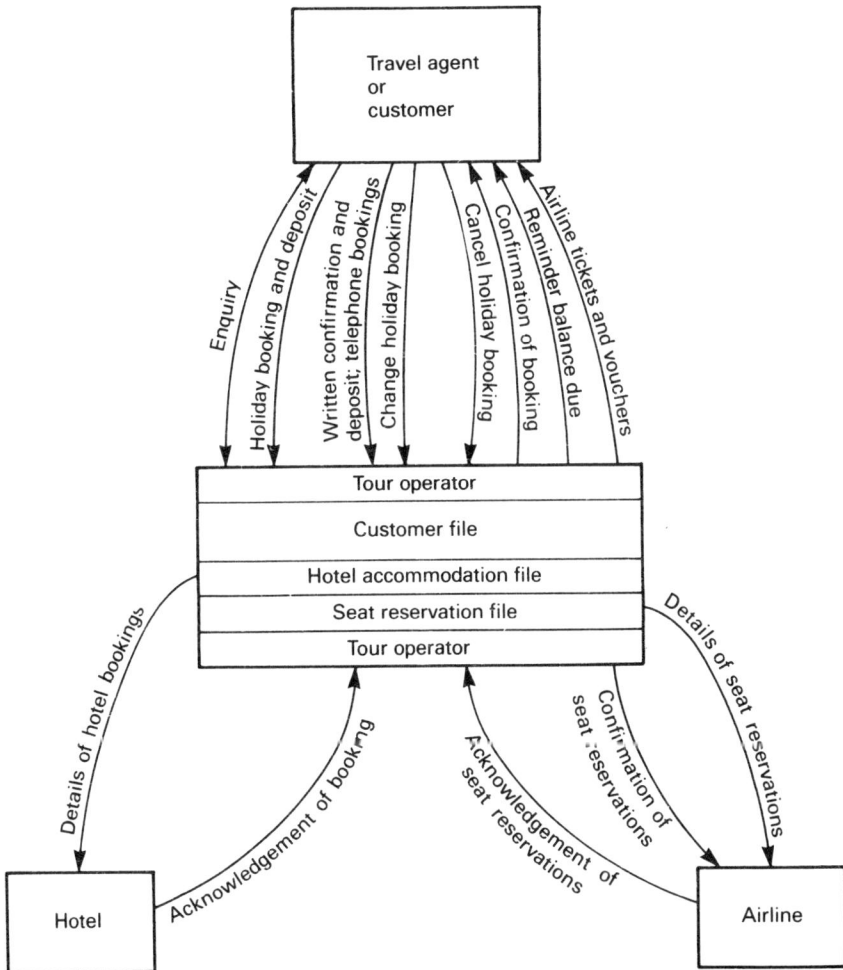

FIG. 9.5   *Context diagram of a tour operator system (same as 8.5)*

DATA FLOW DIAGRAMS: COMPLEXITY OF DATA FLOWS

Fundamental considerations

Data flow diagrams are very important for portraying a system when a top-down, data-driven approach is adopted for system development. It presents a visual representation of the elemental structure of the system including entities, processes, data flows and data stores (files). It is a flexible method of portraying a system because it can be used to show high level data flows outlining the system in very broad terms, which may then be subjected to partitioning or levelling to portray data flows in increasing levels of detail down to the ultimate level of what is known as a *functional primitive* (see construction, below).

It is important to appreciate that a data flow diagram differs from a program or system flowchart as it does not show control factors such as GET record or OPEN file, nor does it show physical system aspects relating to the movement of materials in and out of the stores or manufacturing departments, for instance. A data flow diagram shows how data moves through a system; it is an advantage to plot data flows in the sequence in which they occur, thus providing an extension to the logical approach and subsequently saving valuable time when constructing a flowchart of the logical structure of a system. This was the adopted approach when preparing the case studies on a structured basis. Data flow diagrams provide a simple graphical method of portraying the flow of data through a system and it is important to appreciate that they show only the logical view of the system. Most of the details required to develop a new system can be summarised in a data flow diagram, which may render any supporting narrative unnecessary, unlike system flow charts, which require detailed narrative in order to improve their comprehension.

Construction

One of the approaches to the preparation of data flow diagrams is to commence with a single process box representing the complete system in terms of inputs and outputs and then progressively decompose this into a number of separate transforms. This aspect is shown in Fig. 9.5, which shows a context diagram of a tour operator system.

Data flow diagrams can be constructed either using the 'bottom-up' approach or a 'top-down' approach. The bottom up approach commences with data flows to or from a user and progresses upwards to the higher level data flows. The top-down approach commences at the top level functions showing the data flows in and out of these. The construction of this type of diagram is concluded when each process box corresponds to a single task. Each of the major functions can be further analysed and shown in more detail on individual diagrams. The generally used method of constructing data flow diagrams may be based on the guidelines outlined below.

a All processes, data flows, entities and stores should be clearly named and given identifiers.

b All data flows must pass through at least one process.

c Each process box may be broken down (decomposed) into its component, more detailed processes. Net flows into and out of the lower level DFD must equal those into and out of the process depicted at a higher level. Process 1 is broken down into processes 1.1, 1.2, 1.3 etc. Refer to Transforms.

d When constructing a data flow diagram, it is sometimes necessary to duplicate data stores (files) and entities to avoid excessive crossover of data flow lines. This is illustrated in Fig. 8.6.

e Data flow diagrams should be constructed from left to right in a similar way to the preparation of a flowchart except that this is constructed from top to bottom commencing with the input data flows and terminating with the output data flows.

Sources and sinks

Data flow diagrams establish data origination points and destinations. The point where data is originated is known as the *source* and the point of destination as the *sink*. A source of data may also be a sink as shown on Fig. 9.6. A source or sink may be shown by an action box (a rectangle) which contains the name of the source. Sources and sinks are located outside the area of the system under development; Fig. 8.6 clearly shows this factor by means of a rectangle formed by broken lines. The various processes are shown by a process symbol which is a rectangle with curved ends. The diagram clearly shows the data flows entering and leaving the system and their points of origin and destination. If we examine an integrated order processing system the source of the data is the customer sending in an order for the supply of goods. The ultimate destination of data flows is also the customer who receives despatch notes, invoices and statements of account. If it is considered necessary to expand the scope of the system then new sources and sinks will be created. This may apply if it is required to expand the system to embrace the buying office activities.

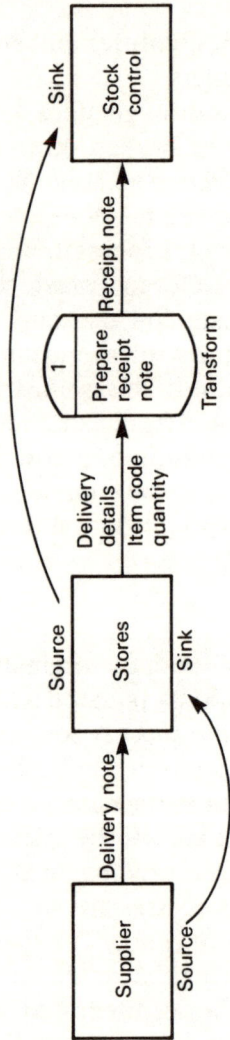

FIG. 9.6   *Dataflow diagram indicating source and sink*

Symbolic representation of data flows
The symbolic representation of data flows vary according to specific sources and the points of view of the authors of design methodologies. Whichever symbolisation is used data flow diagrams usually consist of four components:

a entities which send or receive data flows-sources and sinks
b processes which transform or alter the structure of data
c data store.
d arrow with name of data flow superimposed.

In order to demonstrate the use of such symbols a segment of an order processing system is adopted which is used throughout each demonstration of symbolisation for comparison purposes.

General symbolisation
One method, as shown in Figures 9.7 and 9.8, is to show 'entities' which send or receive data from the system by a 'terminal' symbol; activities or processes which alter the data structure are represented by an 'action box'; data storage may be represented by a 'storage' symbol and data flows are shown by an arrow with the name of the data flow superimposed.

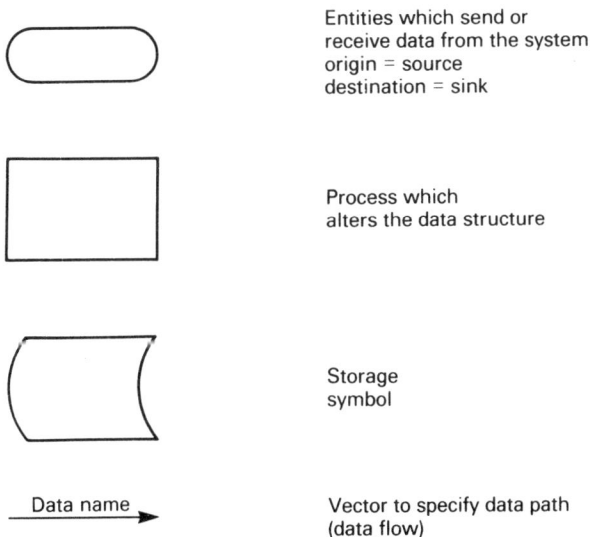

Entities which send or
receive data from the system
origin = source
destination = sink

Process which
alters the data structure

Storage
symbol

Data name

Vector to specify data path
(data flow)

FIG. 9.7   *General symbolisation for the construction of data flow diagrams*

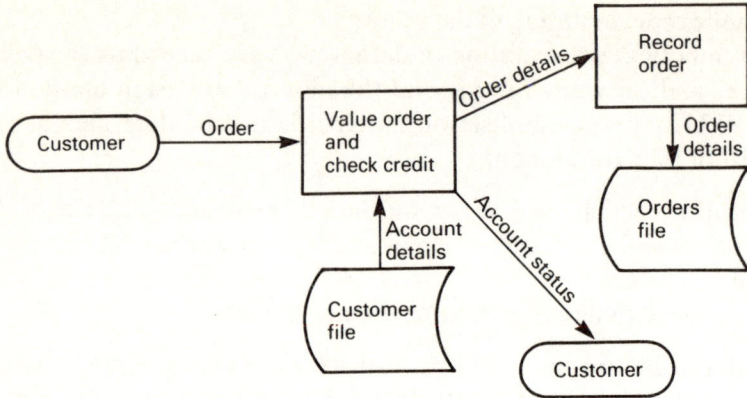

FIG. 9.8   *Example of the use of general symbols*

Alternative symbolisation

The alternative symbols are shown in Figures 9.9 and 9.10. An arrow with the name of the data flow superimposed is used in the usual way to denote the data path; a vertical rectangle with curved ends is used to represent a process which transforms data; an open-sided rectangle with a sub-section for a prefix to denote the type of store

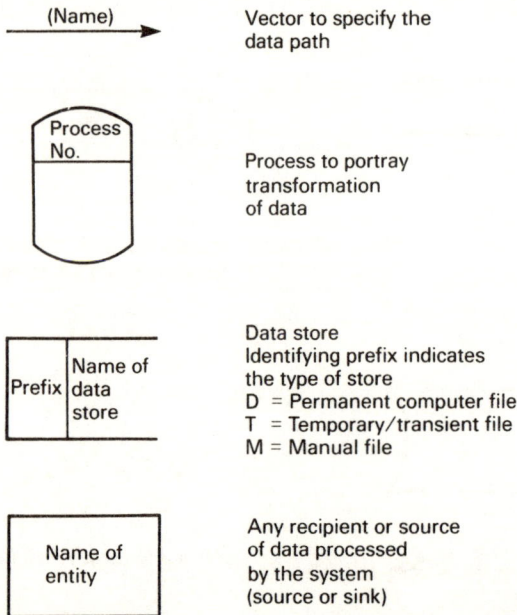

FIG. 9.9   *Alternative symbolisation for the construction of data flow diagrams*

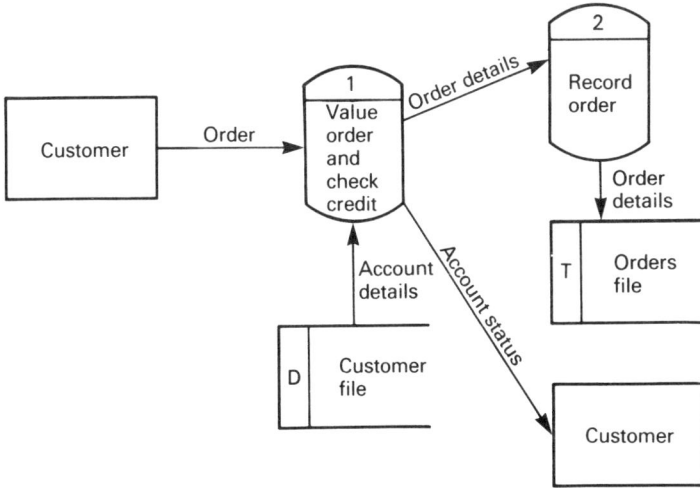

FIG. 9.10   *Example of the use of alternative symbolisation*

and a section to indicate the name of the data store and finally, a rectangle to denote the recipient of source (the entity) of data.

Gane and Sarson as applied by Knowledgeware Inc.

Symbolic representation used by KnowledgeWare Inc. utilises a terminal symbol for a process; an open ended rectangle for a data store; an arrow for a data flow and an action box (rectangle) for an entity. These are shown in Figures 9.11 and 9.12. Each symbol is

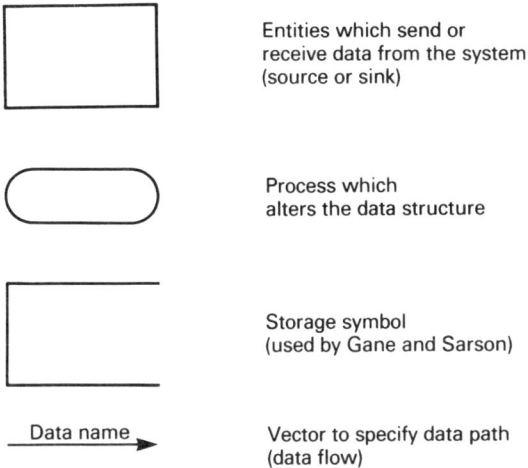

FIG. 9.11   *Gane and Sarson Symbolisation for the construction of data flow diagrams; representation used by Knowledgeware Inc.*

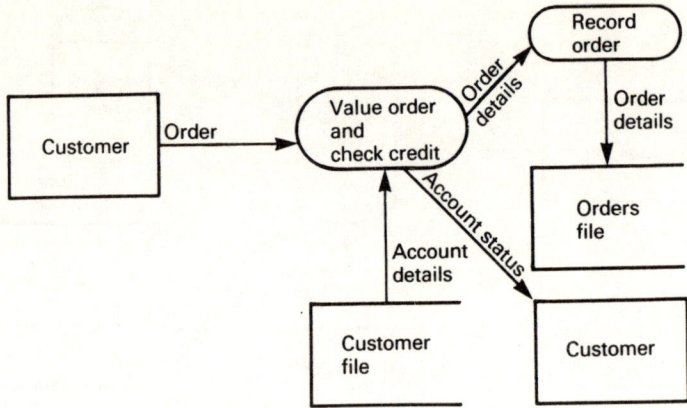

FIG. 9.12   *Example of the use of Gane and Sarson symbolisation*

allocated a name which is used for cross-reference to the system documentation.

DeMarco symbolisation

An alternative method used by DeMarco, uses the notation shown in Fig. 9.13. An arrow with the name of the data flow superimposed; a circle to denote a process which transforms data; a square to represent a source or sink; a star or asterisk (*) to represent a conjunction operator (AND) which indicates that two inward data flows are required in the example, one for the details of the order sent in by the customer and the other consisting of account details for checking the credit status of the customer. In addition a small circle enclosing a cross(+) represents a disjunction operator (OR), used to

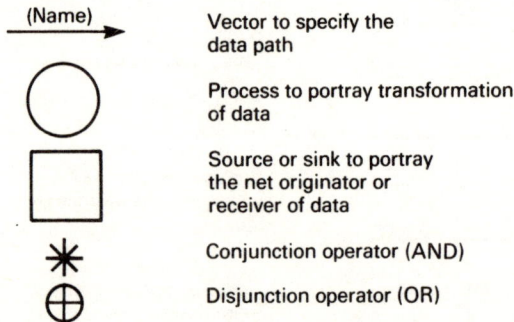

FIG. 9.13   *DeMarco symbolisation used for the construction of data flow diagrams*

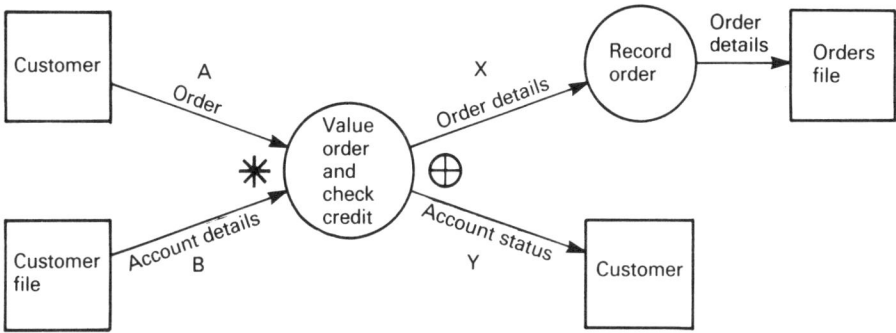

FIG. 9.14 *Example of the use of DeMarco Symbolisation*

show alternative data flows which, in the example, consist of order details for storing on the order file (a sink) and the other indicates an unacceptable account status to the customer (also a sink). The use of the symbols is demonstrated in Fig. 9.14 which shows that input A when processed with input B produces either output X or Y.

LBMS symbolisation
The symbols used by LBMS are outlined in Fig. 9.15 which indicates that an external entity is shown as an oval symbol containing the name of the entity; a process is shown by an action box (rectangle) which provides for the insertion of the process number, subject and the process; an open-sided rectangle with a sub-section for inserting a prefix which identifies the type of store-D for a permanent computer file, T for a temporary/transient file and M for a manual file. An arrow with data name superimposed is used to indicate the direction of the data flow. Fig. 9.16 provides an example of the use of LBMS symbolisation.

Transforms and levelling
The technique of levelling refines a top level data flow diagram into more detailed DFDs by successive levels of detail to assist the analysis and/or development process. There is no strict ruling on the number of transforms that should be included in a DFD but obviously too many will cloud the issue and make the interpretation of data flows more difficult to follow. This is the reason for implementing the technique of levelling. The term 'transform' is a synonym for process and is used to describe an activity which converts an input data flow from one form to another. In other words, a process receives a data flow of one structure and transforms it into an output data flow of

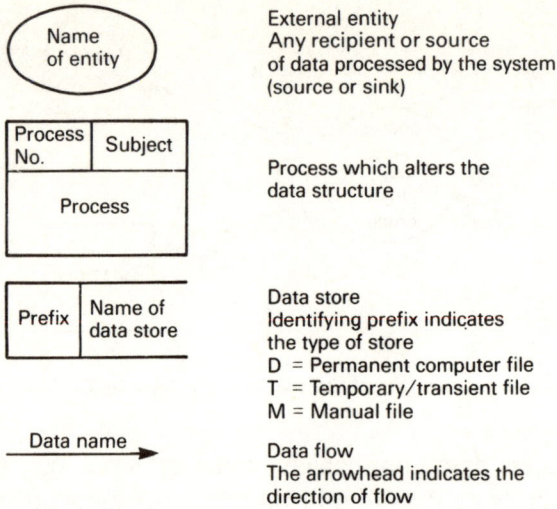

Name of entity	External entity Any recipient or source of data processed by the system (source or sink)
Process No. / Subject / Process	Process which alters the data structure
Prefix / Name of data store	Data store Identifying prefix indicates the type of store D = Permanent computer file T = Temporary/transient file M = Manual file
Data name →	Data flow The arrowhead indicates the direction of flow

FIG. 9.15 *Symbolisation used by LBMS for the construction of data flow diagrams*

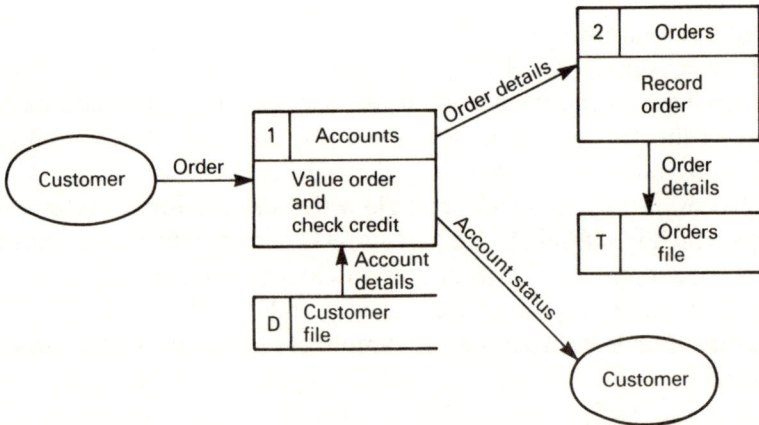

FIG. 9.16 *Example of the use of LBMS symbolisation*

another structure. Each transform should be allocated a name which states its purpose. Each transform should be numbered, those at the top level being numbered 1, 2, 3, 4, 5 and so on. Figure A.6. in the case study at the end of the book relates to a stock control system and shows the top or first level DFD; this is a comprehensive outline of the data flows in the system. Second level transforms for process 7 are numbered 7.1, 7.2, 7.3, 7.4 (see Figures A11–A14). Second level transforms for process 3 are numbered 3.1 and 3.2 (see Figure

A7–A8). Third level transforms of process 7 would be enumerated as 7.3.1 and 7.3.2 (see Figures A15 and A16). The process of levelling is carried out on every transform until functional primitives are attained.

Transforms: transaction analysis
Transaction analysis is necessary when a transform separates an input data flow into several distinct output data flows. This occurs when processing transactions of different types, e.g. in a stock control system. In this case an initial diagram may record input data flows relating to stock transactions as one stream which is then separated into several outputs streams as shown in Figure 9.17. The first transform is to separate the streams of input data flows into separate flows by the process of testing for the transaction type. After this is done a further transform updates a stock record by defined rules in accordance with the transaction type.

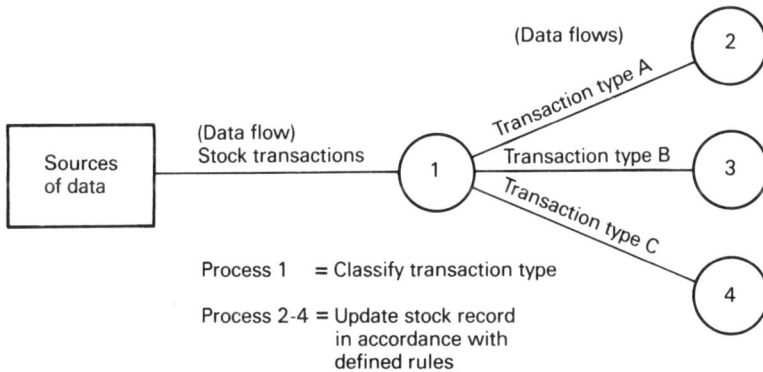

FIG. 9.17   *Transaction analysis*

FUNCTIONAL DECOMPOSITION

Most modelling and structured design techniques use a form of hierarchical construction, known as functional decomposition, for breaking down (refining) a high level definition of a task, process or function into more detailed processes (successive levels of detail) which can then be subjected to further analysis to provide even more details of the various processes. The diagram of this refinement process forms an inverted tree structure. Refer to Figures A23–A28 and B27–B28 in the case studies at the end of the book.

SUMMARY OF KEY POINTS

- A feasibility study determines if a system should be subjected to further development.
- Analysis of the current system provides details of its characteristics, operational efficiency, data flows and processes (transforms).
- Entities are identified together with their attributes (data items) and relationships.
- The need to analyse data within the system.
- The need to identify events which occur in the environment and trigger specific actions.
- The purpose and importance of a conceptual model.
- The nature and purpose of data flow diagrams (DFDs).
- The nature and purpose of sources and sinks.
- The various ways of representing data flows symbolically.
- The nature and need for levelling.

SELF-TEST QUESTIONS

1 What is the purpose of a feasibility study?
2 What is an entity and what does it represent?
3 List details you would collect about data in a system during the course of data analysis.
4 What effect do events have on a system?
5 What is the purpose of a conceptual model and what elements of a system does it contain?
6 What is an entity life history diagram? What does it contain and what purpose does it serve?
7 A transaction history diagram provides details of the time dependent behaviour of a system. Discuss.
8 Before preparing a detailed data flow diagram it is good practice to construct a context diagram. What benefit does it serve?
9 How is a dataflow diagram constructed?
10 What is the purpose of levelling?

FURTHER READING

Business information systems, Chris Clare and Peri Loucopoulos, Paradigm, London, 1987.
Chapter 6, Structured process analysis, provides an introduction to the subject.

Practical systems design, Alan Daniels and Don Yeates, Pitman Publishing, London, 1986.

Chapter 4 Structured methodologies, provides a general outline of the subject.

Structured systems analysis, Gane and Sarson, Prentice Hall. 1977. Provides a detailed treatment of the subject.

Practical guide to structured system design, Meilir, Page-Jones, Yourdon Press.

Provides a detailed treatment of the subject.

Structured systems development techniques: Strategic planning to system testing, Garfield Collins and Gillian Blay, Pitman Publishing, London, 1982.

Provides a detailed treatment of subject.

Systems analysis, design, and development with structured concepts, Perry Edwards, CBS College Publishing, Holt-Saunders International editions, 1985.

Provides a wide treatment of system analysis, system design and system development.

CHAPTER 10

Data Modelling

LEARNING OBJECTIVES

This chapter indicates the nature and use of entity models for data modelling. The need to be aware of entity interrelations and dependencies is also stated. Of particular importance is the need to be aware of the various types of entity relationships such as one to many; many to one; many to many; one to one; hierarchical, network and relational. Of particular significance is the need to know about relational data structures because they form the basis of relational databases. The technique of normalisation must also be appreciated as it plays an important part in the development of relational databases by ensuring that all non-key data items in each relation are directly and fully dependent on the entire prime key. It is also important to understand the nature of two-dimensional tables and the significance of prime and composite keys. Awareness of the purpose of a data dictionary is a necessity because it provides a precise definition of all data represented in the various models.

DATA MODELLING

Entity model: logical data model

An entity diagram or model is in effect a logical data model demonstrating the relationships between different types of data within the system and how it can be accessed (see Fig. 9.1). It is necessary to analyse the system under development to identify those items which represent a data group – an entity. Entity models consist of three basic components – entities, attributes and relationships. An entity diagram identifies the principal entity types involved in running a business, e.g. materials, employees, suppliers, customers, functions, locations, products and assets about which records need to be maintained, and determines the major relationships among them. Entity diagrams are used for both top-down data planning and detailed data modelling. Top-down planning identifies the principal entity types.

An entity model is used to identify entry points and access paths to data. They can be developed using logical data structuring techniques (LDST), known as entity modelling, or by using the result of third normal form (TNF) data analysis. See normalisation, p. 128. A choice is possible between the two common methods of denoting entity relationships using either arrows or 'crows feet' on the lines. Standard rectangles or Chen 'diamonds' can also be selected to represent associative entity types.

Dependency
The various entities which exist in an application environment will be interrelated either directly or indirectly. In order to show which entity is dependent upon another the convention may be adopted of showing dependency by defining which data group is a master and which is a detail. The determination of dependencies is a matter of systems analysis. Fig. 9.1 uses crows feet, pointing from the Master entity to the Detail entity which is based on the question 'Will an A entity own more than one B entity and will a B entity own more than one A entity?' If the answers are Y and N respectively then A is the master and B the detail. If the answers are N and Y then B is the master and A the detail. A one-to-one relationship applies if the answers are N and N. It is also necessary to assess if A can be related to B without the relationship being described in terms of some other entity. An entity which is a master in one relationship can be a detail in another as entities can exist in either role. Before entities can be precisely defined as 'master' or 'detail' it is necessary to study the operating environment in which the system functions to state rela-tionships precisely. It is also useful to keep in mind that transaction histories show how entities change with time and there is a definite link between entities in the entity model and the data stores on a data flow diagram because, it must be remembered, that entities are specific data groups requiring the storage of attributes relating to them. Entity relationships (refer to Fig. 9.1.):

1 *One to many*
  a one customer may have many orders on a supplier.
  b one supplier may have orders from many customers.
  c one order may have many items.
  d one part may appear on many orders.

2 *Many-to-one*
  Many order items may be recorded on one invoice.

3 *Many to many*
   a many of the same products may be supplied by many suppliers.
   b many products in a range utilise many of the same parts.

4 *One to one*
   a one invoice relates to only one customer.
   b one special order relates to one customer.

5 *Hierarchical*
   The entities in a hierarchy take the form of an inverted tree structure consisting of the main trunk from which stem main branches and which in turn have smaller branches (sub-branches) emanating from them. Access starts at the top and proceeds downwards through the hierarchical structure. Each entity may be related to any number of entities at any level below it but only one element above it. A customer entity, for instance, may have several order entities each of which may have several order lines. Hierarchical data structures are often used for the storage of data in databases. See Figure 10.1.

6 *Network structure*
   This type of structure is complex as it resembles the logical data relationships existing in the real world of business. It is structured

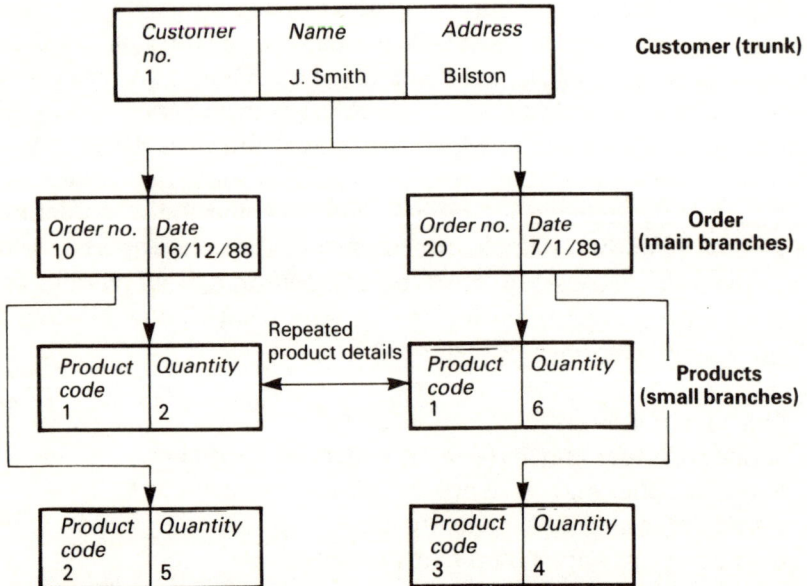

FIG. 10.1   *Hierarchical structure (contrast with network structure)*

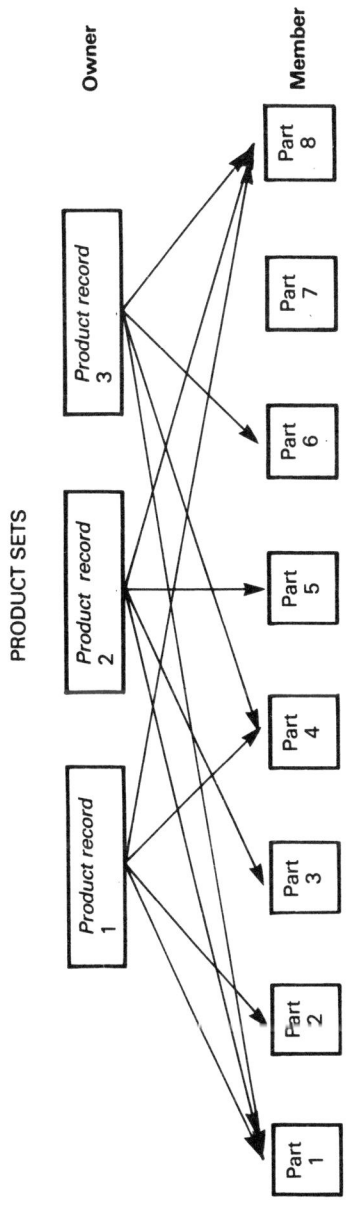

FIG 10.2   *Network structure*

1. The product 1 set consists of members which are part records.
   The number of part records required for this set
   are 1, 2, 4, 8.

2. The product 2 set consists of members which are also part records.
   The number of part records required for this set
   are 1, 3, 5, 8.

3. The product 3 set consists of members which are also part records.
   The number of part records required for this set
   are 1, 4, 6, 8.

around the concept of a set which is a relationship between two record types, e.g. a product and a component. This type of structure is also used in the construction of databases. See Figure 10.2.

7 *Relational structure*

A data structure used for the construction of relational databases is based on what are referred to as 'relations' which are two-dimensional tables of data consisting of columns and rows. A 'relation' is also known as a 'record'. The columns, which are also generally known as data elements, attributes or fields, store specific categories of data containing values relating to a particular relation which may be a customer, stock item or employee record. Relational data analysis describes a relation by listing its columns. A customer relation contains data categories (columns) called Customer number and Customer name, etc. An employee relation contains categories called Employee number and Employee name, and so on.

Each row in the relation (table) contains one value of Customer number and one value of Customer name, etc. A 'tuple' is one occurrence of related column values of an entity. Thus Smith, Brown, Jones and Quasimodo are all occurences of the entity, employee. This is analogous to records in a file where the file is comparable to a table of relations and the fields are comparable to the columns.

It is important to appreciate that no two rows may be identical in terms of their total column values, implying that a combination of one or more columns can form a key whose combined values in any given row are unique across all rows. The order of rows cannot be significant and each column must be uniquely identified. See Figure 10.3.

NORMALISATION

Data models define the structure of files and assist in obtaining an appreciation of the data needs of a business. They facilitate the segregation of data into separate files or integrate data structures when developing databases. An initial requirement is 'normalisation', the process for obtaining the final result of having all non-key data items in each 'relation' directly and fully dependent on (related to) the entire Prime key. See relational above. It is especially suited for the design of relational databases. Tables and lists of data are

Columns

Relation: machines			Machine = Entity
Machine type	Cost (£)	Location	
Capstan	1000	1	
Driller	500	2	
Lathe	5000	3	
Shaper	300	3	
Profiler	8500	3	

Tuples (rows)
- Occurrences of a relation
- Each row is a record
- A tuple is one occurrence of related column values

Relation: machine maintenance				Machine maintenance = Entity
Machine type	Location	Date	Cost (£)	
Capstan	1	1/1/88	200	
Driller	2	20/12/87	50	
Lathe	3	–	–	
Shaper	3	30/11/87	25	
Profiler	3	30/9/87	100	

Tuples (rows)

Relationships between two-dimensional tables are defined by one or more common fields for example, machine type and location

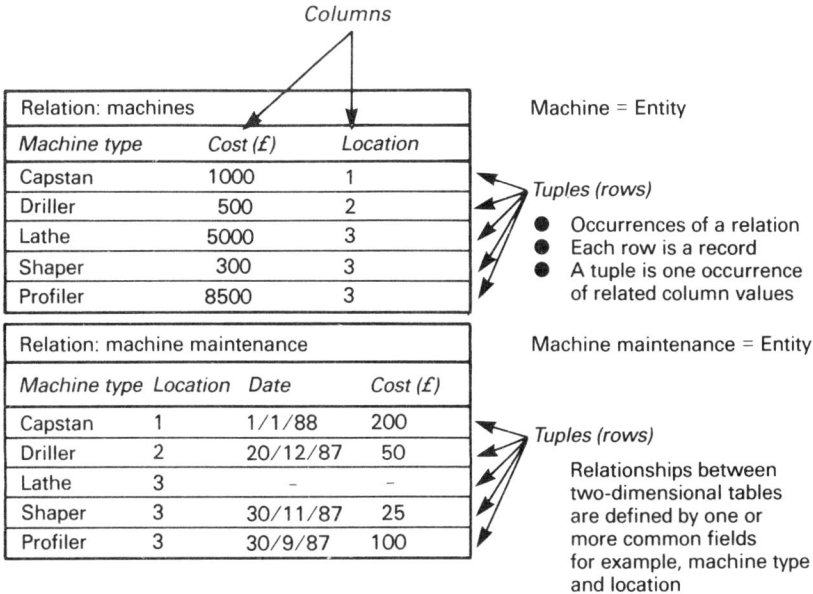

FIG. 10.3   *Relational structure: two dimensional tables*

analysed into relations according to precise rules. The data passes through three stages known as first, second and third normal form.

Stages of normalisation

First normal form
This first stage removes from each 'relation' all 'repeating groups' consisting of elements which may take more than one value in respect to a single value of the Prime key.

Second normal form
This stage removes from each 'relation' all data items which depend on a subset of the elements of the Prime key part-key dependencies. Each non-identifying attribute (non-key field) depends fully upon the identifying attribute (key field).

Third normal form
The final stage removes from each 'relation' all items which do not directly relate to the full Prime key, but on some other data item(s) which are directly related to the Prime key. No dependency between non-identifying attributes.

Refer to the Order processing case study for an example of

normalisation. See Figures B18–B21.

Keys

Logical key
In respect of an entity in a logical data structure, or a relation, the data item or items whose contents, in any given occurrence (row) will be different from all other occurrences thereby providing uniqueness. There are several classifications of logical keys as indicated below.

Prime key
The key which uniquely defines an entity or relation. It is possible for more than one key to provide uniqueness but the Prime key is the one chosen to represent the entity or relation.

Composite key
A key containing more than one data item (key) so related that one of the data items (keys) is meaningless unless qualified by another or others. For example, a database storing relations containing information about books may have a composite key consisting of a book identifier and chapter number where chapter number is assigned sequentially within each book. A key consisting of only the chapter number would be meaningless.

Courting
This process is concerned with finding data which will be held twice to eliminate unnecessary redundancy. This could apply in a stock control system whereby one data structure stores 'basic stock data' and another stores 'usage history data'. They would both contain common fields, i.e. item code and description. In addition, when items are issued from the stores it affects the field 'quantity in stock' in the 'basic stock data' store and the 'usage to date' field in the 'usage history data'. Both could be merged which would avoid inputting the same unit of data twice. When common keys occur in data structures as in this case it is probable that the same entity is under consideration from two points of view which, in this instance, relate to stock issues or usage. This is indicative that the structure should be reviewed to assess if there is a case for merging. The important point to consider is 'relationships', i.e. courting. See p. 235.

DATA DICTIONARY

A data dictionary provides textual support to give a precise definition of all data represented in the various models. It achieves this by defining the meaning (semantics), composition (syntax) and important characteristics of flows and stores on data flow diagrams and also objects and relationships on entity diagrams. The dictionary serves as a central definition catalogue that provides uniformity of expression among analysts and simplifies future analysis and revision. A dictionary can be compiled by Computer-Aided Systems Engineering (CASE) tools automatically when preparing diagrams or by direct entry to dictionary screens, etc. The data dictionary is expanded throughout system design to include new or modified record structures and their relationships, including reference keys, size of data elements, data validation requirements and a description of data items. Most dictionaries are computerised forming an element of database management systems.

SUMMARY OF KEY POINTS

- An entity model is a logical data model.
- An entity model demonstrates the relationships between different types of data and how it can be accessed.
- Entity models consist of three elements: entities, attributes and relationships.
- Entity models are used for top-down data modelling.
- An entity model identifies entry points and access paths to data.
- The various entities in an application are interrelated either directly or indirectly.
- It is necessary to define which entity is a master and which is a detail.
- Entity relationships can be of various forms.
- Normalisation ensures that all non-key data items in each relation are directly and fully dependent on the entire prime key.
- A data dictionary provides a precise definition and facts of all data represented in the various models.

SELF-TEST QUESTIONS
1 State the nature and purpose of an entity model.
2 What are the constituent elements of an entity model?

3 What principal entity types are involved in running a business?
4 How would you determine the dependency of entities in a given application?
5 Define the various entity relationships which may occur in a system.
6 What are relations?
7 How is a relation described in relational data analysis?
8 What is the purpose of normalisation?
9 What are the stages of normalisation?
10 What is a prime and composite key?
11 Define the term 'courting'.
12 What is a data dictionary?
13 What details are contained in a data dictionary?

FURTHER READING

Business information systems, Chris Clare and Peri Loucopoulos, Paradigm, London, 1987.
Chapter 7 Data analysis, provides an introduction to the subject giving details relating to entities, entity relationships and normalisation.
Systems analysis, L. Antill, A. T. Wood-Harper, Heinemann Ltd, London, Made Simple Computer Books, 1985.
Chapter 4 Information modelling, provides an introduction to entities and entity models.
Structured systems development techniques: Strategic planning to system testing, Garfield Collins and Gillian Blay, Pitman Publishing, London 1982.
Chapter 13 Data analysis, provides details relating to relational data analysis, logical data structuring and identification of access requirements.

Part 4

Automated Structured Development Techniques

CHAPTER 11
LBMS Structured Development Method (LSDM)

LEARNING OBJECTIVES

The objective of this chapter is to demonstrate the nature of a proprietory automated structured development method using Computer-Aided Systems Engineering (CASE) tools. In this instance the proprietory structured development method outlined is that of Learmonth and Burchett Management Systems Limited.

APPROACH TO SYSTEM DEVELOPMENT

The LBMS Structured Development Method – LSDM, and the UK Government equivalent SSADM (developed jointly by LBMS and the CCTA), have become a widespread and successful means of performing the analysis and design of information/data processing systems. LSDM facilitates the initial view of a system which can be input in the form of diagrams and simple descriptive text. The initial input is modified and expanded during the project life cycle as more information becomes available until the final logical design is expressed in terms of a complete set of diagrams and forms. Design information is continually checked on input.

ARCHITECTURE OF LSDM

Six stages of systems analysis and design
Systems analysis and design is undertaken in six stages each of which is broken down into steps and each step has associated with it a detailed task list. There are clearly defined interfaces between steps in the form of working documents and criteria for review and project reporting. See Fig. 11.1.

Stages of system analysis
1 Analysis of current system and identification of problems. Commences with the building of a detailed representation of the

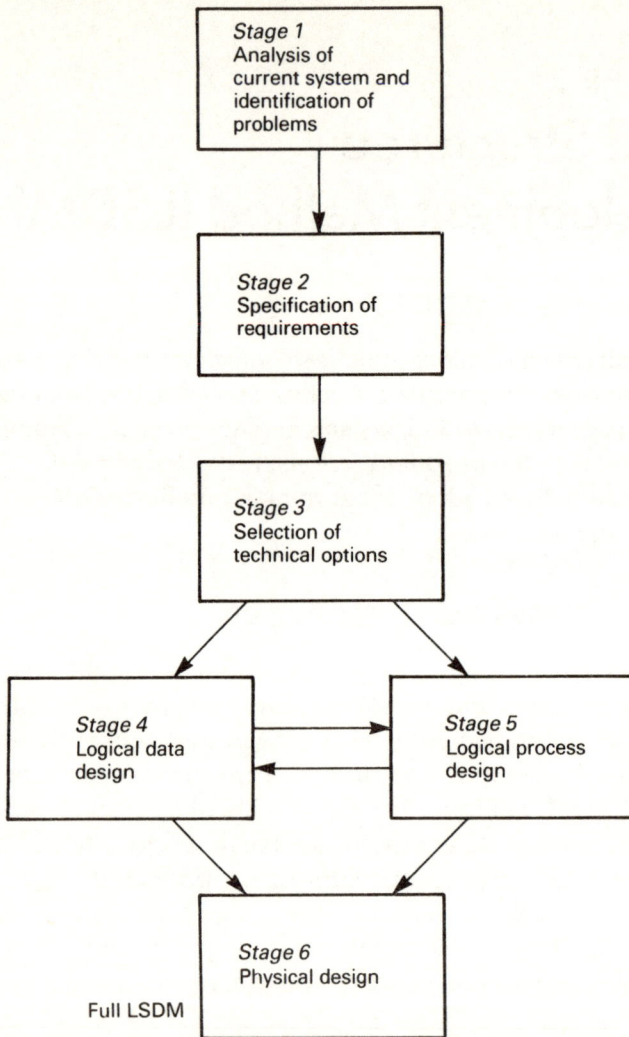

FIG. 11.1   *Stages of systems analysis and design (courtesy of LBMS)*

current physical system which serves the users and the identification of problems and shortcomings. See Fig. 11.2.

2 Specification of requirements. This stage is concerned with producing a logical view of the system and extending it with further services required by the users. This is then expanded into a required system specification (i.e. what it should do, rather than how it should work). See Fig. 11.3.

3 Selection of technical options. This stage is concerned with taking

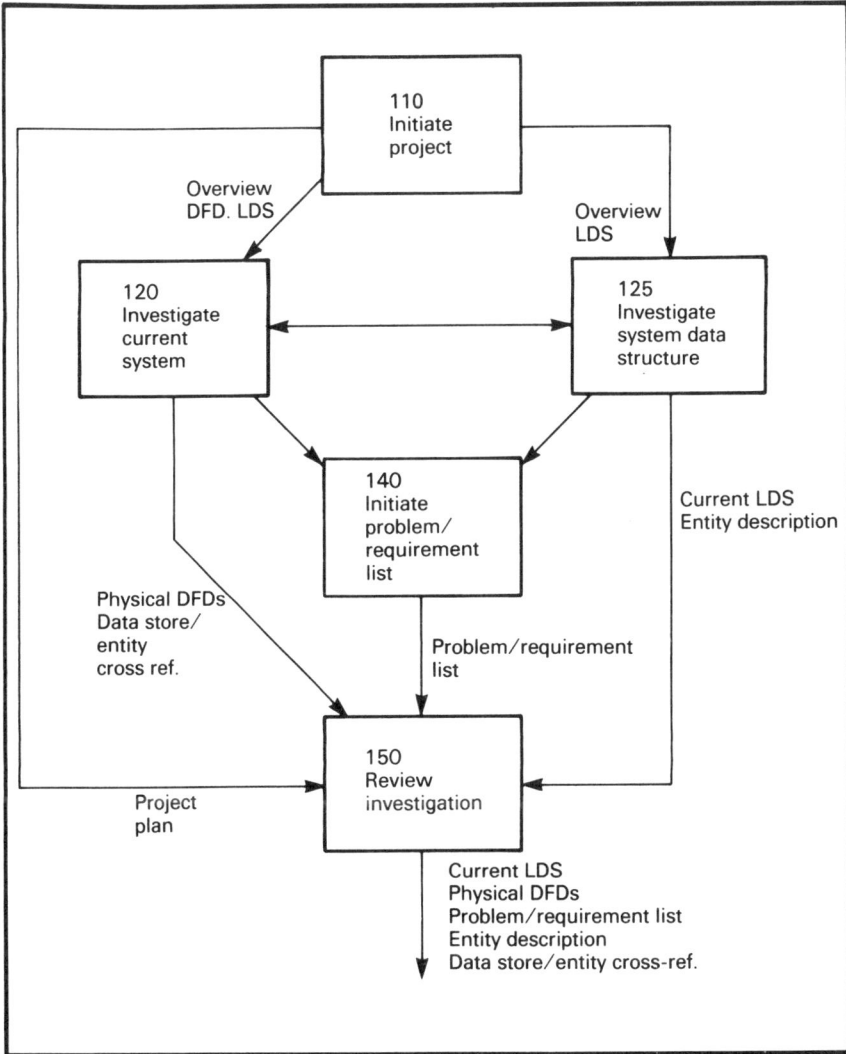

FIG. 11.2   *Stage 1: analysis of current system and identification of problems (courtesy of LBMS)*

the specification and creating a short menu of implementation options, each providing different levels of service (e.g. speed of response, ad-hoc availability of data, flexibility) with each having different costs and delivery times. These are then presented to the users. The users, with technical assistance from the development team, then choose which option is to be implemented. See Fig. 11.4.

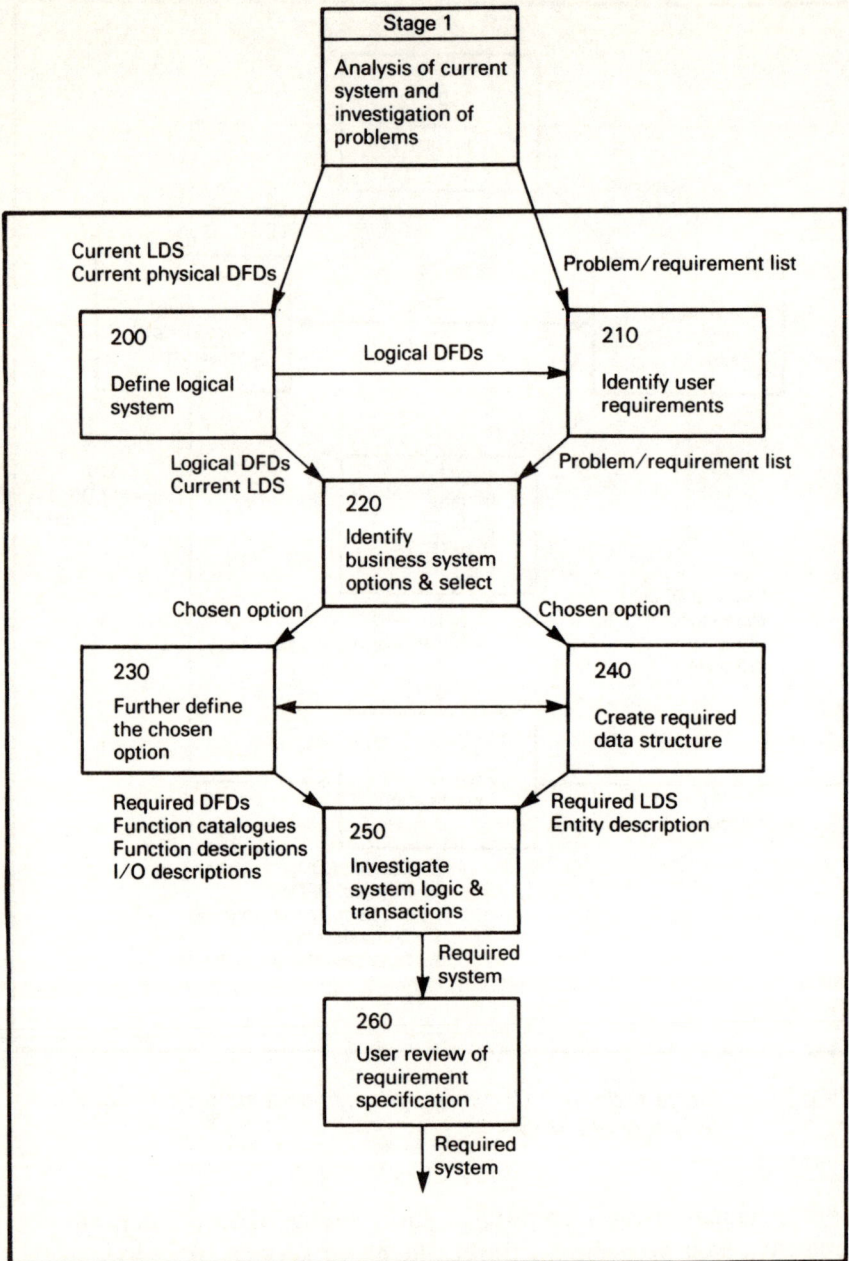

FIG. 11.3 *Stage 2: specification of requirements (courtesy of LBMS)*

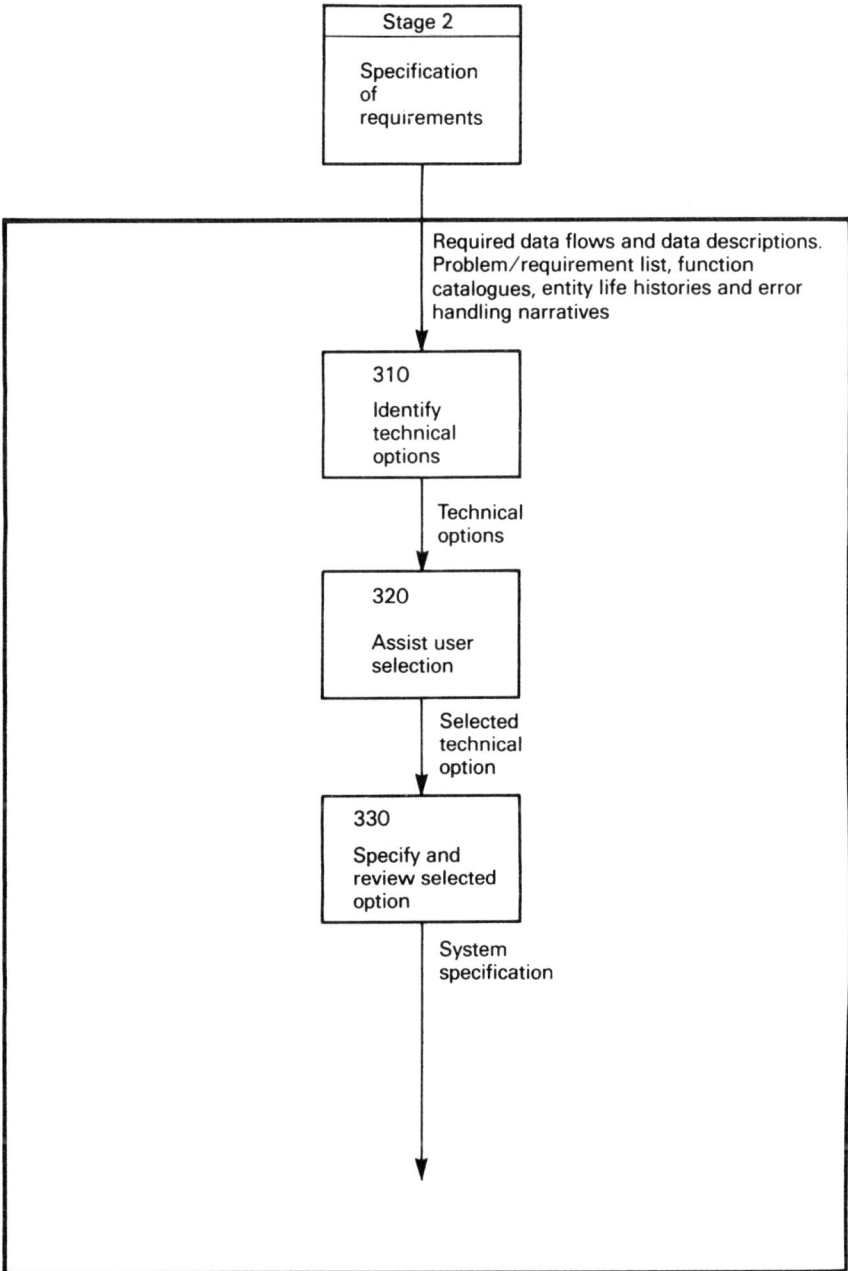

FIG. 11.4   *Stage 3: selection of technical option (courtesy of LBMS)*

Stages of system design

4 Logical data design. A detailed logical data structure is built. See Fig. 11.5.

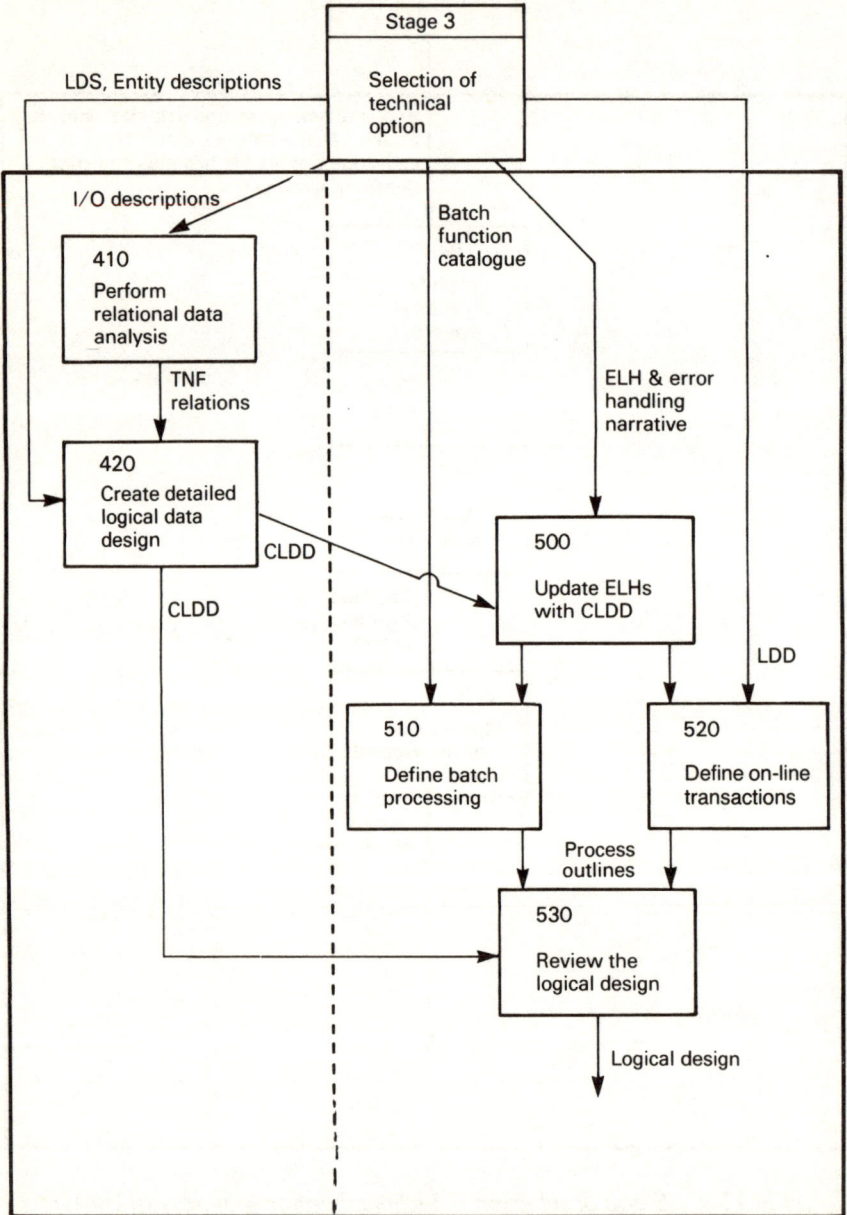

FIG. 11.5 *Stage 4: logical data design. Stage 5: Logical process design (courtesy of LBMS)*

5 Logical process design. Transactions are defined.
6 Physical design. The logical data structure is converted to a 'first cut' file or database design, by application of relatively simple rules which are provided as part of LSDM. This is implementable in the file handler or DBMS to be used but is almost certainly not optimal for performance. The first-cut data design is used to convert the major transactions into a set of first-cut program specifications. See Fig. 11.6.

Before the creation of the remaining program specifications and specifications of file definitions, the first-cut data design and program specifications are put through Physical Design Control, which is a tuning exercise carried out while the design is still on paper. This procedure applies a number of optimisation techniques, using standards provided as part of LSDM, to ensure that the system will meet its performance objectives. After the final design is created by the design control process, the LSDM outputs can be consolidated. LSDM separates logical and physical design. While the conceptual stages of analysis and design are being undertaken, the developer and user are not concerned with any aspect of physical systems. The technique provides a method of checking and proving system logic during the analysis and design phases. The techniques of Entity Life Histories and Process Outlines provide a systematic approach to identifying the events that cause changes to the system's data; identifying the correct sequence(s) of those events; specifying the processing required to handle each event; forcing the analyst and user to consider the system implications and actions required, if notification of events are presented out of sequence; producing a simple-to-use description of processing, error handling and validation requirements for each event (process outlines). LSDM utilises a number of key techniques to provide three views of a system. These are data structure, information flows and events specifying their proper sequence and their associated processing in the system cycle. In the working documentation these three views are represented as entity models, data flow diagrams and entity life histories.

LBMS AUTO-MATE PLUS

Learmonth and Burchett Management Systems Limited market system development software CASE tools known as Auto-Mate Plus, part of a family of software tools aimed at supporting the techniques, documentation and control of LSDM projects. LBMS

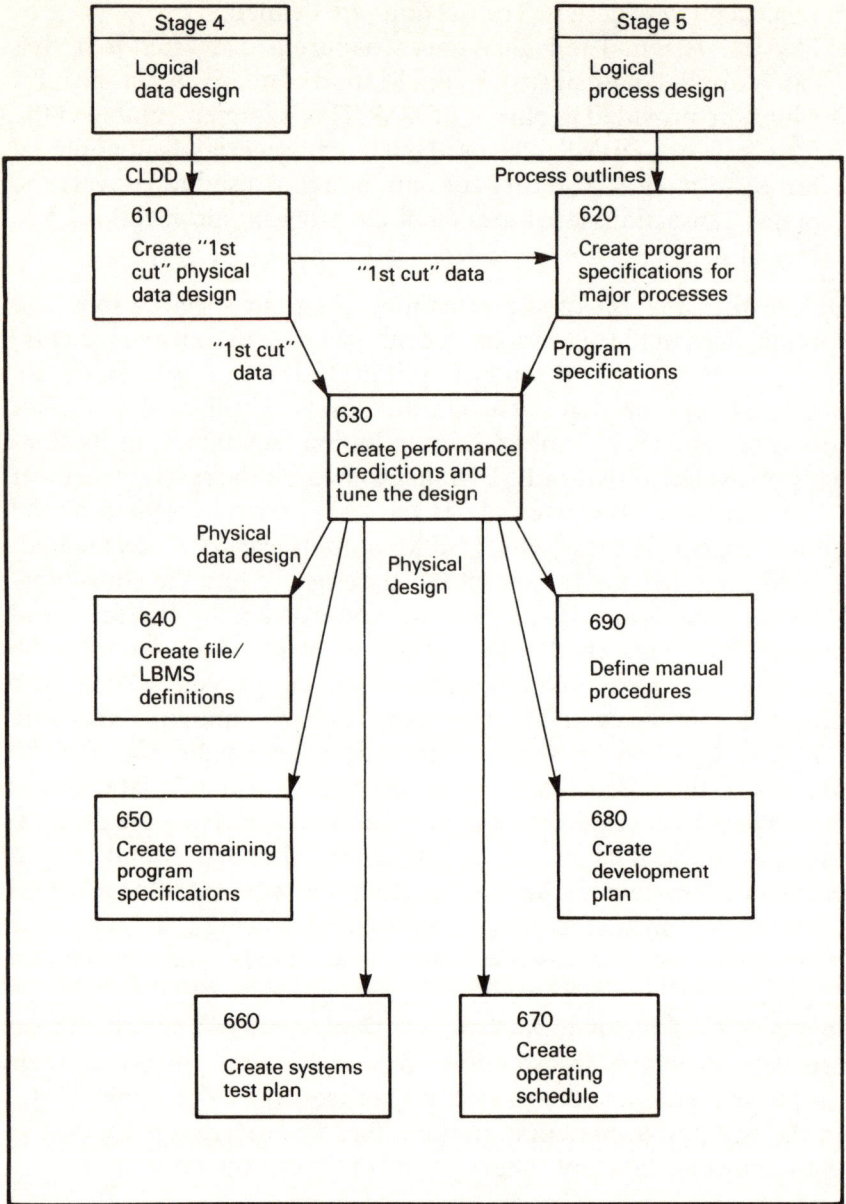

FIG. 11.6 *Stage 6: physical design (courtesy of LBMS)*

Auto-Mate Plus is equally appropriate to SSADM projects. It can be used by systems analysts, designers, database administrators and possibly by users to develop computer systems.

Screen input
The system provides facilities for on-line input of design information which is held in the design database ready for instant retrieval. Input is facilitated by the provision of screen displays including:

- function catalogue
- entity descriptions
- data item descriptions
- process descriptions
- process outlines
- event catalogue

Design database
At the heart of the system is the design database including the data inventory. This holds all the information that has been collected about the system under development – the *target system* as it is called. Using database technology design information can be input, modified and retrieved quickly and reliably. Extensive cross-checking of input data ensures consistency of information relating to the system – which entities use a particular data item, for instance.

Interactive graphics and Diagram Editor
A major advantage of LSDM is the use of discrete diagrams to depict independent views of the system. The maintenance of diagrams places a heavy workload on system design staff but the use of this automated system increases productivity immensely by the provision of a single Diagram Editor that supports Data Flow Diagrams (DFD), Logical Data Structure (LDS) Diagrams and Entity Life History (ELH) Diagrams. The interactive mouse driven selection of actions and shapes enables pictures to be modified and plotted within minutes.

From pictures to systems design
Logical Data Structures and Data Flow Diagrams provide a basis for the system representation and LBMS Auto-Mate Plus follows that philosophy by using the contents of these diagrams to provide the system skeleton. The Diagram Editor supports incomplete pictures for the purpose of system views; diagrams are loaded into the Design Database and verified only when required. Once these diagrams have been loaded into the database further design input is checked against the diagram contents as an aid to consistency. Several Logical Data Structure and Data Flow Diagrams can be maintained on the Design Database to reflect the evolution of the system design.

Reports
Standard reports can be produced through a special report menu.

Hardware
LBMS Auto-Mate Plus operates on IBM PC and compatible machines and a range of printers, plotters and graphics modes are supported.

AUTOMATED DATA ANALYSIS

Data analysis concepts
Data analysis is essential for the effective design of information systems. It is realised that data analysis performed correctly will ensure that delivered systems are flexible and accord with the strategic data planning objectives. LBMS Auto-Mate Plus, part of a family of Information Technology products, aids the analyst with the task of Data – Analysis both in Entity Modelling and in the more formal and rigorous Third Normal Form (TNF) Analysis.

Entity modelling using Auto-Mate Plus
A Diagram Editor is used for the creation and maintenance of entity model pictures and provides the productivity benefits associated with an easy to use but highly advanced CASE tool. The software also facilitates the recording of the Entity Model picture contents on the Design Database; provides a menu driven system for adding Entity, Relationship and Data Inventory descriptions and Entity Model merging at the picture and Database levels. Where several possible Entity models are being postulated, the Data Inventory provides the essential 'where used' information to allow model comparison. A data dictionary based set of entities and relationships can be imported into the design database to produce an entity model in pictorial form. Different entity models may be merged to form a single model with facilities to merge or copy entity information within the design database.

Third Normal Form (TNF) analysis
Auto-Mate Plus revolutionises the approach to TNF data analysis (see Case study B and Figs. B18–B21) by means of an expert-like relational analysis engine for data normalisation. It provides the following features:

* interactive input and maintenance of I/O Descriptions (raw relations)*

- automatic generation and updating of the underlying Data Inventory
- the choice of guidance through the normalisation process in novice or expert 'decision support' mode
- full backout support at any point during the normalisation process
- optimisation of TNF relations into a non-redundant group
- automatic generation of the TNF structure diagram
- a Diagram Editor for picture modification

*New I/O descriptions may be input to the system at any time as the Auto-Mate Plus automatically takes the results of this through to the Optimised set without the need to review existing work and the final TNF Data Structure is automatically analysed.

A unique feature of the software is the ability to produce a picture of the TNF data structure. Amendments to topology may be performed using the Diagram Editor.

Reports and data inventory
Reports can be generated at any time to review the current state of normalisation and sections, or all, of the data inventory may be displayed to provide an interactive method of working. The data inventory holds information about all data items (attributes) and in addition to the easy access facility may be used to enforce naming standards. Interfaces to data dictionaries provide an additional means of standardisation.

Design interchange
The design interchange facility allows the porting of design results to a mainframe for input to software tools such as DBMS, compilers and 4GLs. The DIF also allows the transfer of data between the design database and an existing central dictionary.

SUMMARY OF KEY POINTS
- LSDM is undertaken in six stages.
- Stage 1 is concerned with the analysis of the current system and identification of problems.
- Stage 2 produces a logical view of the system determining what it should do, not how it should work.
- Stage 3 considers implementation options each providing different levels of service.
- Stage 4 – building of a logical data structure.

- Stage 5 – definition of transactions.
- Stage 6 – the logical data structure is converted to a 'first cut' file or database design.
- LSDM applies techniques to obtain three views of a system – data structure, information flows and events.
- The three views are represented as entity models, data flow diagrams and entity life histories.
- The system provides facilities for on-line input of design information which is held in the design database.

SELF TEST QUESTIONS

1 List the six stages of LSDM.
2 Define the three ways in which a system may be viewed.
3 What type of models, diagrams or other technique is used to represent the three views?
4 What is a design database and what purpose does it serve?
5 What type of screen displays are available using LBMS CASE tools?

FURTHER READING

Further details of this proprietory system of structured development methodology may be obtained from:

Learmonth & Burchett Management Systems Limited, Evelyn House, 62 Oxford Street, London W1N 9LF. Telephone: 01-636-4213.

A similar methodology is described in: *Structured systems analysis and design methodology*, G. Cutts, Paradigm, 1987.

This book includes an extensive case study which demonstrates in detail how these systems operate.

CHAPTER 12

Automated system building: information engineering

LEARNING OBJECTIVES

The objective of this chapter is to demonstrate the nature of a proprietory automated structured development method using Computer-Aided Systems Engineering (CASE) tools. In this instance the proprietory structured development method outlined is that of Knowledge Ware, Inc. The system is known as Information Engineering Workbench.

INFORMATION ENGINEERING WORKBENCH (IEW)

Arthur Young, a worldwide leader in Management and Information Technology Training, market KnowledgeWare Inc's Information Engineering Workbench (IEW) which uses advanced Computer-Aided Systems Engineering (CASE) tools. These are as important to information systems development as the CAD/CAM (computer-aided design and manufacturing) techniques which revolutionised the design of cars, missiles and semi-conductor chips. Analysts will be able to create, verify and revise diagrams on a computer screen. The IEW will run on enhanced IBM PC/AT, its diagramming fully integrated by the Encyclopaedia and its Knowledge Coordinator. It will operate via mouse-driven commands, pull-down menus and standard commands; the IEW will display diagrams and related information in 'windows' that can be manipulated on the screen. The user can look at several diagramming windows at once to see the same information in different forms. The contents of any window can be printed. Colours assist the identification of the type of diagram appearing in each window. User-selectable diagramming symbols ensure that the diagrams conform to established standards. A password security provision protects data from unauthorised use. These topics are further expanded upon in the following sections.

EXPERT SYSTEM

Encyclopaedia: knowledge base

IEW incorporates an encyclopaedia, a knowledge base which stores the meaning of each diagram created. It stores information only once, regardless of the number and type of diagrams in which it may appear – consequently any changes made in a diagram will automatically be reflected in all other representations of the information. The diagrams are merely a display format for entry and retrieval of the information in the encyclopaedia. The IEW retrieves current information from the encyclopaedia each time it generates a display and updates the encyclopedia each time anything is changed in a diagram.

Knowledge Coordinator: expert system

In between the encyclopaedia and the diagramming tools there is a Knowledge Coordinator, an expert system module which performs a number of vital functions. It takes the meaning of a diagram from the encyclopaedia and automatically redraws that information in any other selected format. It reconstructs the diagrammatic representation of the information every time a diagram is requested. This means that diagrams and their definitions are inseparable – any change to either is always reflected in the other. This avoids having to draw another diagram if the information is required to be seen in more than one format. The expert system uses hundreds of structured logic rules to check the correctness of analysis. If an attempt is made to violate the rules of any of the common diagramming methods the analyst is alerted of the error.

GRAPHICS AND WINDOWS

Graphics

Direct, on-screen graphics manipulation simplifies the drawing of diagrams as computerised design technology allows the most complex systems to be fully and accurately described and changes are recorded effortlessly. To build a diagram a mouse is used to point to the location where a diagram symbol is to appear. Each diagram is displayed in a 'window'. Associations between symbols can be defined simply by 'drawing' a line between them. IEW prompts the user for names and descriptive information as appropriate. The mouse can be used to highlight a symbol and then delete or move it, to request a detail window to display more information about the symbol, or to change any information shown on the screen. Changes are instantly reflected in the diagrams. Automatic coordination of diagrams through the Knowledge Coordinator allows any object in a diagram to be described in more detail by creating another type of diagram about it.

To more fully describe the contents of a data store appearing in a data flow diagram, for instance, an entity diagram could be created that shows the details associated with the data store. In instances when one diagram's content is implied by the contents of another the IEW can generate it automatically. When, for instance, a set of levelled data flow diagrams are created they imply a function decomposition of a business activity. The IEW can automatically generate a corresponding decomposition diagram using information that was created in the encyclopaedia when the data flow diagrams were created.

Multiple windows
The system also has complete windowing capabilities – see Fig. 12.1. Several diagrams can be displayed on the screen at one time to allow the flow of information from one diagram to the next to be seen. When it is necessary to see, for example, the hierarchy of sub-processes that comprise a process box on a data flow diagram, the hierarchy can be displayed in a second window on the same screen as the original data flow diagram. This provides a better understanding of the interactions among the different parts of the system. Because each diagram type is colour coded, the required diagram can speedily be located. By using a mouse the user can move the windows around on the screen, scroll around the diagram within a window and call up various menu items to construct and modify diagrams. The system allows a diagram to be retained on the screen while scrutinising a definition of some object from the diagram.

Tracing facilities
Tracing facilities assist in clarifying the meaning of a diagram by highlighting the relationship between objects even when they are physically far apart on a complex diagram. The 'neighborhood' command allows the suppression of all parts of a diagram that are not directly connected to the object or objects of special interest. The 'path' command can be used to suppress all objects and relationships that do not lie on a path between the two objects specified. These features are useful for understanding complex diagrams.

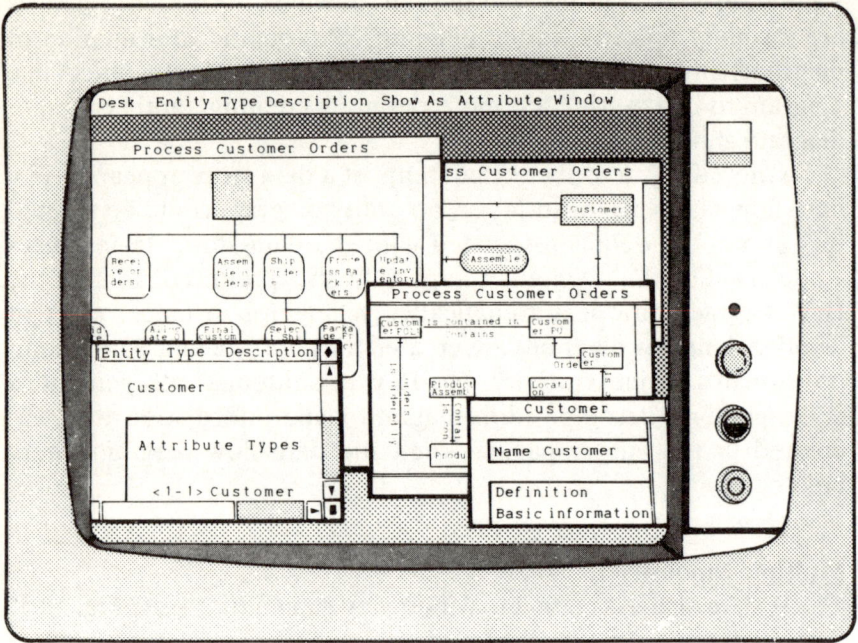

FIG. 12.1   *Multiple window screen.* The ability to view several diagrams at once
when using the Information Engineering Workbench/Workstation means
you can more easily track the flow of data or the sequence of operations
through several diagrams. Because each diagram type is colour coded,
you can locate the diagram you need quickly. Using a mouse, you can
move windows around on the screen, scroll around the diagram within a
window, and call up various menu items to construct and modify
diagrams. (Courtesy of KnowledgeWare Inc.)

DIAGRAMS

The building of diagrams that represent an information system is a
task fundamental to systems analysis. Diagrams help in clarifying the
interrelationships between activities and data and the sources and
uses of information. IEW enables various diagrams to be drawn and
reports to be produced as outlined in the following notes.

Decomposition diagrammer
Most modelling and structured design techniques use a form of
hierarchical construction by breaking down (refining) a high level
definition of an activity into more detailed tasks (successive levels of
detail) which can then be subjected to further analysis to provide
even more details of the various tasks. The diagram of this refinement
process forms an inverted tree structure – the further out on a branch

of the tree, the finer the detail revealed, see Fig. 12.2. The decomposition diagrammer assists in the creation and maintenance of hierarchy diagrams of subject areas, activities and organisational units. When a new child is created the mouse is used to draw a line from parent to child thereby maintaining the elements of a hierarchy. If the child has a subtree, the entire subtree moves with the child. If the object is deleted all of its 'children' move up to its parent. The objects in an hierarchy are automatically numbered based on their position. The rules of decomposition are automatically enforced, to detect a circular relationship among objects, for instance.

Entity diagrammer
Entity diagrammer assists in creating and maintaining entity diagrams which identify the principal entity types involved in running a business and assists in determining the relationships among them. Entity diagrams are used for both top-down data planning and detailed data modelling. Top-down planning identifies the principal entity types, such as materials, employees, suppliers, customers, functions, locations, products and assets about which records need to be maintained, and determines the major relationships among them. Data modelling further refines the entity model created during planning, using details collected from specific end-user information needs. This tool works with entity types, relationships between entity types and attributes, see Fig. 12.3. A choice is possible between the two common methods of denoting entity relationships using either arrows or 'crows' feet' on the lines. Standard rectangles or Chen 'diamonds' can also be selected to represent associative entity types. It is also possible to specify both a minimum and a maximum cardinality (position or rank) for a relationship in both directions, allowing optional relationships to be distinguished from mandatory ones. For a detailed description of an entity a window can be called for displaying the entity's definition, attributes and relationships. The window will also allow additions or changes to attribute information. An entity diagram can be used to define in more detail the data requirements of a decomposition or data flow activity, the contents of a decomposition diagram subject area or the contents of a data store, data flow or external agent in a data flow diagram. Through the Knowledge Coordinator the IEW can automatically construct an entity diagram for the integrated entity model implied by the individual entity diagrams declared for specific activities, data flows, data stores and so on.

Subject area decomposition

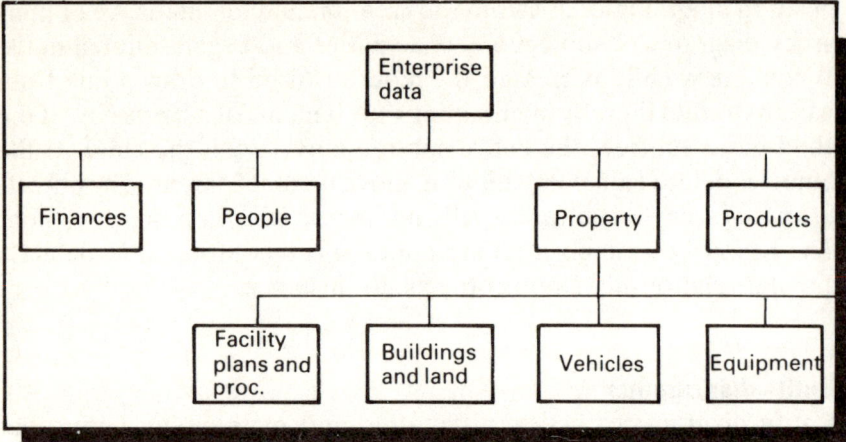

Functional decomposition

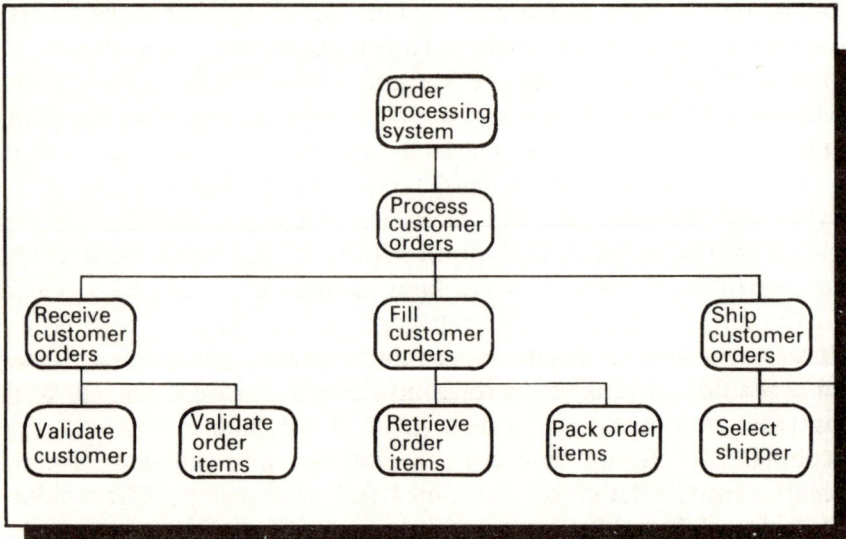

FIG. 12.2 *Decomposition diagram.* Helps you create and maintain a hierarchy diagram for subject areas, activities, and organisational units. When you create a new "child" you use the mouse to draw a line from parent to child. If the child has a subtree, the entire subtree moves with the child. It automatically enforces the rules of decomposition, alerting you to circular relationships among objects. (Courtesy of KnowledgeWare Inc.)

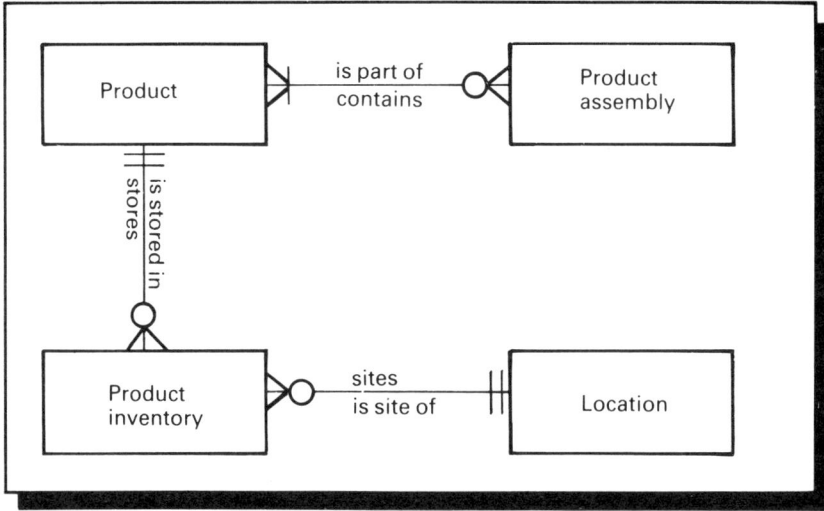

FIG. 12.3 *Entity diagram.* Diagrams the principal entity types involved in running a business and helps you determine the relationships among them. You can specify both minimum and maximum relationship cardinalities to distinguish optional relationships from mandatory ones. It can use information implied by individual entity diagrams for specific activities, data flows, and data stores to automatically construct an entity diagram for the integrated entity model. (Courtesy of KnowledgeWare Inc.)

Data flow diagrammer

The data flow diagrammer assists in the creation and maintenance of data flow diagrams. A dataflow diagram shows the overall flow of information through a business or computer system. Each diagram displays one level of decomposition of an activity, including the sub-activities, data stores, junctions, external agents and data flows that are part of it, see Fig. 12.4. Symbols which can be used include Martin, Yourdon and Gane and Sarson symbols. Yourdon-like data flow expressions may also be used to describe flow contents. The data flow diagrammer provides for detailed descriptions of objects in a data flow diagram with other diagrams. Detailed descriptions of objects in a data flow can be created using other diagramming methods. Using an entity diagram, for example, the data requirements of an activity, data flow or external agent can be defined more completely. An activity on a data flow diagram may be further decomposed using either another data flow diagram or a decomposition diagram. There is no limit to the number of levels.

Activities are automatically numbered based on their position in the activity hierarchy. Additionally, a full-levelled set of 'skeleton' data flow diagrams can be generated automatically from the activities in a decomposition diagram, with one data flow diagram corresponding to each object in the decomposition diagram. Each of these data flow diagrams will already be populated with symbols for the sub-activities that comprised the node in the decomposition diagram.

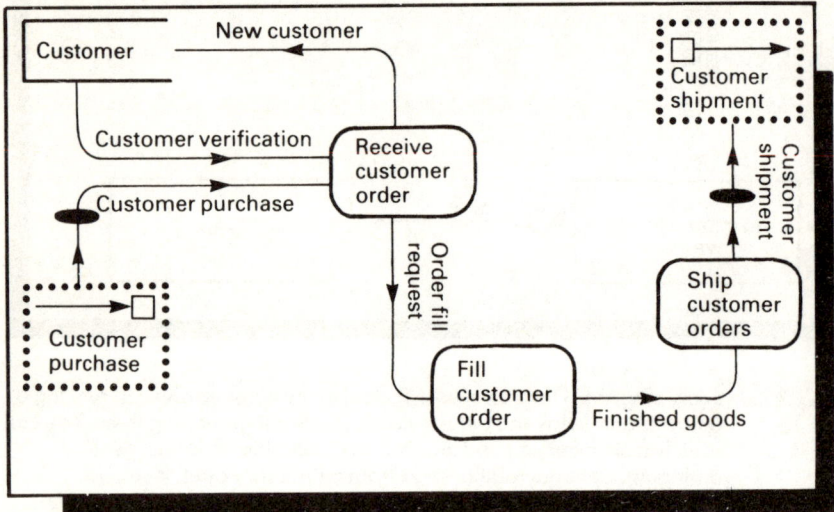

FIG. 12.4 *Data flow diagram.* Diagrams decomposition activities, subactivities, data stores, junctions, external agents, and data flows that are a part of the activity. You can automatically generate a fully-levelled set of data flow diagrams; one for each object in the decomposition diagram. Each of the data flow diagrams generated is populated with symbols for the sub-activities of the node in the decomposition diagram. (Courtesy of KnowledgeWare Inc.)

Action diagrammer

Action diagrams can be used for structuring the logic of a system much more precisely than structured English alone and may be used for mini-specs on a data flow diagram. Action diagrams are comprised of graphic and narrative notation that is complete and rigorous enough to represent both high-level overviews and detailed program logic. These notations represent hierarchical structure, repetition, case structure, exits, database actions and common subprocedures – see Fig. 12.5, action diagram.

Brackets are the basic building blocks of action diagrams. A bracket can be of any length so it can grow to make space for as much text or detail as is needed. Inside the bracket is a sequence of operations. A simple control rule applies to the bracket which is – do things in sequence – enter it at the top; do the actions in a top-to-bottom sequence and exit at the bottom. There may be other brackets inside a bracket. The nesting of multiple brackets indicates hierarchical structure of processes and subprocesses triggered by execution decisions and conditions. Data references in an action diagram must be consistent with the topic activity's view. The encyclopaedia stores action diagram logic details right down to the specific execution conditions and actions. This is the kind of detail that will support code generation. A hard copy of any diagram can be produced on a suitable graphics printer or plotter. The diagrams may be full-sized or reduced.

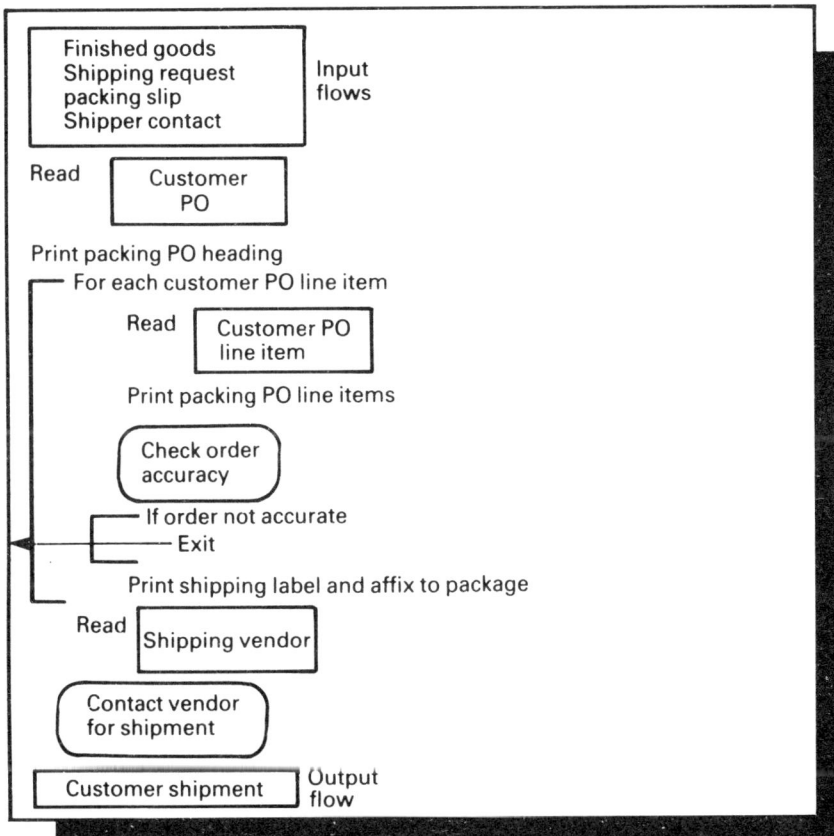

FIG. 12.5   *Action diagram.* Uses graphic and narrative notations to represent hierarchical structure, repetition, case structure, exits, database actions, and common sub-procedures. Nesting of multiple brackets shows the hierarchy of processes and sub-processes triggered by execution decisions and conditions. The Encyclopaedia stores action diagram logic details right down to the specific execution conditions and actions. This is the kind of detail that will support code generation. (Courtesy of KnowledgeWare Inc.)

REPORTS

In addition to providing printed copies of any diagrams the system generates reports to help in the evaluation of every aspect of the analysis. Sample reports are listed below:

1 *View content analysis report.* This report finds and lists the views that contain a given entity type, relationship type, or attribute type. This 'where used' report is especially helpful when it is necessary to know if changes to an entity, relationship or attribute will affect operations in another area of the system.

2 *Data flow course analysis report.* Using this report feature it is possible to trace the course of data from source to destination – regardless of the number of levels the data traverses. All points along the course can be reported or only the ultimate source and destination.

3 *Flow expression report.* Lists data flow expressions for the object instances selected from a diagram. It is also possible to request flow expressions for data flows, sources, destinations, contents or activities selected independent of any diagrams.

4 *Connectivity analysis report.* The first step in designing a consistent model of data flows is making sure each flow is connected to something. This report assists in the location of unconnected flows and highlights flows that are not connected to valid sources of destinations. It is possible to generate a connectivity report for the entire encyclopaedia, or just the diagram being worked on or selected data flows within the diagram.

5 *Data conservation analysis report.* To ensure that data inputs and outputs balance the system can automatically check data conservation of the entire encyclopaedia, a selected data flow diagram, or selected data flow nodes. The system checks for conservation based on internal rules for data stores, junctions, external agents, and activities. The analysis can consider entities, attributes and relationships individually, in valid combinations only, or in valid combinations with their cardinalities.

6 *Object summary report.* This report can be tailored to provide just the information needed on a specific object, a group of objects, or all objects in the encyclopaedia. An important benefit of this report is the ability to determine when an object was last revised and by whom. It is also possible to choose all or a limited number of properties and associations listed for each object.

SUMMARY OF KEY POINTS

- Information engineering workbench (IEW) applies Computer-Aided Systems Engineering (CASE) tools.
- Analysts are able to create, verify and revise diagrams on a computer screen.
- The system functions via mouse-driven commands, pull-down menus and standard commands.
- The user can look at several diagramming windows on the screen simultaneously.
- The contents of any window can be printed.
- IEW incorporates an encyclopaedia, a knowledge base which stores the meaning of each diagram created.
- A Knowledge Coordinator, an expert system module, takes the meaning of a diagram from the encyclopaedia and automatically redraws that information in any other selected format.
- On-screen graphics manipulation simplifies the drawing of diagrams.
- The system provides diagramming facilities for creating and maintaining entity, data flow and action diagrams.
- The system generates reports to assist in the evaluation of every aspect of the analysis.

SELF-TEST QUESTIONS

1 What operational facilities are available for operation of the system?
2 What facility does the system provide for the display of diagrams and related information?
3 How is it possible to ensure that diagrams conform to established standards?
4 What is the nature and purpose of an encyclopaedia in the context of IEW?
5 What is the nature and purpose of a Knowledge Coordinator?
6 How is on-screen graphics manipulation facilitated?
7 What purpose do multiple windows serve?
8 What type of diagramming facility does IEW provide?
9 What types of report does IEW provide?

FURTHER READING

Further details of this proprietary system of structured development
   methodology may be obtained from:
KnowledgeWare Inc., 3340 Peachtree Road, N.E., Atlanta GA 30326.
or International office, KnowledgeWare Inc., St Alphage House, 2 Fore
   Street, London EC2Y 5DA.

CHAPTER 13

The Oracle Approach to System Development: 4th Generation Environment

LEARNING OBJECTIVES

The objective of this chapter is to demonstrate the nature of a proprietory 4th generation environment combining modern systems methods and software which provide the tools for system development. The 4th generation environment is marketed by ORACLE Corporation UK Limited.

The world is now tending to accept a standard method for the development of systems which is usually based on the following stages (see Fig. 13.1):

1 Strategy – determine what needs to be done and how much it should cost
2 Analysis – specify the user requirement (specified in terms of what functions a business needs to do and what information is needed to support these functions)
3 Design – decide what the systems should look like and what methodology and tools should be used
4 Implementation
  - build – develop the system
  - documentation – write the user handbook
  - Transition – implement actions to smoothly changeover to the new system
5 Production – live with the system and create an environment for ongoing maintenance and enhancements.

The details which follow are based on the products and services available from ORACLE Corporation UK Ltd, a company providing a full range of software and services encompassed in what is referred to as the ORACLE 4th Generation Environment.

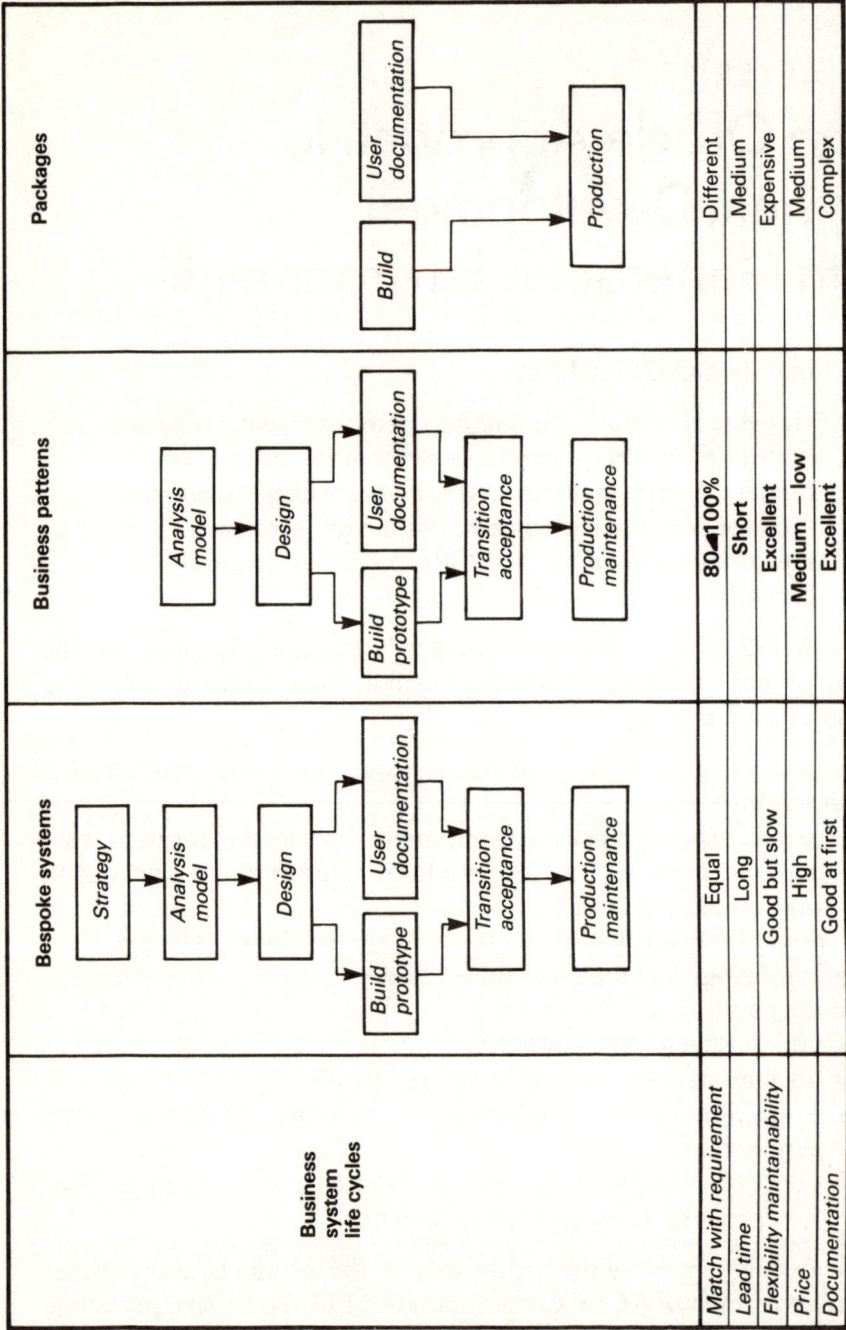

Business system life cycles	Bespoke systems	Business patterns	Packages
Match with requirement	Equal	80—100%	Different
Lead time	Long	Short	Medium
Flexibility maintainability	Good but slow	Excellent	Expensive
Price	High	Medium — low	Medium
Documentation	Good at first	Excellent	Complex

FIG. 13.1 Approaches to system development in the 4th generation environment (courtesy of Oracle Corporation UK Ltd)

APPLICATION PACKAGE: BUSINESS PATTERNS

Of particular relevance to system development is an application package from ORACLE known as business patterns covering a particular subject area, accounting, business assets and personnel, for instance. It comprises:

- A working system built entirely using the ORACLE 4th Generation Environment which can be put into immediate production. This includes the database, screens, reports and user instructions.
- A full system specification which describes the analysis of the business area and the way in which the package has been designed and implemented.
- A comprehensive developer's guide which describes how the business pattern can be readily extended to meet a particular customer request or be integrated with other systems in the installation. See Figure 13.1.

Ways of using business patterns
There are three different ways of using business patterns:

1 *The package approach.* This approach is simply to use the product unchanged. The application screens, batch programs and reports are packaged into a hierarchical menu, and the clear, concise operating instructions enable users to obtain immediate operation.
2 *The prototyping approach.* This approach reviews the application screens and reports and then uses the power of the ORACLE 4th Generation tools and the SQL enquiry language to make any changes that the users request prior to going live.
3 *The system development approach.* This approach uses the system specification as a basis for agreeing requirements with the users. The specification, which is documented in the System Development Dictionary (SDD), can be updated to reflect the agreed requirements. These updates then create a fully customised system with accurate documentation.

Meeting requirements
Traditionally, users have had to compromise their real requirements either because of cost or because of timescale constraints. The business pattern user can select an early implementation date by using the product unchanged which enables the system to go live in a very short period of time.

On the other hand if the prototyping approach is adopted it is only necessary to make cosmetic changes. If the system development approach is adopted the full systems specification may be used as a speedy means of discussion and agreement with users. As previously indicated the systems specification describes the analysis of the business area and the way in which the package has been designed and implemented. The business pattern is delivered with full documentation:

- requirements specification providing details of the system as if the user had personally analysed the system
- design documentation is complete, including reasons for all the decisions
- implementation manual providing the technical details of each application program, screen or report including full source code listings, see Fig. 13.1.

SYSTEM DEVELOPMENT USING SYSTEM DEVELOPMENT DICTIONARY (SDD)

SDD is a structured system to monitor and control the development of applications systems at all stages of their development, from initial analysis of the function through to live operation and maintenance. It provides a definitive record of what the target system is to achieve and how it achieves it. SDD is a computerised database system which holds and actively manages all the information collected and derived during the development and production running of a business system. It provides the mechanism to undertake continuous consistency and quality checks throughout the analysis and design process and then optionally to automatically generate relational database structures. SQL (a powerul easy-to-learn language with English-like syntax) statements to create tables, views and indexes are generated directly from the business specification.

SDD can be grouped into three major categories:

- development support
- usability
- ORACLE related

Development support
SDD consists of over 50 on-line application screens, reports and programs which maintain the SDD database and provide a combination of working documents and management information.

Input and query screens
These screens which have comprehensive validity and creditability checks include:

- function and entity definitions
- relationships and attributes, including domain validation
- volumes and frequencies
- table definitions, columns, sizes, identifiers
- user views of data
- performance indexes
- application, screen, report and program definitions

Working documentation
SDD produces working documentation which can form the major part of a requirements specification and includes:

- function hierarchy
- project activity schedule with customisable gearing factors
- database sizing

Usability
The System development dictionary provides several features to ensure that users attain maximum value from its use. The features include:

- screen driven prompted data entry
- all access to functions is via a menu
- bulk data, if it already exists, can be loaded into SDD
- full back-up and recovery features are included
- comprehensive HELP and user documentation
- synonym support
- interpretation of certain data (e.g. relationship names) is displayed at data entry time so that early high quality is ensured
- provision for ad-hoc queries
- user-defined reports to fit in with their existing standards

ORACLE-related
SDD is built exclusively using the ORACLE 4th Generation Environment. All SDD data is stored in the ORACLE relational database which automatically provides other ORACLE facilities to SDD users:

- extensive input validation
- query-by-example enquiry facilities for selective data searching

- powerful mechanisms for granting database access privileges and preventing unauthorised access
- ad-hoc reporting using the SQL language
- identical SDD versions run on IBM, DEC, Data General and other micro, mini and mainframe systems and can therefore co-operate in a distributed development environment

SUMMARY OF KEY POINTS

- Business patterns comprises the ORACLE 4th Generation Environment consisting of a database, screens, reports and user instructions.
- Business patterns may be used in three different ways: the package approach, the prototyping approach or the system development approach.
- SDD is a structured system to monitor and control the development of systems.
- SDD is a computerised database system which holds and manages the information collected during development.
- SDD provides for consistency and quality checks throughout the analysis and design process.
- SDD optionally generates relational database structures.
- SDD consists of over 50 on-line application screens, reports and programs which maintain the SDD database.

SELF-TEST QUESTIONS

1 Business patterns may be used in three different ways. List and describe the three different ways.
2 What is the purpose of SDD?
3 What is the nature of SDD?
4 List seven different input and query screens facilitated by SDD.
5 The System Development Dictionary provides a number of features to ensure the user attains maximum benefit from its use. Specify several of these features.
6 What database facilities does SDD provide?

FURTHER READING

Further details of this proprietory Fourth generation environment may be obtained from:

ORACLE Corporation UK Limited, UK Headquarters, Thames Link House, 1 Church Road, Richmond, Surrey TW9 2QE.

Case Studies demonstrating Structured Methodology

Stock Control

The details contained in the following text are for the purpose of demonstrating the structured approach to the development of systems. Chapter 8, Structured Development Methodology (SDM) provides an introduction to the structured approach and Chapters 9–13 provide a greater depth of detail.

The approach adopted to designing the system is primarily a top-down, input-to-output, data-driven approach as it is considered that data flows are the predominant factors around which the system should be structured. The meaning of these terms are outlined in Chapter 3. The stages of the adopted structured approach are:

1 Obtain terms of reference.
2 Analyse current system including data analysis.
3 Identify entities and construct conceptual model.
4 Analyse entity life and transaction histories.
5 Construct context diagram.
6 Specify data elements (attributes) relating to each input data flow. Specify data elements (attributes) of output data flows and the origin of each output data flow.
7 Specify input and output data flows and an outline of processing activities by means of a comprehensive data flow diagram.
8 Transform analysis – levelling of data flows.
9 Data modelling using an entity diagram to depict the relationship between data items, their entry points and access paths.
10 Functional decomposition of processes.
11 Construct flowchart portraying logical model of the system.
12 Initial design of physical system – first sketch.

DETAILS OF EACH STAGE

Stage 1 Terms of reference

Management require a system which will optimise stocks by efficient stock management techniques, i.e. application of stock control parameters, the use of minimum, maximum and reorder levels and the computation of reorder quantities to avoid storing excessive quantities, to minimise shortages and to optimise the investment in stocks. Stock optimisation is also necessary to minimise the use of storage space which is a critical factor, as additional space for the storage of stocks is unavailable. If storage space was to run out a costly building extension project would need to be undertaken which management wish to avoid due to a shortage of liquid funds and the need to avoid overdrafts or loans until the business becomes more profitable.

The proposed system is to incorporate an audit trail which the current system does not have. With the increasing levels of stocks it is considered necessary to have a greater degree of independent control of the system. The current system does not record details of orders placed. This is considered to be an essential, if not imperative, feature of the proposed system, in order to be aware of orders outstanding for a particular part, by reference to the relevant stock record. The stock controller is to be provided with a daily stock schedule, which will necessitate a daily updating frequency. A weekly schedule is considered inadequate for effective control because of the envisaged increase in stock levels due to an anticipated increase in the volume of sales. The new system is to incorporate a decision making routine for automatically printing items which have reached the reorder levels on a reorder list. This will enable the buying office to place replenishment orders for bought out items with a minimum of delay and without omissions.

Although the proposed system is primarily for the effective control of stocks of parts it has a number of interfaces with related functions (sub-systems). They include the recording of parts to be reserved for specific jobs/orders, as directed by the production planning function. The stores provide details of receipts from suppliers, providing the interface between the external and internal environment. The stores also interface with the production function (manufacturing sub-system) by providing details of issues and returns to stock control. The stock control system interfaces with the buying office (purchasing sub-system) by the provision of a re-order list and the buying office provides details of purchases to stock control by means of a copy of the purchase order. The stock control system also interfaces with the audit function by providing a list of transactions and amendments processed, i.e. an audit trail. Refer to Fig. A2 outlining entity relationships.

Stage 2 Analyse current system including data analysis
This activity is concerned with collecting and analysing facts about

the current system in order to obtain an appreciation of its nature, characteristics, problems and weaknesses. Data analysis is a very important aspect of systems analysis and it is primarily concerned with defining the attributes (fields) of each entity and the relationships which exist between them. Data analysis collects details as outlined below:

1 The data originating point
2 How the data is used, by whom and for what purpose
3 The frequency of preparation and access
4 Data validation requirements
5 Volume information:
   Anticipated volume of transactions:
   - issue notes 3500 per day
   - goods received notes 400 per day
   - returns to stores notes 100 per day
   - returns to supplier notes 30 per day
   - purchase orders 350 per day
   - stock reserve notes 30 per day
   Anticipated volume of amendments:
   - addition of new items to stock file 25 per week
   - deletions of obsolete items from stock file 10 per week
   - amendments to stock records 150 per week – mainly adjustments to quantities in stock due to physical differences to book stocks. Amendments provided by the audit section as a result of stock checks.

Nature and size of files:
The system will initially have only one file consisting of stock records the details of which are:
   Number of stock records:
   - current 3000 records
   - anticipated 4500 records (increased range of parts in relation to an expanded product range).
   Events:
   An analysis of the events which cause things to happen include:
   - Receipt of file amendments: this event generates a variety of functions. For instance, it is necessary to add new stock records to the file, delete obsolete records and amend records with new attributes relating to revised stock levels, etc. Later on in this case study Figs. A24 and A25 give a fuller idea of the functions involved.

- Receipt of transacitons: this event generates functions which include data validation, computing values relating to the trans- actions for recording on the relevant stock records. Before this can be accomplished, however, it is necessary to classify each transaction in order to establish the way in which the record is affected. Fuller details can be found later on in the case study (Figs. A26, A27 and A28.)
- Checking stock levels: this event triggers off the recomputation of stock control parameters (stock levels) to accord with current requirements. This then generates the function of stock re-ord- ering as the stock level has reached the point where an order should be placed. It is necessary to take lead time into account when establishing the re-order level.

Stage 3 Identifying entities and construct conceptual model

Conceptual model
A conceptual model, as previously discussed, see chapter 9, can be used for portraying a panoramic view of a system identifying the various entities and their relationships; the primary processes to be performed and their sequence. The model also shows sub-system interfaces which includes suppliers, the buying office, internal audit, production and production planning. The boundary of the system being developed is also shown. A conceptual model of the stock control system is shown in Fig. A1 which shows the data flows which will subsequently be analysed. It is important to appreciate that the directional arrows are for showing the direction of data flows – not physical movement of materials from the stores, for instance, which is an outward flow of materials but an inwards flow of data.

Entity diagram
See chapter 10 for initial explanation of entity models. The entities shown in Fig. A2 are listed below:

External entity supplier
Subject   stock file
Department   production, producting planning, buying
                 office, internal audit, stores and stock
                 control (stock controller)

Each entity is shown as a box containing the entity identifier. The attributes of each entity are expressed in terms of data flows, which are superimposed on the relational lines. The entry point and access

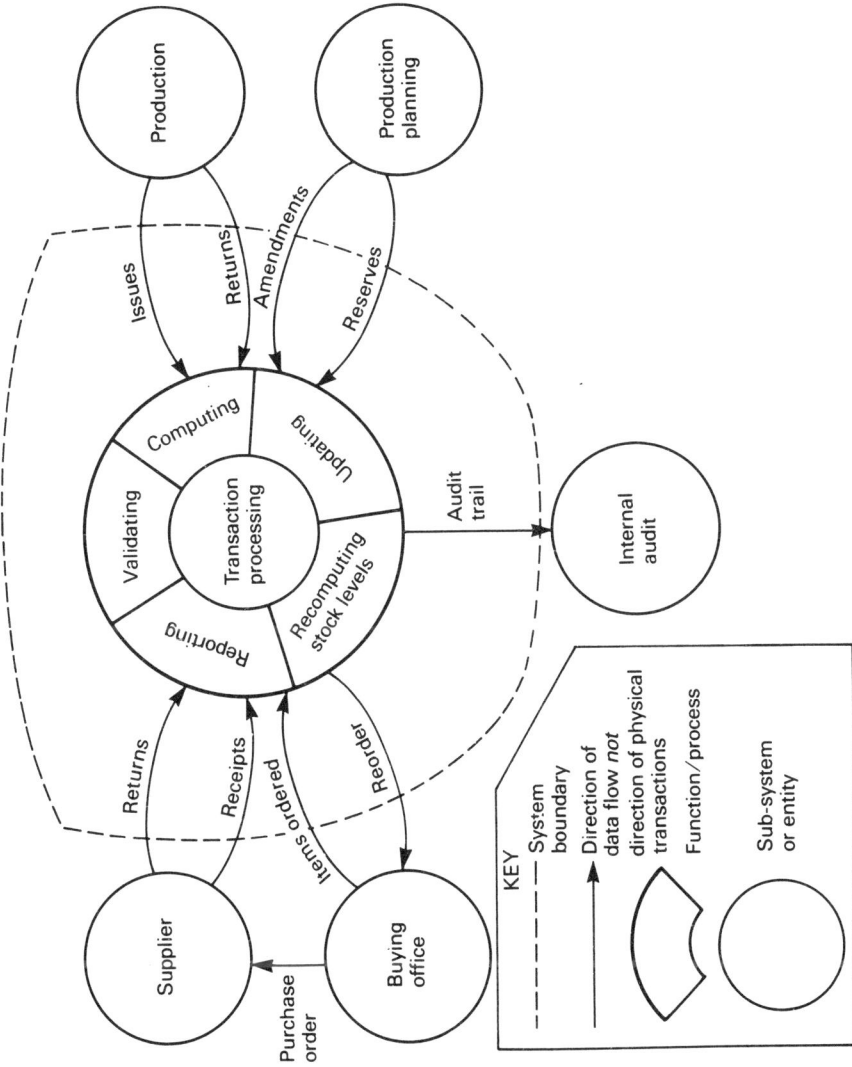

FIG. A1 Conceptual model of a stock control system emphasising functions and data flows

path between entities is clarified by means of a directional arrow. If we examine the entity diagram it will be observed that supplies of many stock items are received from many suppliers, i.e. a many-to-many relationship. Many transactions are also received from the various departments, again a many-to-many relationship. With regard to the reorder list supplied to the buying office this is a one-to-one relationship. The stock schedule and transaction list supplied to the stock controller and internal audit department respectively are also one-to-one relationships, as one report is provided in each case. See Fig. A2.

Stage 4 Analyse entity life and transaction histories

Entity life history
This has already been defined in Chapter 9. In respect of stock control a new entity is created by the addition of a new stock item to the stock file (addition). This event is triggered off when a new item is required for use in the manufacture of a product in the factory. A file amendment form would be provided for this purpose. A purchase order is produced for items to be ordered from outside suppliers. Details of the order are recorded on the relevant stock record (insertion). A further entry is made when the order is received, details of which are then recorded (insertion) on the stock file. The stock item is then active but during its life cycle specific details (attributes) of the entity (stock item) may be changed as when changes are implemented amending the control parameters (amendment). Subsequently the item becomes inactive and no current transactions occur, in which case a notification to delete the obsolete item from the stock file will be provided (deletion). See Fig. A3.

Transaction history
This term has been defined in Chapter 9. In respect of the stock control system the stock file is the entity in question which consists of stock items. The transaction history diagram (see Fig. A4) indicates the correspondence between entities and how a stock item changes with time. At one moment of time it is brought into existence by the placing of the item on the stock file as discussed above. The placing of an order on a supplier triggers off a receipt which may consist either of the full order quantity or only a part order quantity. Either may be rejected or accepted depending upon its adherence to a defined specification. If it is rejected it is returned to the supplier. When accepted the quantity is held in the stores where it is a stock item.

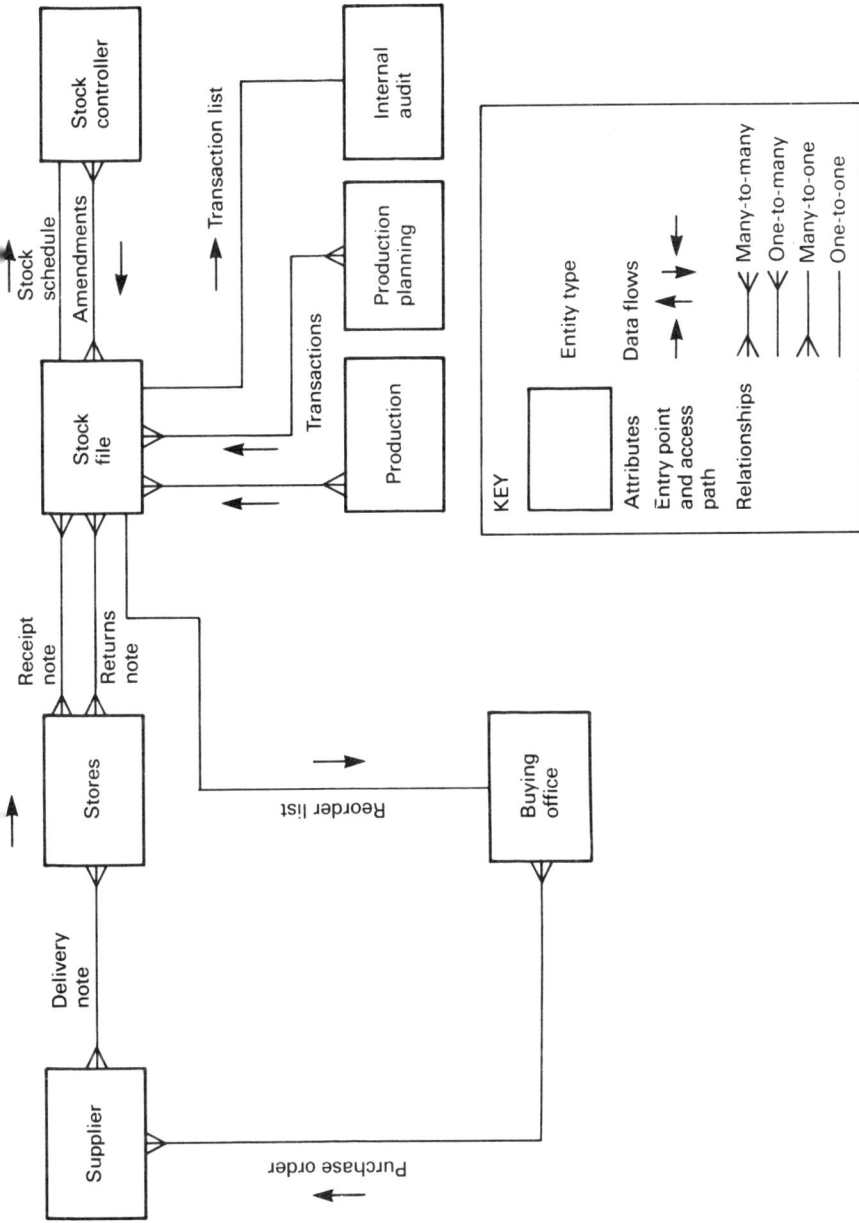

FIG. A2 *Entity diagram: stock control system*

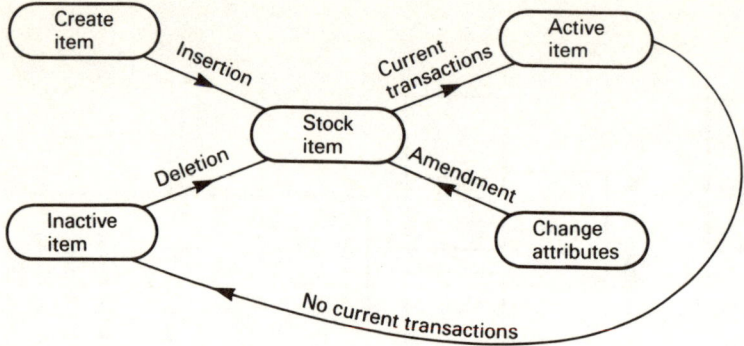

FIG. A3   *Entity life history for a stock item*

When the item is issued to production it may have caused the quantity left in the stores to be reduced to its reorder level, in which case it is recorded on a reorder list which triggers the placing of a purchase order. If only a part quantity is issued this may be due to an unforeseen stock shortage, in which case the reorder routine would also be triggered off. The issue may be in excess of requirements in which case the surplus is returned to the stores. Items may also be reserved for a special order which subsequently becomes an issue and so the transaction history continues.

Stage 5 Construct context diagram
The context diagram in Fig. A5 takes the form of a high level flowchart providing an overall view of the system. It portrays the primary inputs and outputs. It provides a panoramic overview which may be used as a vehicle for further detailed analysis and development. See Chapter 9 for further details.

Stage 6 Specify data elements (attributes) relating to each input data flow:
- purchase orders
- issues to production
- receipts from suppliers
- returns to suppliers
- stock reserves for special orders
- returns to stores
- stock adjustments

The data elements relating to each of the above data flows are listed below. The data elements specify the composition of each data flow

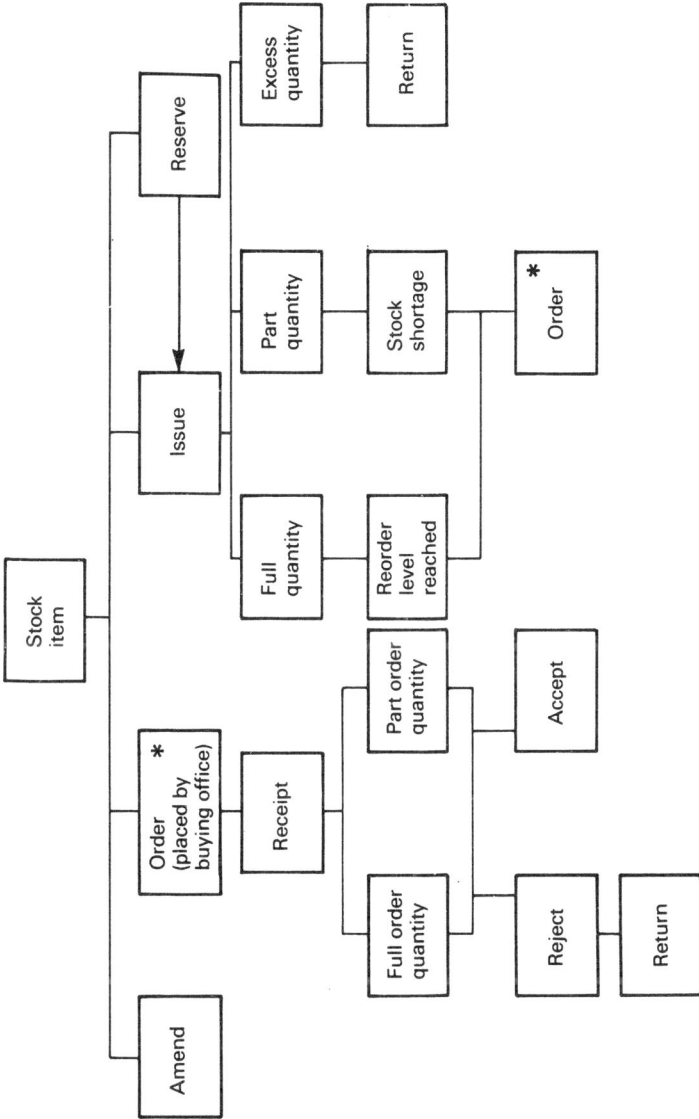

FIG. A4 *Transaction history diagram: stock item*

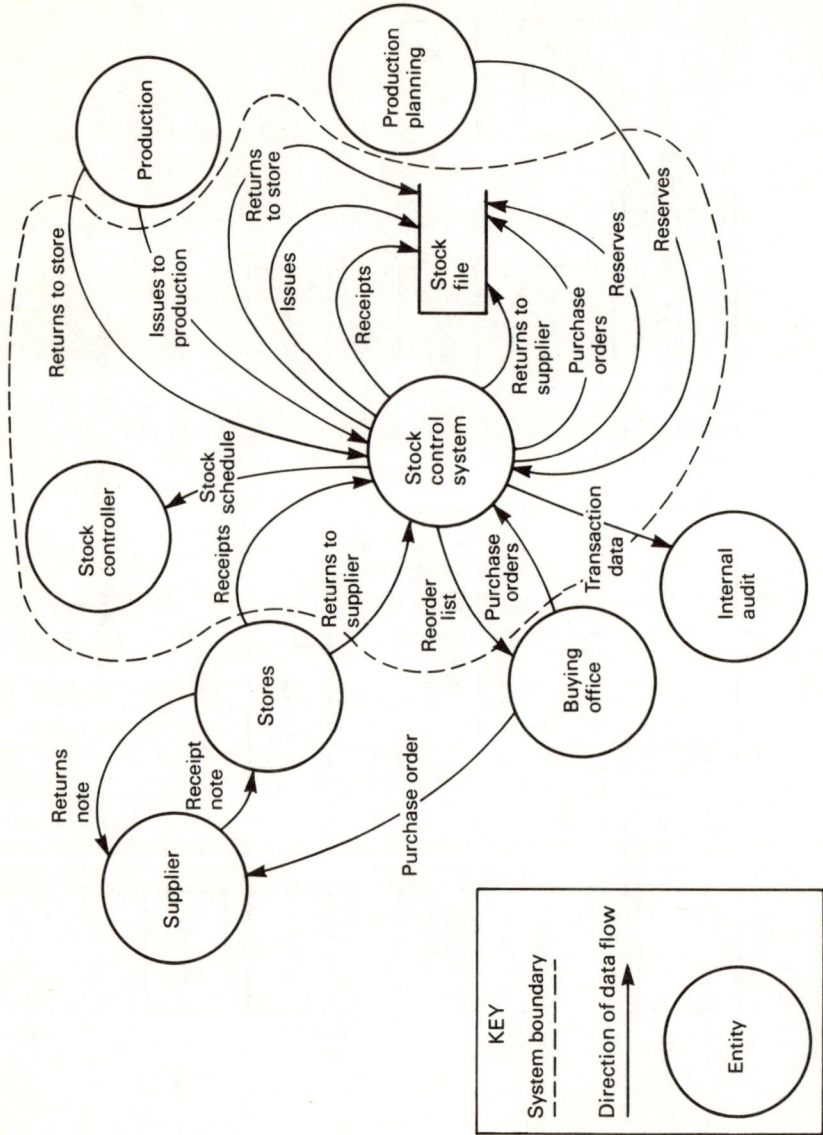

FIG. A5   *Context model of stock control system*

which is essential information for the subsequent design of forms and data modelling as a prerequisite to the design of file structures.

Data element
1 Item code
2 Date
3 Reference number
4 Transaction type
5 Quantity

The data elements relating to purchase orders are as indicated below:

Purchase orders
1 Item code
2 Description
3 Re-order quantity
4 Price

This document specifies requirements to the supplier. Date and details relating to the supplier are added by the buying office (purchasing department). Other details are obtained from the re-order list.

Specify data elements of output data flows and the origin of each output data flow
This detail facilitates the information which must be held in data stores (files) for subsequent retrieval either for random enquiries or for the preparation of reports

Stock schedule:
- item code
- description
- quantity in stock
- value of stock
- re-order level
- stock reserves
- free stock
- quantity on order
- maximum stock quantity
- minimum stock quantity

These details provide information to the stock controller relating to the status of each item in stock to enable appropriate action to be taken to modify stock levels and to deal with slow-moving and obsolete items.

All of the details on this report are recorded from data stored on the stock file.

Re-order list:
- item code
- description
- re-order quantity

This report provides details of stocks to be replenished to the buying office and is used as a basis for preparing a purchase order.

The details on this report are recorded from data stored on the stock file.

Audit trail: transactions:
- transaction type
- transaction reference
- item code
- description
- quantity
- value
- total value of issues
- number of issue notes
- total value of receipts
- number of goods received notes
- total value of returns to store
- number of RTS notes
- number of reserve notes
- number of order copies

These details are obtained from the transaction file which enables the internal auditors to be aware of the system's transactions and verify if all transactions have been processed, by comparison of pre-computed control totals with totals generated during processing. A random sample of records from the master file will verify the integrity of file processing. Details of processed transactions are recorded, together with details relating to the number and value of transactions.

Audit trail: file amendments:
- amendment type
- amendment reference
- number of amendments

These details enable the internal auditors to be aware of the amendments which have been implemented. The details required for this report are those relating to changes to records including additions, deletions and amendments.

Error report:
- transaction reference
- transaction type
- item code
- type of error
- the error report is referred to the originating department and corrections are re-input

Returns to supplier note:
This document is prepared by the stores department which records the relevant data elements.

Stage 7 Specify input and output data flows and an outline of processing activities

Refer to previous notes in Chapter 9 relating to data flow diagrams and their construction. The data flow diagram shown in Fig. A6 is a visual representation of the flow of data in the stock control system. It clearly shows the entities which send or receive data, the processes which alter the composition of the data; and the data stores (files) required to store details of entities. It must be appreciated that this diagram is meant to outline primary processes and data flows.

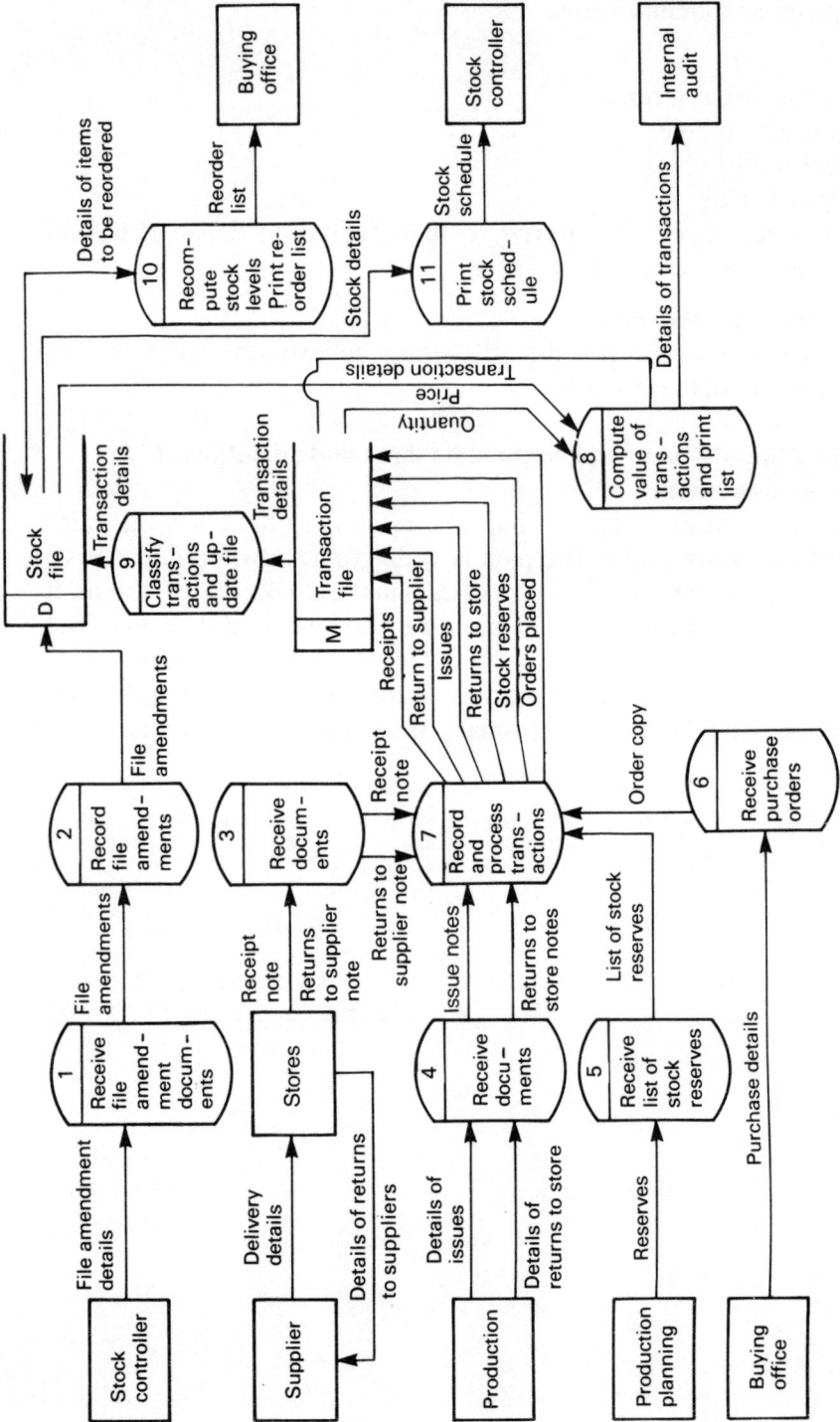

FIG. A6   First level data flow diagram: stock control overview

Stage 8 Transform analysis: levelling of data flows

When data flows are shown on separate diagrams it allows each stage of the system to be closely examined to ensure there is no duplicated or omitted data flows. It also enables a close examination to be undertaken of the entities which send or receive data (sources and sinks), the processes (transforms) which alter the structure of data and the data stores which hold data.

Sources and sinks are located outside the area of the system under development but the flow of documents is of extreme importance to the effective logical design of the system.

Summary of levelled data flows

Process	Source	Data flow	Sink
Level 1 (See Fig. A6)			
1 and 2	Stock controller	File amendments	Stock file
Level 2 (See Figs. A7 and A8)			
3.1	Stores	Receipt notes	Stock control
3.2	Stores	Returns to supplier notes	Stock control
Level 2 (See Figs. A9 and A10)			
4.1	Production	Issue notes	Stock control
4.2	Production	Returns to stores notes	Stock control
Level 1 (See Fig. A6)			
5	Production planning	List of stock reserves	Stock control
6	Buying office	Purchase Orders (copy)	Stock control
Level 2 (See Figs. A11 to A14)			
7.1	Stock control	All transactions	Stock control
7.2	Stock control	Transaction details	Transaction file
7.3	Transaction file	Valid transactions	Valid transactions file
		Invalid transactions	Relevant entity
7.4	Transaction file	Sorted transactions	Transaction file

Process	Source	Data flow	Sink

Level 3 (See Figs. A15 and A16)

Process	Source	Data flow	Sink
7.3.1	Relevant entity	Corrected transactions	Stock control
7.3.2	Stock control	Valid transactions	Valid transactions file
		Invalid transactions	Relevant entity

Level 2 (See Figs. A17 and A18)

Process	Source	Data flow	Sink
8.1.	Stock file	Valued transactions	Transactions file
	Transactions file	Transaction details	
8.2	Transactions file	Transaction list	Internal audit

Level 2 (See Figs. A19 and A20)

Process	Source	Data flow	Sink
9.1	Transactions	Classified transactions	Transform 9.2
9.2	Classified transaactions	Transaction details	Stock file

Level 3 (See Fig. A20)

Process	Source	Data flow	Sink
9.2.1	9.1	Purchase order transaction details	Stock file

or

Process	Source	Data flow	Sink
9.2.2	9.1	Issue transaction details	Stock file

or

Process	Source	Data flow	Sink
9.2.3	9.1	Receipt transaction details	Stock file

or

Process	Source	Data flow	Sink
9.2.4	9.1	Returns to supplier transaction details	Stock file

or

Process	Source	Data flow	Sink
9.2.5	9.1	Returns to store transaction details	Stock file
or			
9.2.6	9.1	Stock reserve transaction details	Stock file

Level 2 (See Figs. A21 and A22)

10.1	Stock file	Recomputed stock levels	Stock file
10.2	Stock file	Reorder list	Buying office

Level 1 (See Fig. A6)

11	Stock file	Stock schedule	Stock controller

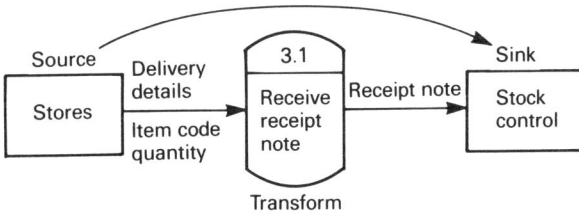

FIG. A7   *Second level transform: data flow diagram for process 3*

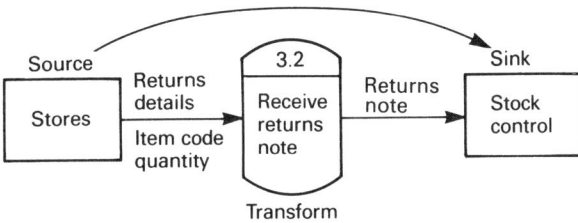

FIG. A8   *Second level transform: data flow diagram for process 3*

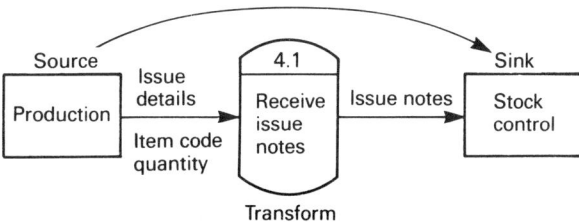

FIG. A9   *Second level transform: data flow diagram for process 4*

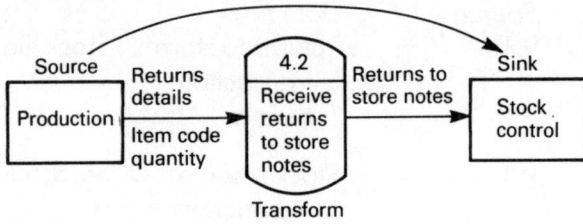

FIG. A10   *Second level transform: data flow diagram for process 4*

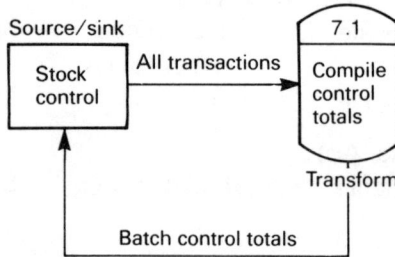

FIG. A11   *Second level transform: data flow diagram for process 7*

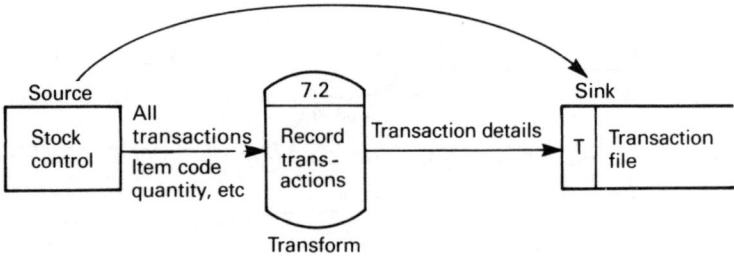

FIG. A12   *Second level transform: data flow diagram for process 7*

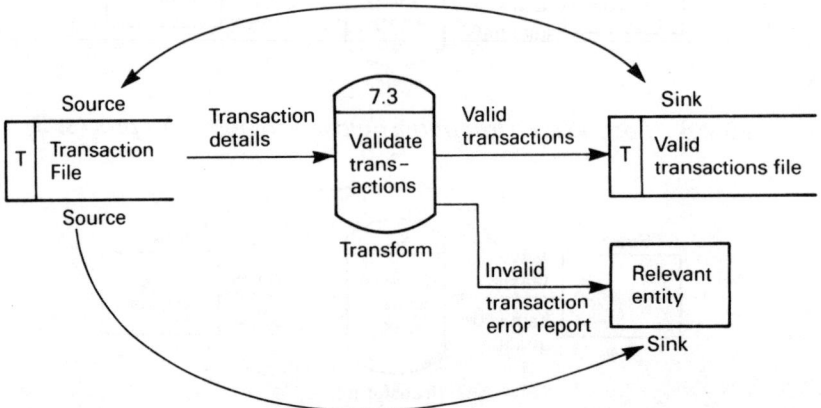

FIG. A13   *Second level transform: data flow diagram for process 7*

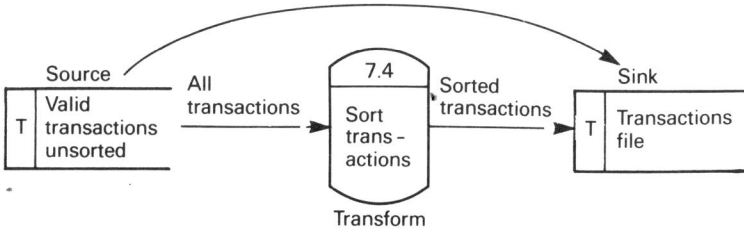

FIG. A14   *Second level transform: data flow diagram for process 7*

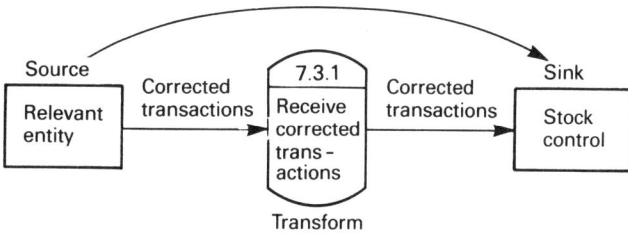

FIG. A15   *Third level transform: data flow diagram for process 7*

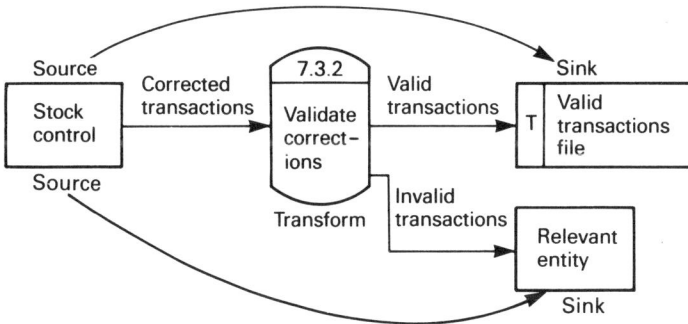

FIG. A16   *Third level transform: data flow diagram for process 7*

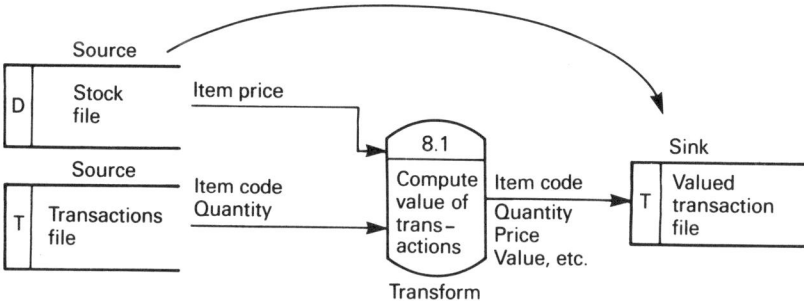

FIG. A17   *Second level transform: data flow diagram for process 8*

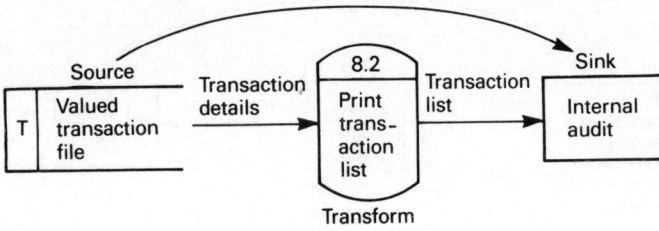

FIG. A18 *Second level transform: data flow diagram for process 8*

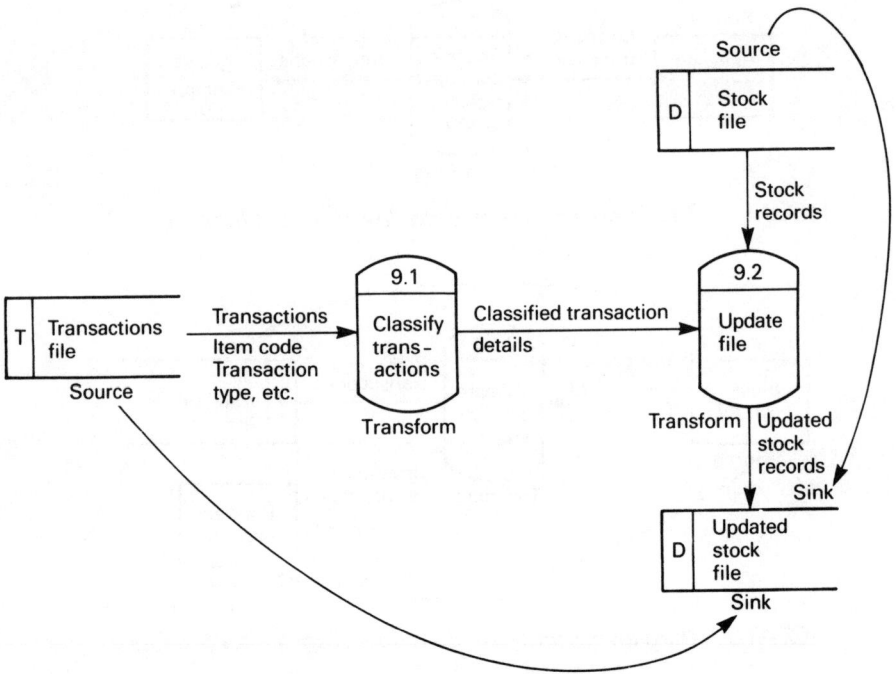

FIG. A19 *Second level transform: data flow diagram for process 9*

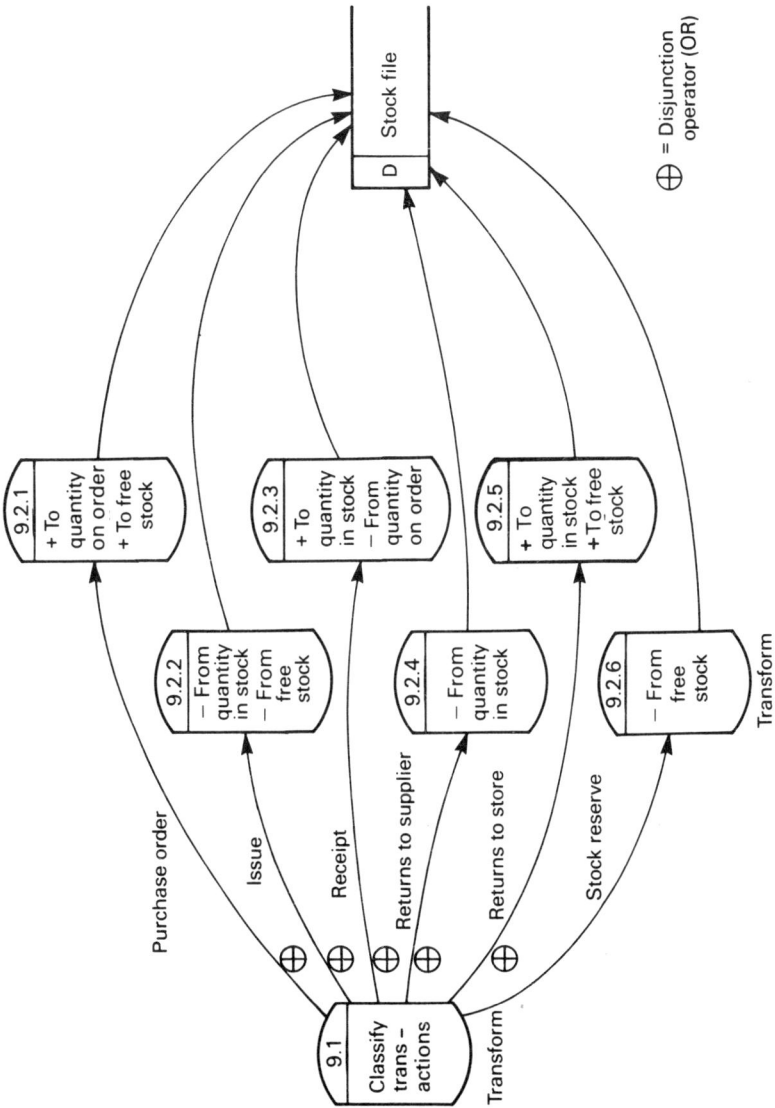

FIG. A20 *Third level transform; transaction analysis: data flow diagram for process 9*

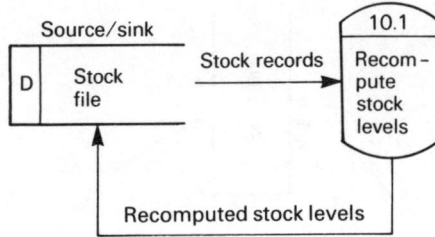

FIG. A21   *Second level transform: data flow diagram for process 10*

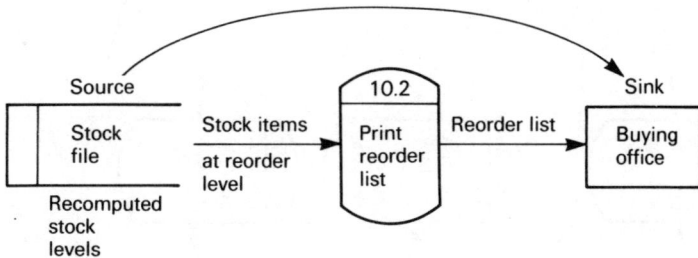

FIG. A22   *Second level transform: data flow diagram for process 10*

Stage 9 Data modelling

An entity diagram is constructed specifying the relationship between different types of data within the system and how it can be accessed. See Fig. A2 and refer to p. 168 for further details. Data models define the structure of files and assist in obtaining an appreciation of the data needs of a business. They assist in segregating data into separate files or integrating data structures when developing databases. An initial requirement is 'normalisation', the process of separating items which are independent of each other into groups. Refer to Chapter 10 for further details. For each category of objective it is necessary to ensure that each store (file) has a 'key' which uniquely identifies an entity which the data describes. Relationships between fields must be established, e.g. the relationship between the key field and the other fields of an entity. All details should be recorded in a data dictionary. In respect of the stock control system being discussed each of the transactions has two fields: 'item number' and 'description'. These can be used as alternative keys. Given either of these two keys all the other fields can be determined as the fields are dependent upon the key. This stock control system has only one store, i.e. the stock file which stores details relating to stock data. In some instances, however, a record relating to an entity may have two or more distinct groups of data which should be segregated into separate stores, i.e. files. This would apply if the purchasing system was fully integrated with stock control.

Contents of stock file:
- item code
- item description
- stores location
- date of transaction
- item reference
- transaction type
- item quantity
- value of transaction
- quantity in stock
- value of stock
- price
- re-order level-quantity
- re-order quantity
- free stock
- maximum stock quantity
- minimum stock quantity
- quantity on order
- stock reserve-quantity
- stock reserve-job number

Stage 10 Functional decomposition of processes

A decomposition diagram is constructed to show the primary activities and/or processes concerned with the stock control function. It analyses high level definitions of a function into more detailed functions for further analysis. The decomposition diagram of this refinement process forms an inverted tree structure – the farther out on branch of the tree, the finer the detail revealed.

Summary of functional decomposition
Level 1 Stock control primary processes (see Fig. A23)
  a file maintenance
  b transaction processing

Level 2 File maintenance (see Fig. A24)
  a compile control totals
  b validate amendments
  c classify and amend records
  d print list of amendments

Level 2 (see Fig. A25)
  a compile control totals
  b validate amendments
  - report errors
  - correct errors
  c classify and amend records
  d print list of amendments

Level 3 (refer to **c** above)
  - add new records
  - delete records
  - modify records

Level 2 Transaction processing (see Fig. A26)
  a compile control totals
  b validate transactions
  c sort transactions
  d compute transaction values
  e classify transactions and update records
  f recompute stock levels
  g print reports

Level 2 (see Figs. A27 and A28)
  a compile control totals
  b validate transactions
  - report errors
  - correct errors
  c sort transactions
  d compute transaction values
  - print transaction list
  e classify transactions and update stock file
  f re-compute stock levels
  g print reports

Level 3 (see **e** above)
  If Purchase order THEN
      + qnty on order
      + free stock ELSE
  IF Issue THEN
      − qnty in stock
      −free stock ELSE
  IF Receipt THEN
      + qnty in stock
      − qnty on order ELSE

IF Returns to supplier THEN
   − qnty in stock
   − free stock ELSE
IF Returns to store THEN
   + qnty in stock
   + free stock ELSE
IF Stock reserve THEN
   − free stock

Level 3 (see **g** above)
  a print re-order list
  b print stock schedule

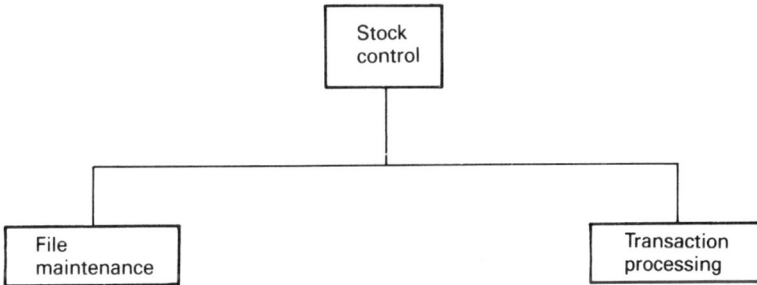

FIG. A23   *Functional decomposition; level 1: stock control primary process*

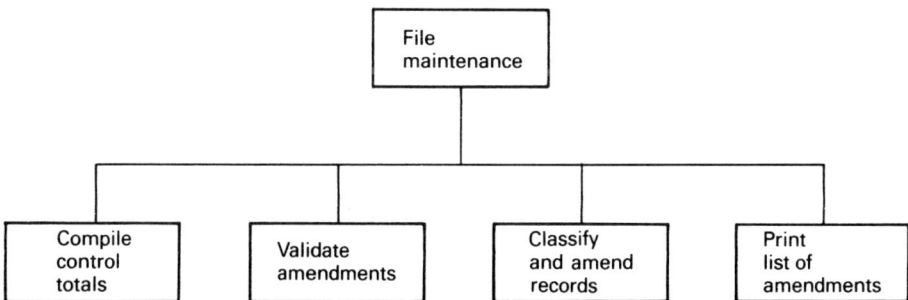

FIG. A24   *Functional decomposition; level 2: file maintenance*

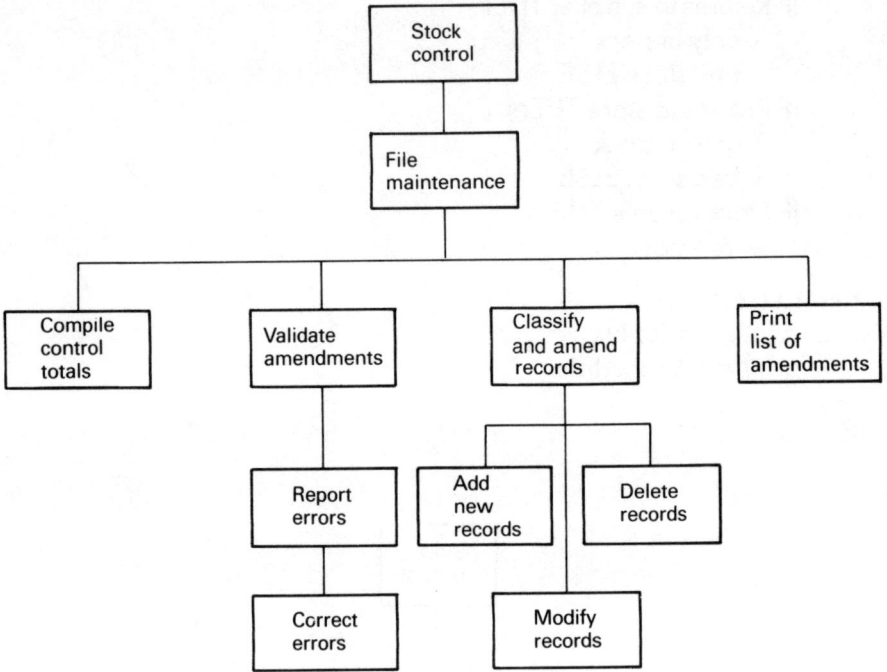

FIG. A25   *Functional decomposition; level 3: file maintenance*

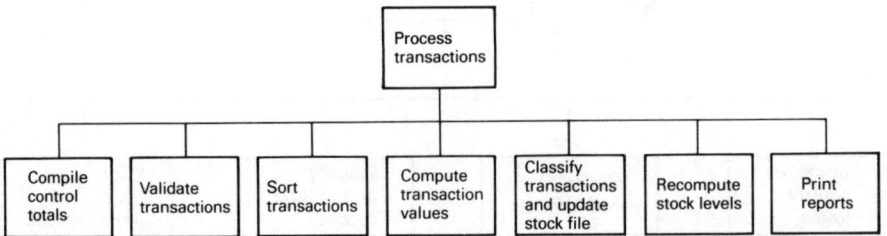

FIG. A26   *Functional decomposition; level 2: transactions*

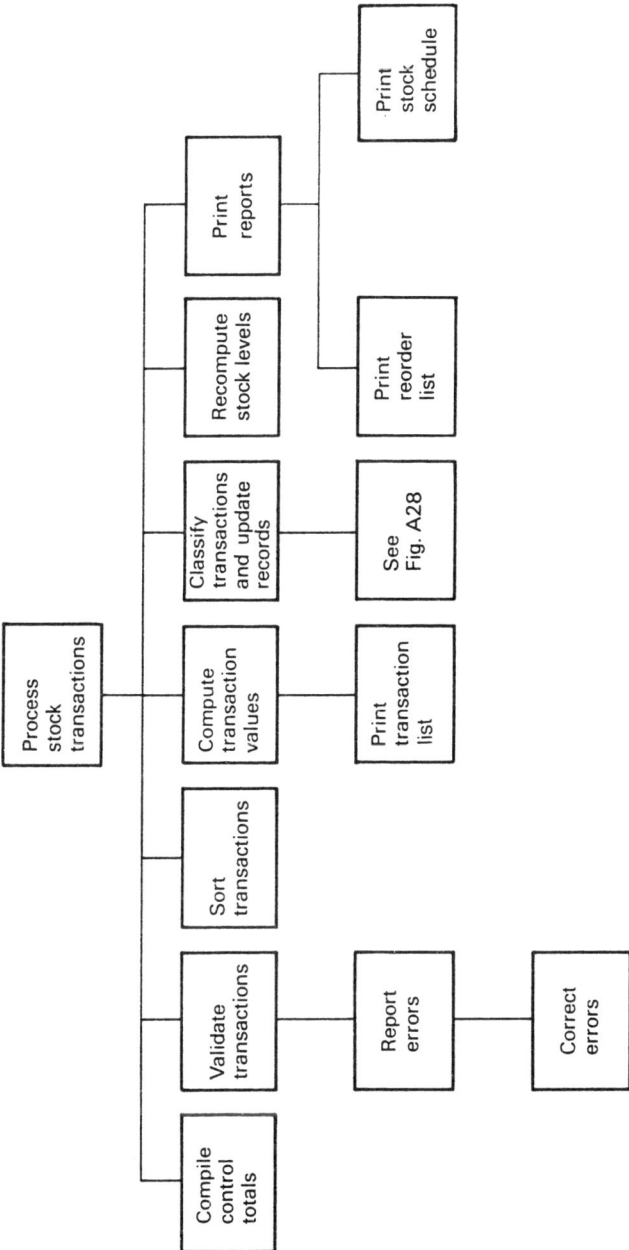

FIG. A27   *Functional decomposition; level 3: transactions*

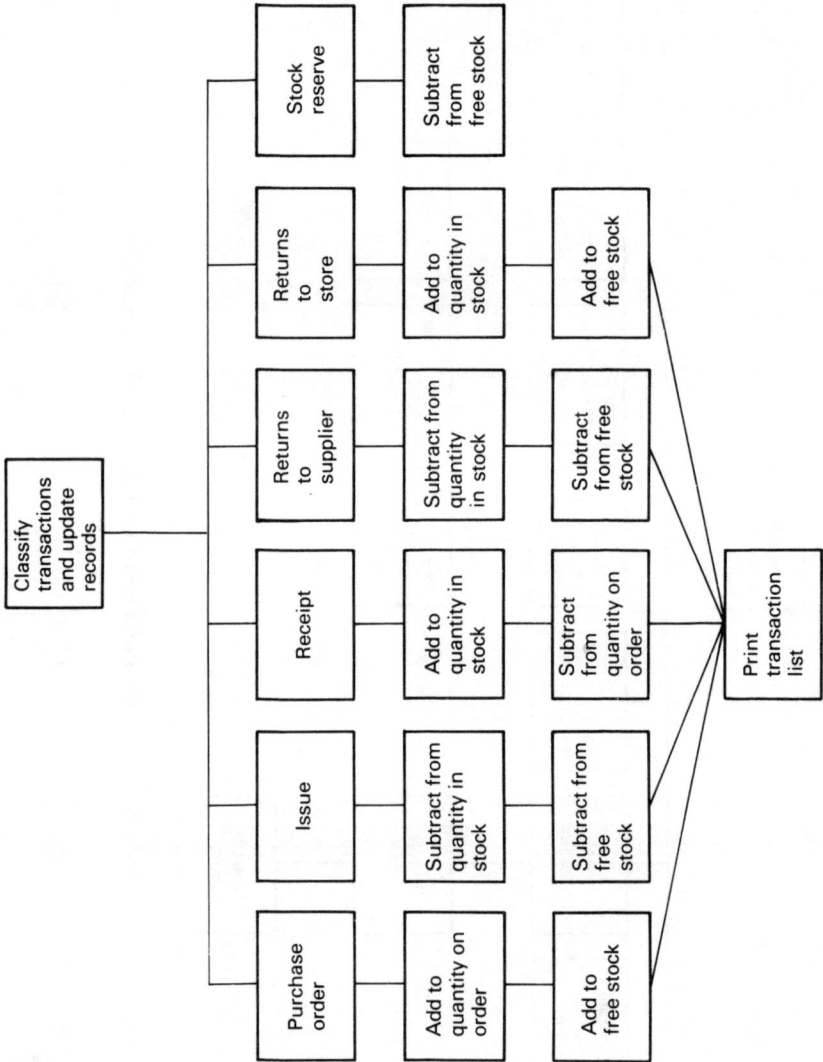

FIG. A28   *Functional decomposition; level 3: transactions continued (see Fig. A27)*

Stage 11 Construct a flowchart portraying a logical model of the system
This can be constructed either from the comprehensive data flow diagram constructed in stage 7, or it may be constructed from diagrams of each data flow prepared in stage 8. The decomposition (levelling) diagrams may also be used for this purpose in order to consolidate data flows and processes. Refer to Fig. A29, which portrays the logical model of this system. Note it does not mention any matter relating to hardware, only the logical sequence of processes and the data flows between file and processes.

Stage 12 Initial design of physical system – first sketch
Having spent considerable time mapping data flows and establishing the logical requirements of users this stage of system development accords to the traditional approach as it is now necessary to consider **how** the user requirements can be met by the use of physical methods and tangible machines and equipment (hardware) and complementary software. The volumes of data to be processed and the number of stock records to be updated implies the use of a small mainframe or minicomputer equipped with hard fixed discs – Winchesters of a capacity of 20–40 Mb. Data is input by means of terminals located in stock control. The initial outline of processes shown on the dataflow diagrams (refer to Figs. A6 to A23) is developed at this stage into a first sketch of the physical system, illustrated by a flowchart outlining the processes required for its accomplishment. The flowchart is not meant to fully illustrate all aspects of the system, but should show sufficient details to appreciate the methodology concerned with the transition from the initial data flow diagram through to a composite logical model of the system. This is then assessed in terms of the best physical way of accomplishing the logical requirements of the system. See Figs. A30 and A31.

After this initial stage of physical design it is necessary to commence the detailed design of the system which follows the normal stages of the system life cycle. See Chapter 7.

SUMMARY OF PROCESSES
File maintenance: (see Fig. A30)
1 Receive file maintenance details in respect of additions, deletions and amendments. Batch transactions and prepare control totals.
2 Check batches and record in control register.

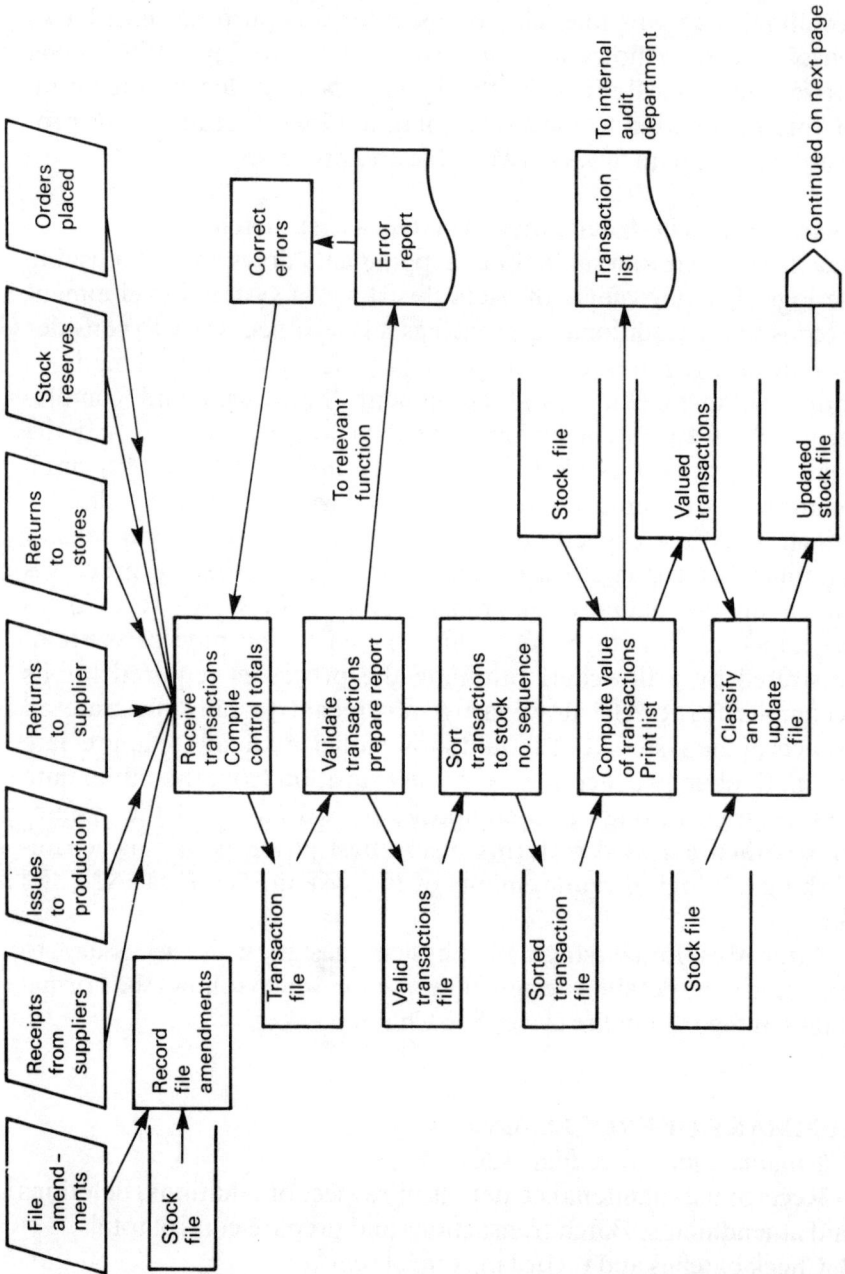

FIG. A29   Logical model: stock control system

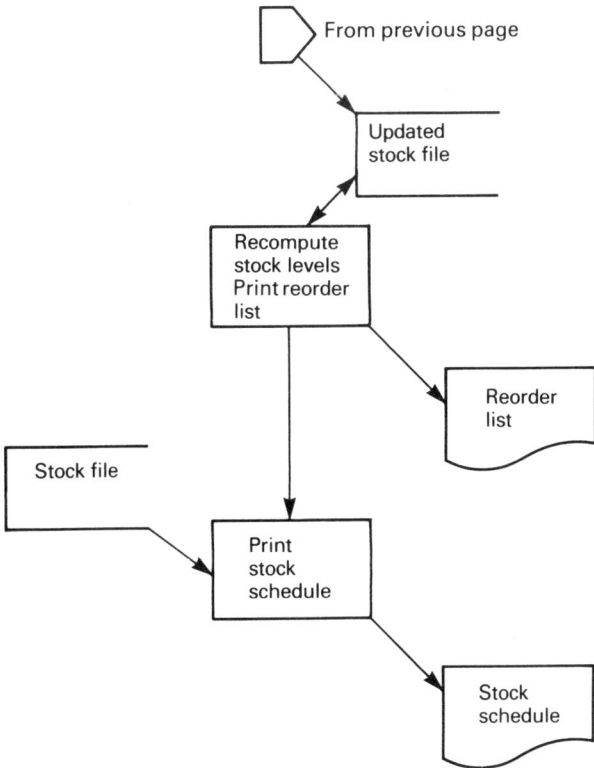

3 Key in data and record file maintenance details on disc. Validate details display errors and reinput corrections. Record valid changes on disc.
4 Sort changes to sequence of stock file, i.e. stock number sequence.
5 Record changes on stock file and print list of changes. Send list (audit trail) to internal audit department.

Processing transactions (see Fig. A31)
1 Receive transactions in respect of orders placed, issues to production, receipts from supplier, returns to supplier, stock reserves and returns to stores.
Receive batches of transactions from the stores, production planning and the buying office in batch control section.
2 Batch documents. Check batches, correct errors and record details in batch control register.
3 Key in data and validate transactions listed on an invalid items reports which is sent back to relevant function for correction. Input

errors are displayed and corrections keyed in. Corrected transactions are recorded on disc.

Corrected transactions are reinput and the above processes are repeated. Valid transactions are recorded on disc.

4 The valid transaction file is sorted into stock number sequence to facilitate efficient file processing by avoiding the need to access the same tracks several times when the same stock number reoccurs. The file is processed with one pass. The sorted file is then recorded on the same or a different disc.

5 The sorted transactions file is then input and transaction values are computed for each class of transaction. Prices are obtained from the stock file and quantities from the transaction file. The transaction details are recorded on the stock file by the process of file updating which records the latest quantity and value of each stock item. A list is printed containing details of all classes of transaction, and is sent to the internal audit department for the purpose of providing an audit trail, to enable the auditors to verify that the system is performing according to accepted procedure and that all transactions have been processed and errors detected and corrected.

The functions of computing and updating are combined for processing efficiency as the file is updated while computed values are stored in the memory. Similarly, details of transactions are printed out whilst the data is stored in the computer's memory.

6 The stock file is input and each item is checked to assess if it has reached the reorder level. Those items for reordering are printed on a reorder list which is sent to the buying office for the purpose of preparing a purchase order. The details of each stock item are stored on a print file for subsequent printing of a stock schedule, which is sent to the stock controller for stock management purposes.

Process

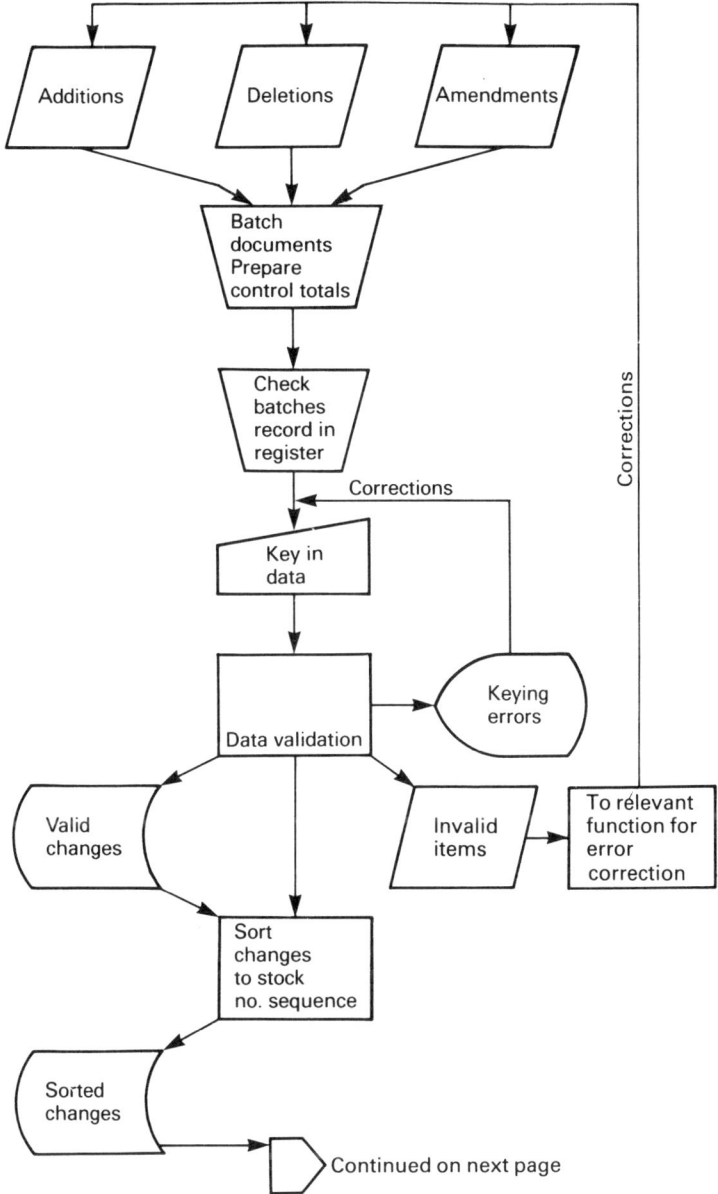

FIG. A30 *Physical model stock control: file maintenance*

Process

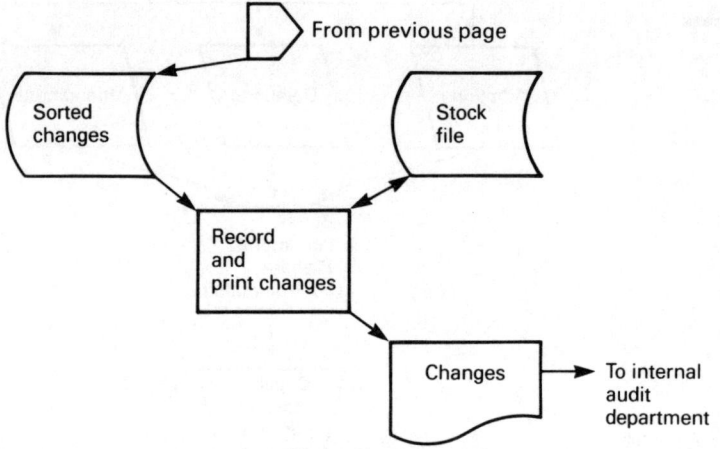

(Fig. A30 *contd*)

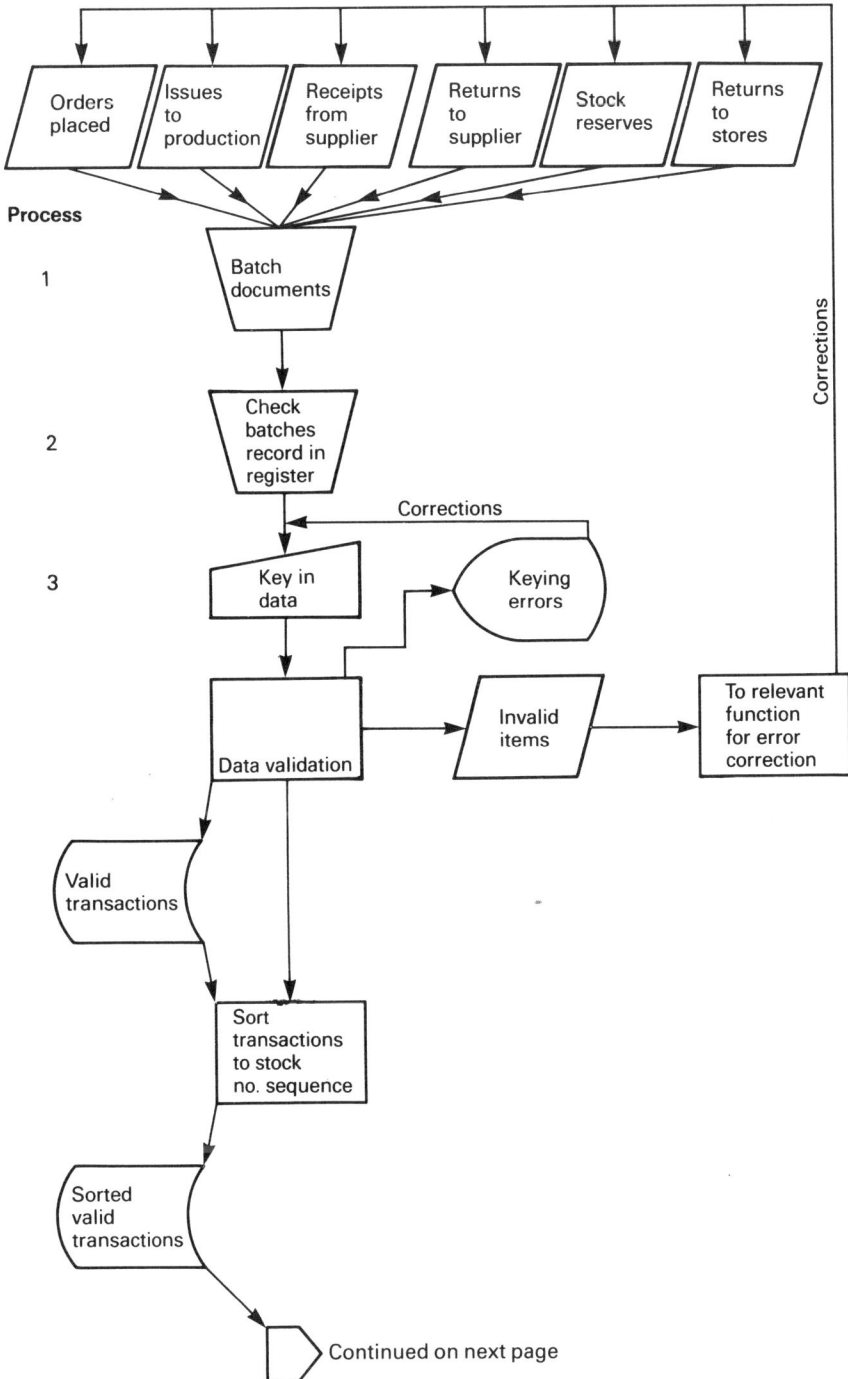

FIG. A31 *Physical model stock control: processing transactions*

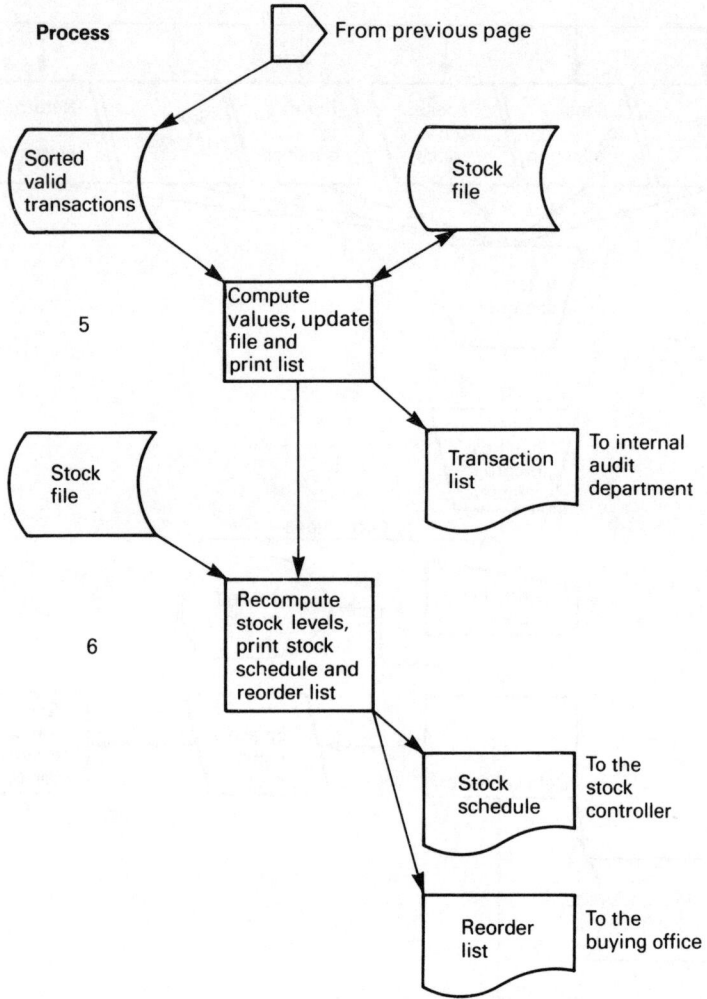

(Fig. A31 *contd*)

CASE STUDY B:
Integrated Sales Order Processing System

THE CURRENT SYSTEM

The business is a wholesale warehouse supplying goods to the retail trade. The name of the company is ABC Supplies plc. The current order processing system is a manually operated system handling a large commodity range, details of which are outlined in Stage 2. The system outlined is restricted to that for order processing and does not include routines for receipts and returns to the warehouse or remittances from customers, neither does it provide for file mainten-ance routines and replenishing supplies for the warehouse. This restriction is merely for keeping the details of the case study in reasonable bounds. The omitted sub-systems would be dealt with by an identical methodology. The primary purpose of the case study is to provide an outline of the main requirements of the structured approach to systems design. The stages of the structured approach adopted for this case study are identical with those applied to the stock control case study which are repeated here for convenience.

1 Obtain terms of reference
2 Analyse current system including data analysis
3 Identify entities and construct conceptual model
4 Analyse entity life and transaction histories
5 Construct context diagram
6 Specify data elements (attributes) relating to each input data flow. Specify data elements (attributes) of output data flows and the origin of each output data flow
7 Specify input and output data flows and an outline of processing activities by means of a comprehensive data flow diagram
8 Transform analysis-levelling of data flows
9 Data modelling using an entity diagram to depict the relationship between data items, their entry points and access paths
10 Functional decomposition of processes
11 Construct flowchart portraying logical model of the system
12 Initial flowchart of physical system – first sketch

Stage 1: Terms of reference

Management are dissatisfied with the current order processing system which is too inflexible and inefficient. It suffers from a number of weaknesses which are now outlined.

The majority of orders from customers are received by telephone and customers expect to be immediately advised of the availability of items required and if there is no current stock, or an insufficient quantity to that required, the alternatives which are available. Sales order forms are compiled by clerks and sent to the warehouse where they are used as picking lists from which despatch documentation is prepared, after amending quantities for stock availability. Delays and inaccuracies in stock recording mean that stock shortages are only apparent at the time the order is being made up from the picking list. This situation prevents the customer being immediately informed, and does not allow discussions on possible substitutes. This is an unacceptable situation as it reduces business profitability. The current system also suffers from incomplete deliveries because of sales orders/picking lists going astray and not reaching the warehouse. In addition, the incidence of bad debts is increasing because the credit of customers is not checked before despatching deliveries to bad payers. Management require a system which will remove the weaknesses of the present system.

Stage 2: Analyse current system including data analysis

Specify data elements (attributes) relating to each input data flow (each objective). Specify data elements (attributes) of output data flows and the origin of each output data flow.

Data analysis
The current system handles a large commodity range consisting of:
  a 5000 lines distributed to approximately 500 retailers
  b on average 200 orders are received each week, i.e. 40 each day
  c the number of order items per order varies between an average of 20 and a maximum of 300
  d the number of lines is expected to increase by 5% p.a.
  e the number of orders is expected to increase to an average of 225 each week, i.e. 45 each day
  f the number of order items per order is expected to remain at the current level

Stage 3: Identifying entities and construct conceptual model

Entities
There is no precise way to define an entity. It is therefore necessary to analyse the system under development to identify those items which represent a data group. In the order processing system being discussed the primary entities fall into two categories as listed below:

1 Data groups: sales order, order item, product/stock item, despatch item, shortage item, purchase item, purchase order.
2 External: customer, supplier entities.

Although the system under discussion is order processing, the entity diagram to be illustrated includes purchasing aspects merely to show the link between sales orders and purchase orders. The purpose of an entity model is to show relationships between entities as the various entities which exist in an application environment will be interrelated either directly or indirectly.

Dependency
In order to show which entity is dependent upon another the convention may be adopted of showing dependency by defining which data group is a master and which is a detail. To do this it is necessary to be aware of the operating environment in which the system functions in order to precisely state existing relationships. These matters have been discussed in Chapters 8 and 9. The order processing system operates in the environment having the following characteristics:

    a Many orders are received from individual customers specifying a one-to-many relationship, although many orders from different customers may be in the system concurrently. The customer entity is the master and the order the detail.
    b A customer's order may contain many different order items which have a one-to-many relationship. In this instance the order, previously a detail, is now a master in relation to order item which is the detail.
    c One stock can supply many order items which become depatch items, providing they are in stock, therefore one stock-to-many order items is a one-to-many relationship. The stock item becomes the master and the order or despatch item the detail.
    d One invoice can contain many despatch items, in accordance with the requirements of a specific order which gives a one-to-many relationship with the invoice as the master and the despatch items the detail.

e Order items out of stock generate shortage items and the relationship is one-to-many on the basis of one stock may have many items out of stock.

The stock item is the master and the shortage item is the detail.

f Many shortage items become many purchase items which is a case whereby an A entity owns more than one B entity and a B entity owns more than one A entity. This is a many-to-many relationship

g Many orders can be placed on many suppliers which is a many-to-many relationship, but only one supplier can have a number of specific orders which is a one-to-many relationship. In the latter case the supplier – entity A, can own more than one purchase order – entity B, the supplier is therefore the master and the purchase order the detail.

Check questions
A number of check questions may now be asked to verify the environment details outlined above:

1 Could many sales orders be associated with one customer?

The answer is *yes*, therefore the customer entity is the master and the sales order the detail.

2 Could many order items be contained on one order?

Again the answer is *yes*, which makes the sales order the master and the order item the detail.

3 Could one stock provide many despatch items?

The answer is *yes*, therefore the stock item becomes the master and despatch item the detail.

4 Could many despatch items be recorded on a single invoice?

The answer is *yes* – usually the items belonging to the same order which makes the invoice the master and the despatch item the detail.

The normal course of action is to prepare an entity cross-reference chart showing the direct relationship of entities (refer to Fig. B1), which is then used as a basis for constructing an entity model as shown in Fig. B2.

Construct conceptual model
The conceptual model of the system is shown in Fig. B3 which identified entities and functions and shows the sequence in which the functions are performed. It also shows the interfaces between various sub-systems which are beyond the boundary of the system with which we are concerned. The customer interfaces with the order processing

system by the placing of an order which triggers off the order processing system. (Refer to events). A number of functions/processes are then performed including:

   a value order
   b check credit
   c check stock
   d stock available – despatch goods
   e stock unavailable – inform buying office
   f invoice goods
   g update accounts

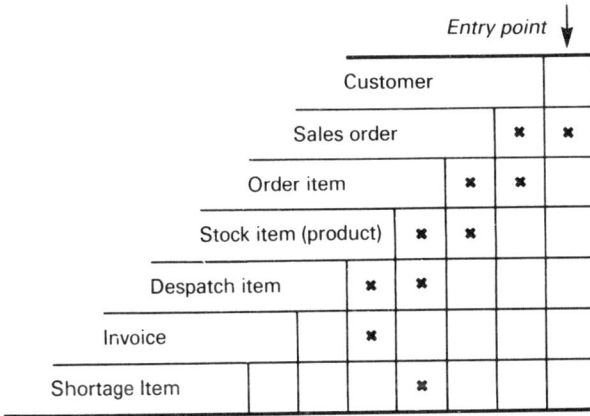

FIG. B1   *Entity cross reference direct relationship chart; order processing only (see Fig. B2)*

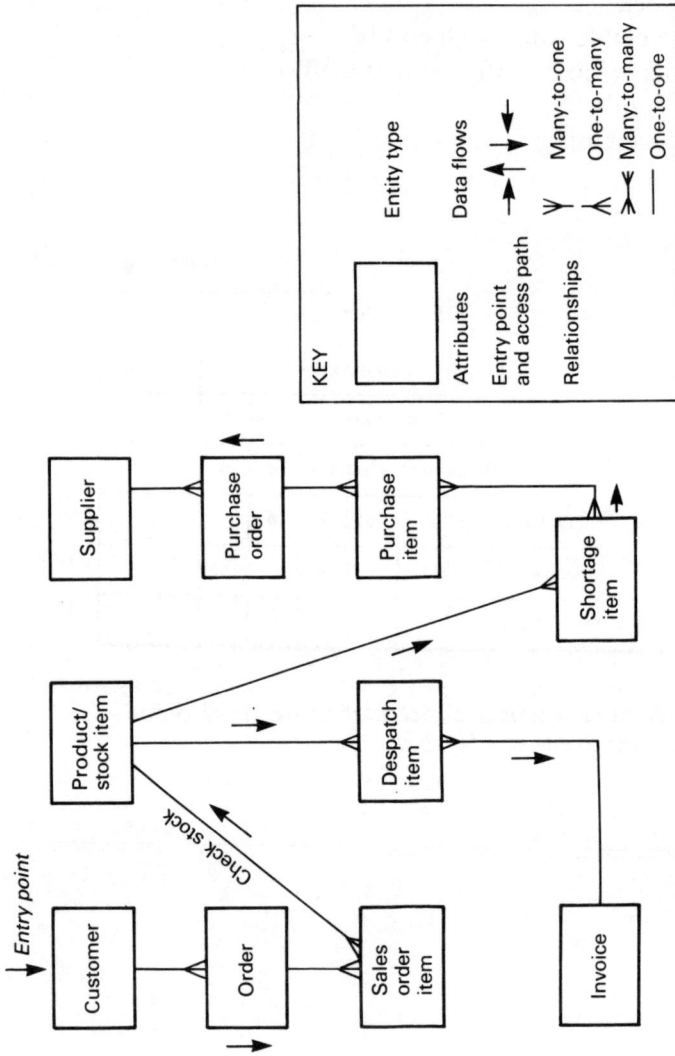

FIG. B2   Entity model integrated order processing system (depicting relationship between data items, entry points and access paths) (see Fig. B1)

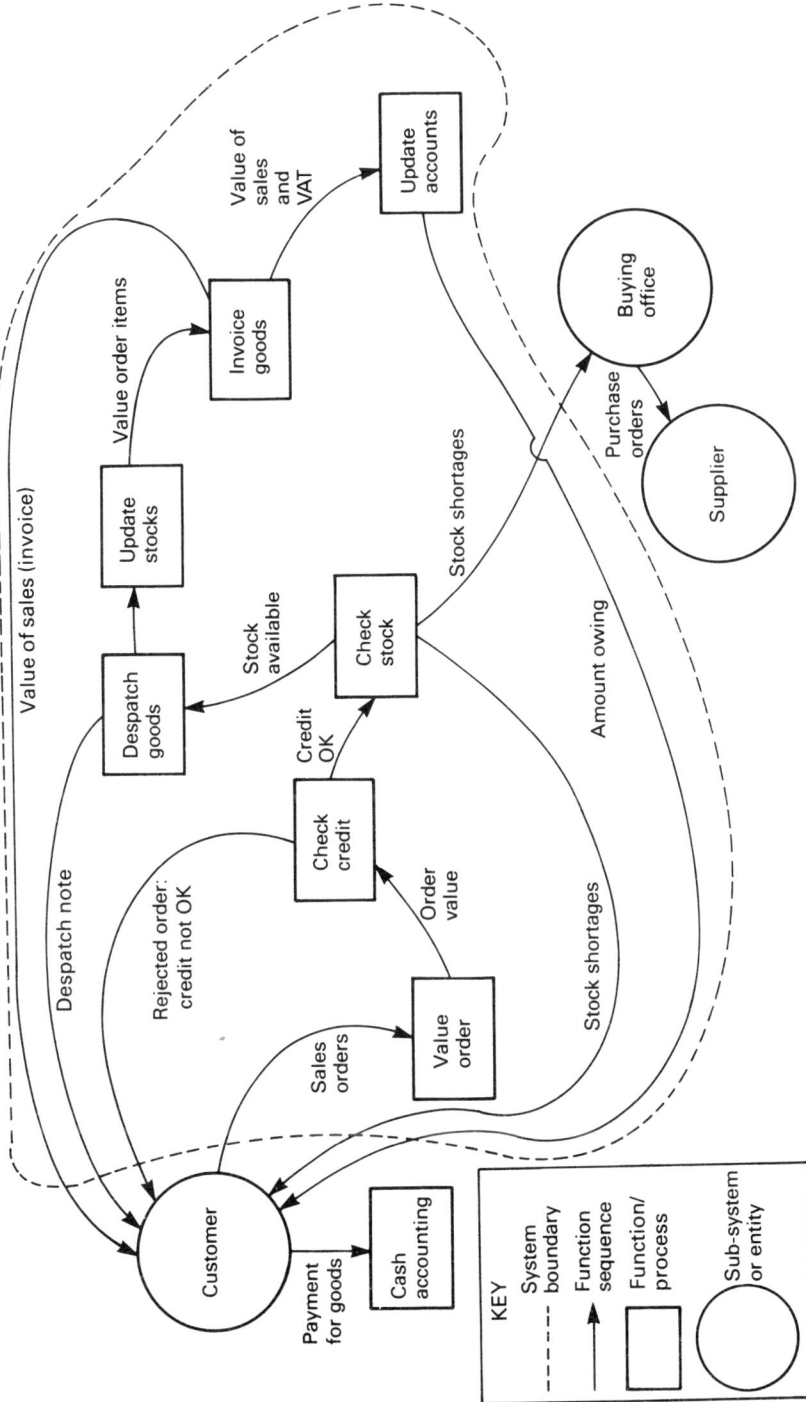

FIG. B3 Conceptual model of integrated order processing system, emphasising functions and their sequence

Stage 4: Analyse entity life and transaction histories

Entity life history: orders
Refer to Chapters 8 and 9 for an introduction to this topic. The primary entity of an order processing system is, of course, the sales order. The life history of this entity is now to be traced as it is important to know how this entity is created, modified and disposed of. Orders are created by a customer which are recorded on an orders file. The status of each item ordered is established after conducting a stock check. Items unavailable are recorded on a back-order file, a transitory file as items will be merged with items to be despatched when they become available. Items for which stock is available are recorded directly on the orders for despatch file. The order items are then checked and modified by the relevant corrections. The file then becomes an amended orders file. The status of the orders file is modified when values are computed for updating the stock file and the preparation of invoices for charging the customer. The file is then purged of the despatched orders items to provide a blank file, which is then used for other purposes including re-use as an orders file.
    The details outlined are illustrated in Fig. B4.

Transaction history diagram: sales order item
This topic has previously been introduced in Chapters 8 and 9. Fig. B5 indicates the various states of each order item. The first event is to check stock availability which indicates if there is sufficient in stock for the full order quantity; sufficient stock for a part delivery or no stock at all. When the status is part order quantity or no stock then two situations arise – to consider alternatives by discussing the situation with the customer and secondly, the need to re-order an item from the supplier. This situation is shown in the transaction history diagram to highlight the close relationship which exists between a stock item and an order item – one becomes the other. The details may be correct or incorrect and it is necessary to check to establish the specific status. The order items then become items for despatch. The items despatched are valued in readiness for producing an invoice to charge the customer and for updating the customer records (accounts) on the customer file. The various control processes need not be shown on the diagram but they have been included to indicate what events affect each order item. The control processes are:
  a Check stock availability
  b Check item details
  c Correct details

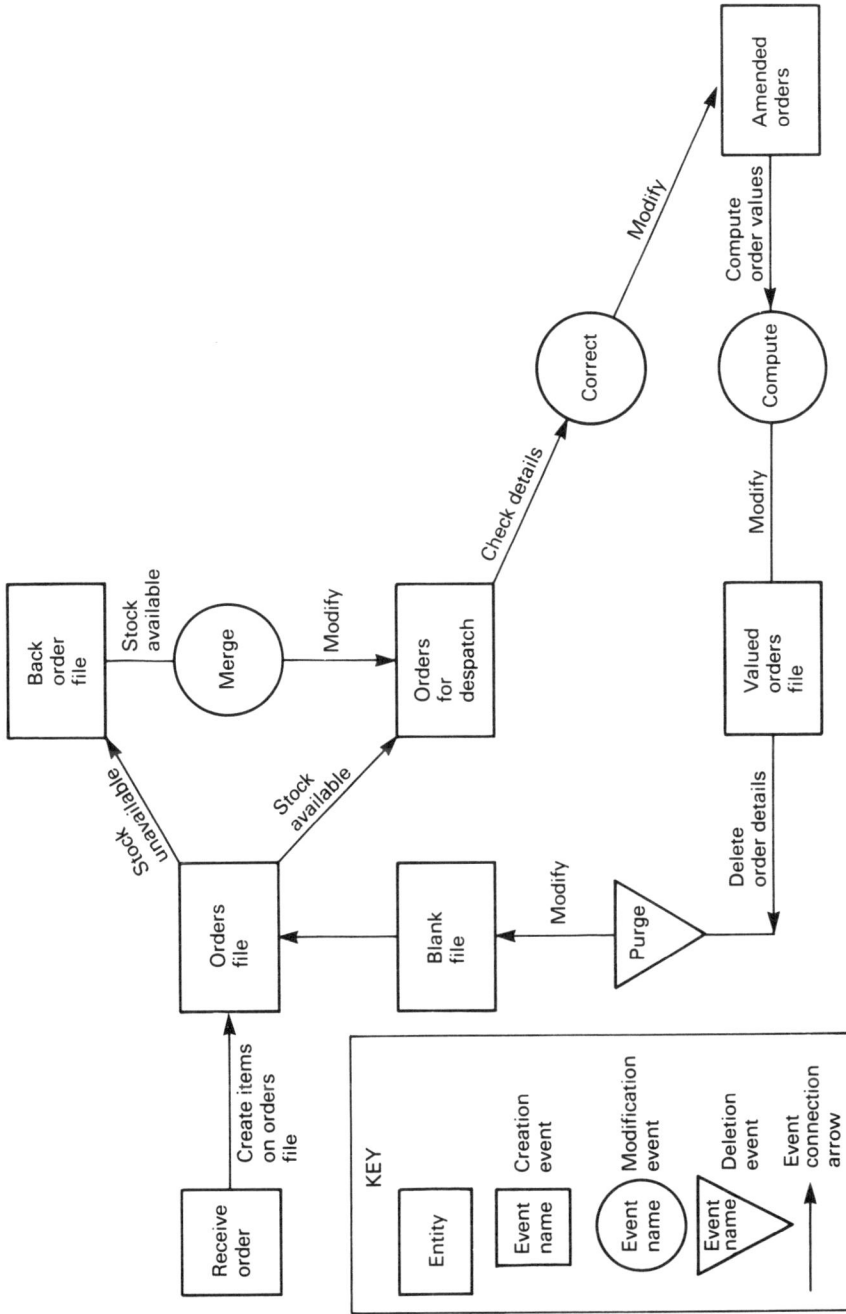

FIG. B4   *Entity life history for an order using LBMS symbolisation*

Events affecting a sales order

An analysis of the events which cause things to happen include:
  a Receipt of order.
    This event generates the function of computing the value of the
    order as a basis for checking the credit status of the customer
    before accepting an order which is a weakness of the current
    system.
  b If as a result of the check on the customer's credit status it proves
    to be unsatisfactory then this event triggers off the routine to
    inform the customer.
  c If the result of the credit check is satisfactory then this event
    triggers off a check on the stock situation.
  d If, as a result of this check, a shortage of stock is apparent then
    this event generates the need to discuss alternatives with the
    customer and the preparation of a record of the shortages.

Other events will become apparent in later stages of the case study.

Stage 5 Construct a context diagram
This diagram portrays the sources of data flows in and out of the stock
control system. This is shown in Figs. B6 and B7, which provide an
overall view of the order processing system and facilitates a framework for more detailed design considerations. Figure B6 provides a
simplified outline while Figure B7 provides a more comprehensive
view of the system.

**Stage 6 Specify data elements (attributes) relating to input and output
data flows**
At this stage the design is expanded to include more detail of the data
flows. It is necessary to specify the data elements comprising each
incoming data flow. Details are entered in a data dictionary. Details
would also be required of the type and number of characters contained in each data element (field) which is not shown in this study.
Details are indicated below of the data originating point. The
frequency of preparation and access of each type of data will depend
upon the nature of the physical system but orders would be dealt with
as they are received on the telephone, throughout the day. Routine
processing is likely to be on a daily basis.

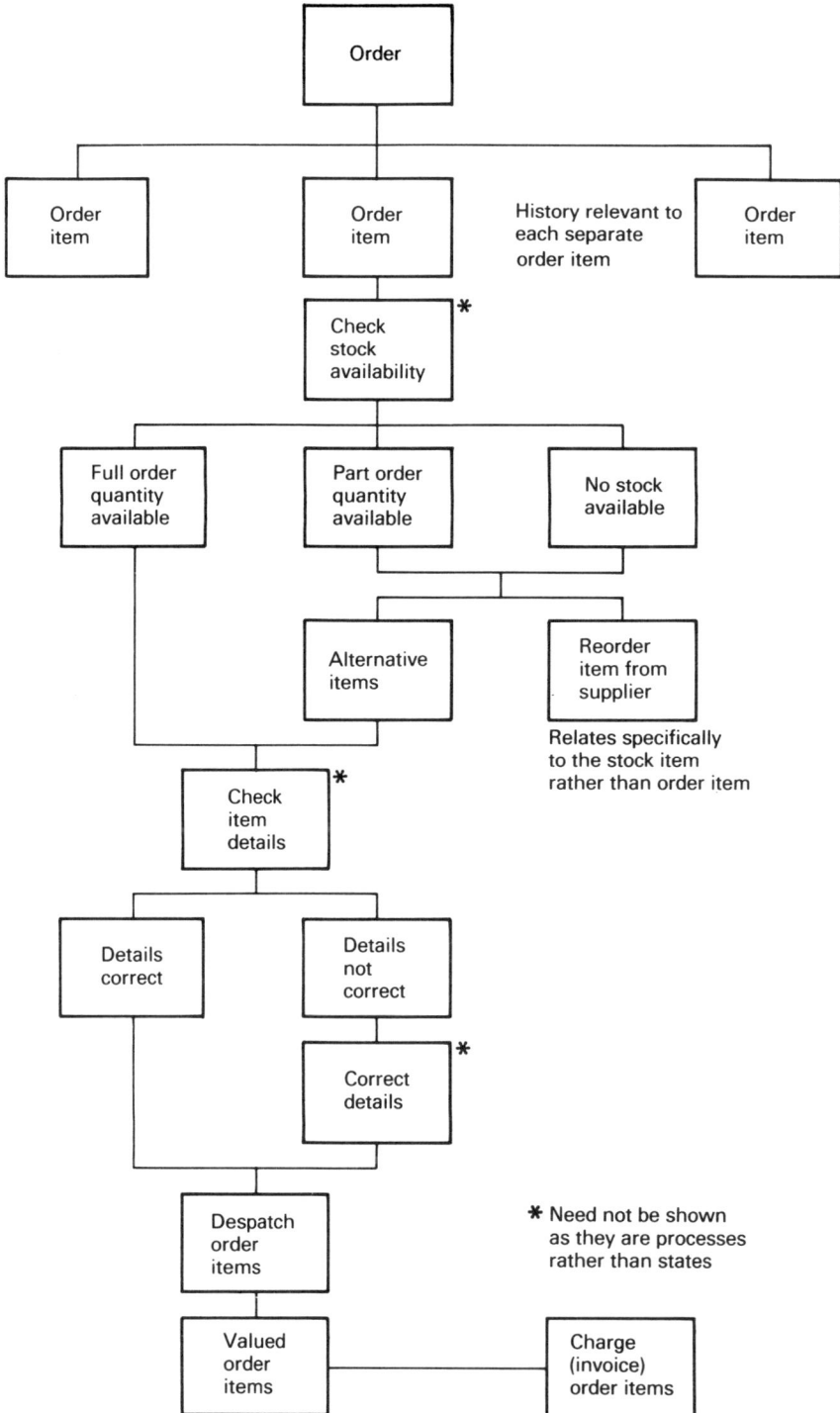

FIG. B5 *Transaction history diagram: sales order item*

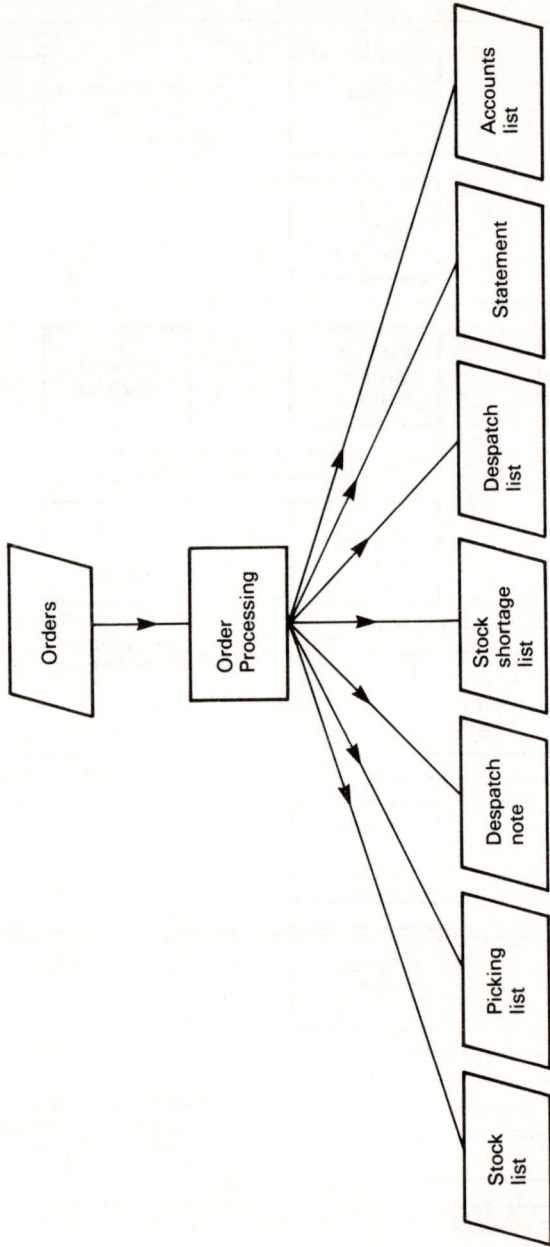

FIG. B6   *Simplified context diagram: integrated order processing system*

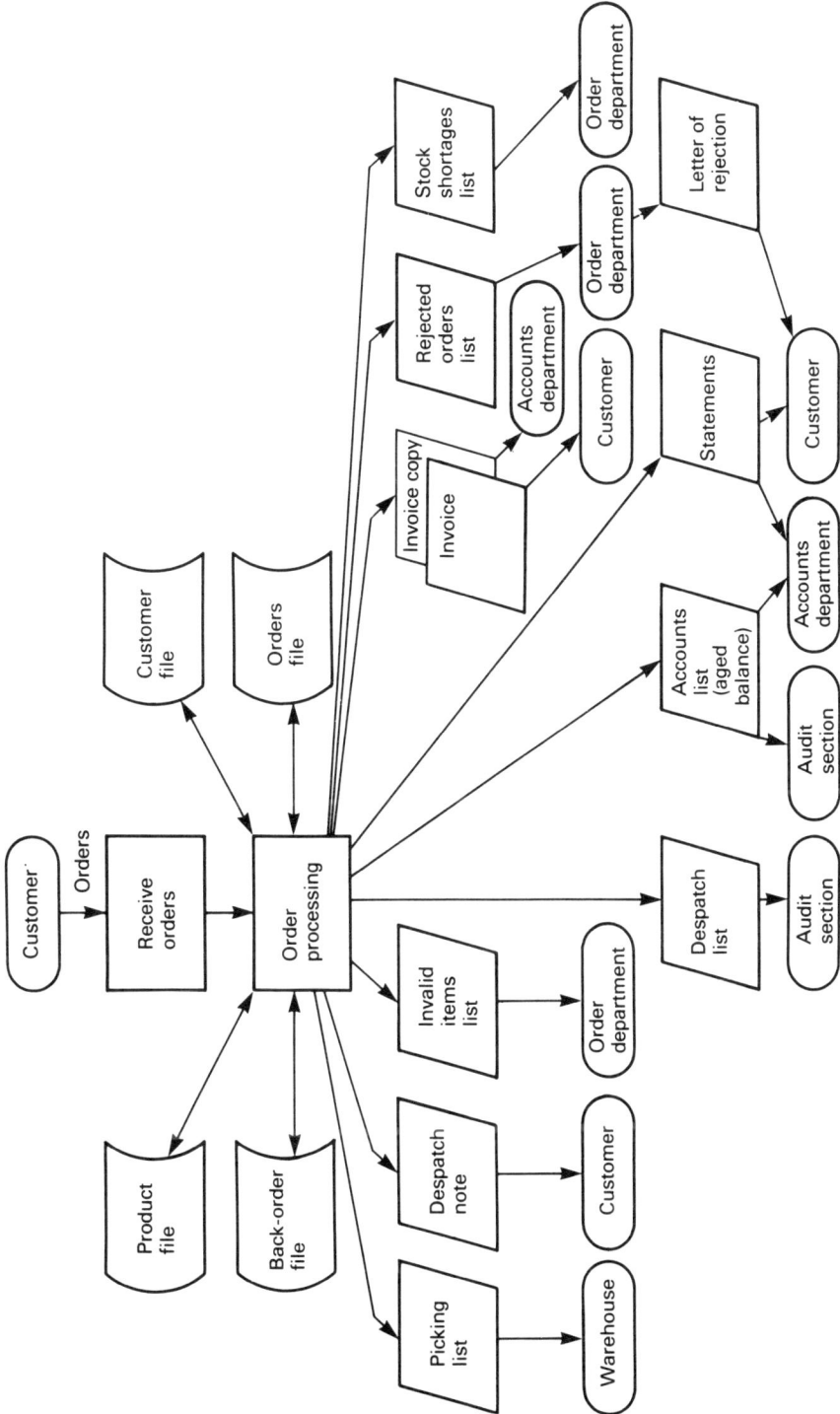

FIG. B7   *Comprehensive context diagram: integrated order processing system*

Input data flows
1 Orders
Data elements (attributes):
   a order number
   b customer code
   c date of order
   d item code
   e item description
   f quantity

Orders are received from customers by the order department. They are then subjected to internal checking procedures to ensure details are correct and complete.

2 Batch control slip
Data elements (attributes):
   a serial number
   b originating department
   c date
   d system
   e number of documents in batch
   f type of documents
   g hash total
   h total value of transactions (if relevant)

Prepared and attached to batches of orders by the order department. It provides data for controlling the processing of orders. Control data on the batch control slip is compared with control data generated during processing. This ensured that any mislaid documents are searched for and any corrupted data is detected and corrected.

Output data flows
1 Picking list
Data elements (attributes):
   a order number
   b customer code
   c date of order
   d item code
   e item description (obtained from product stock item) file
   f quantity

The picking list consists of details of items stored on the orders file containing items for despatch file. Attributes (d) – (f) are repeated for each item.

2 Despatch note
Data elements (attributes):
  a order number
  b customer code
  c date of order
  d despatch address
  e delivery date
  f item code
  g item description
  h quantity despatched

Prepared from stored order details of items for despatch. The despatch address is obtained from the customer file but may have originated on the order details if the address can vary when a business has a number of retail sales outlets. The item description is derived from the product (stock item) file. Attributes (f)–(h) are repeated for each item despatched.

3 Invoice
Data elements (Attributes):
Pre-printed data on invoice form
  a name of document
  b name of business
  c VAT registration number
  d terms of payment

Details generated by system automatically
  e invoice number
  f invoice data

Attributes from customer file
  g customer name
  h invoice address
  i delivery address

Attributes from valued orders file containing items for despatch
  j order number
  k customer code
  l date of order
  m delivery date
  n item code
  o quantity despatched

Attributes obtained from valued order file containing details from the product (stock item) file
  p item description
  g selling price
  r VAT rate %
  s quantity discount rate %
  t carriage charges data

Computed data for each item
  u gross value
  v quantity discount
  w VAT (unless a standard rate applies in which case the total VAT could be computed for all items)
  x net invoice value

Computed data for complete invoice
  y total gross value, total discount, total net value, total VAT and total of invoice

4 Statement
Data elements (attributes)
  a date
  b customer code
  c customer name
  d customer address
  c account balance (either balance forward or open item)
  d balance forward age analysis: current month, 1 month, 2 months, 3 months, 4 months and over
  e credit limit

Compiled from details extracted from customer records (accounts) stored in the customer file which contains details relating to the amount outstanding, i.e. the amount (balance) unpaid to date. Computations are required for producing an age analysis of the balance.

5 Stock shortage list
Data elements (attributes)
  a order number
  b date of order
  c item code
  d description
  e quantity

Compiled from details stored on the back order file relating to items out of stock or for which there is insufficient stock for quantities ordered. The buying office is notified of such shortages so that a purchase order may be placed on suppliers to replenish stocks.

6 Stock list
Data elements (attributes)
    a item code
    b item description
    c quantity in stock
    d value of stock @ selling price
    e value of stock @ cost price
    f reorder quantity
    g reorder level
    h minimum stock level
    i maximum stock level

Prepared from the updated product (stock item) file after items for despatch have been subtracted from the quantity and value of items in stock.

7 Despatch list
Data elements identical with those on the despatch note excluding despatch address

Compiled from the same source as despatch notes relating to orders available for despatch.

8 Accounts list
Attributes are identical with those on the statement produced from the records on the customer file.

Stage 7 Specify input and output data flows and an outline of processing activities by means of a composite data flow diagram
The data flow diagram shown in Fig. B8 presents a visual representation of the flow of data in the order processing system. It clearly shows the entities which send or receive data, the processes which alter the composition of the data and the data stores (files) required to store details of entities.

Stage 8 Transform analysis – levelling of data flows
When data flows are shown separately on separate diagrams it allows each stage of the system to be closely examined to ensure there are no duplicated or omitted data flows. It also enables a close examination to be undertaken of the entities which send or receive data (sources

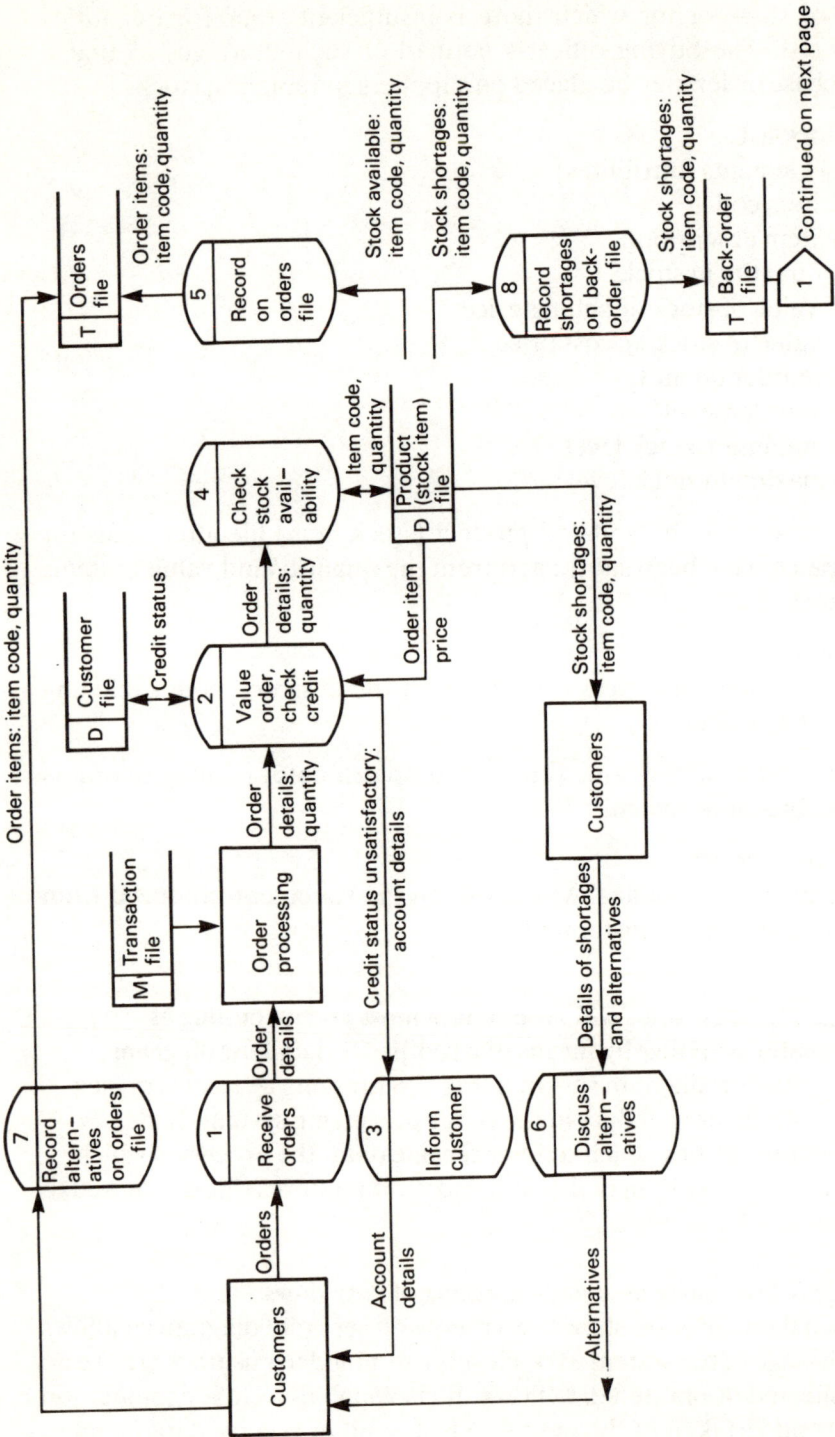

FIG. B8   *Integrated order processing: parent data flow diagram: level 1*

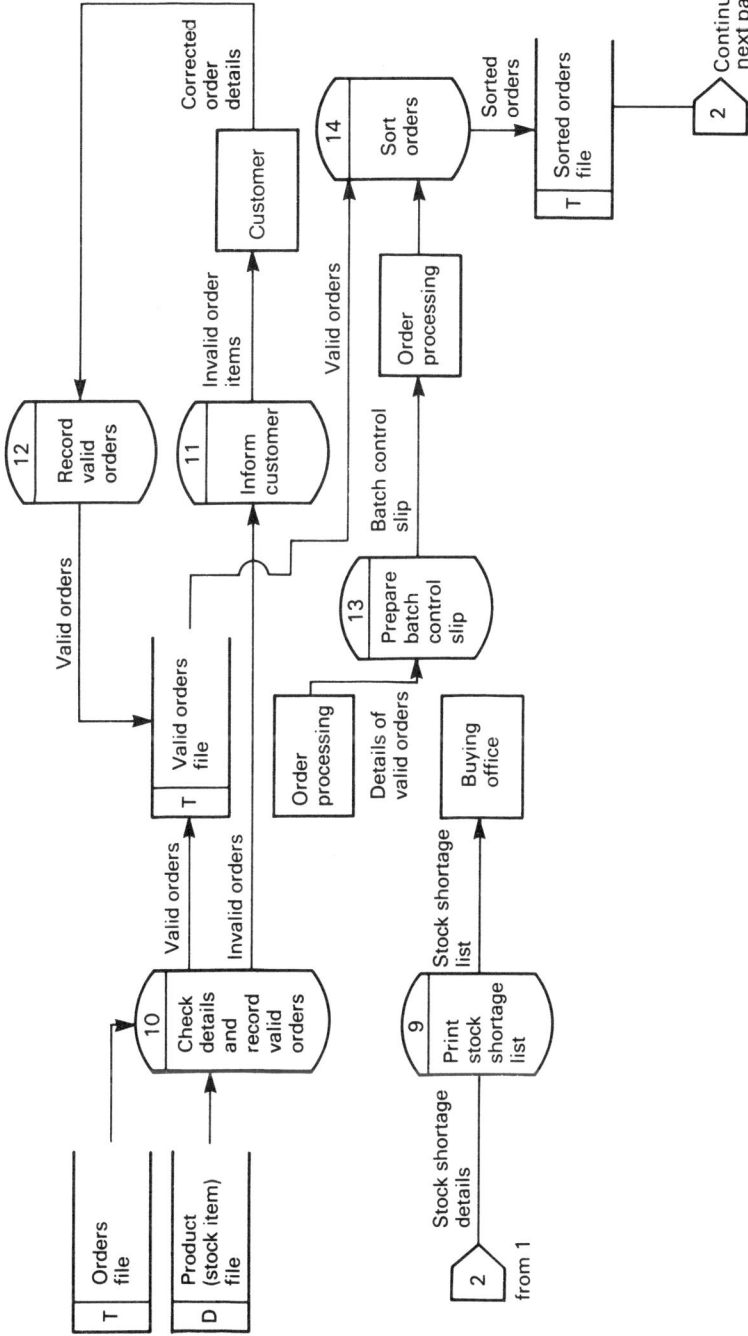

(Fig. B8 contd)

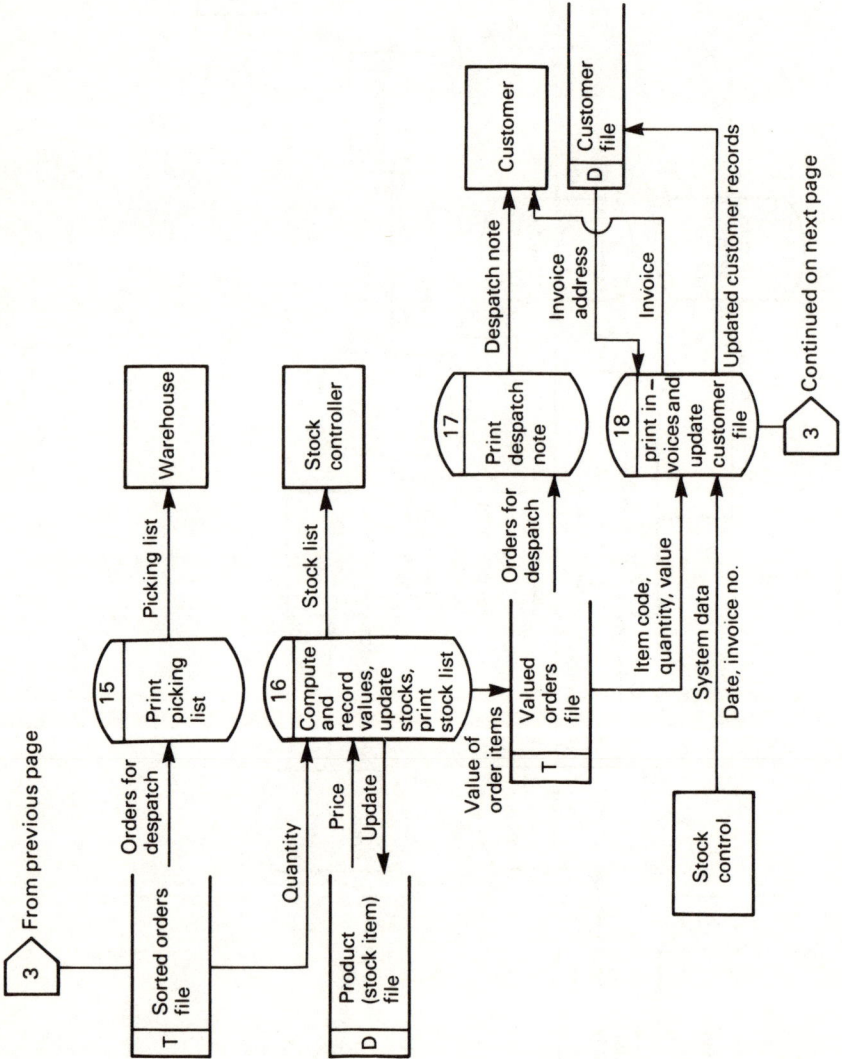

(Fig. B8 *contd*)

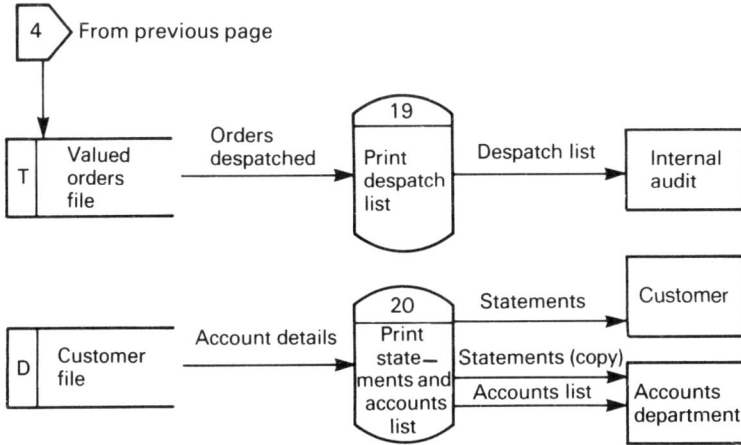

(Fig. B8 *contd*)

and sinks) the processes (transforms) which alter the structure of data and the data stores which hold data.

Sources and sinks are located outside the area of the system under development but the data flows emanating from such entities are of extreme important to the effective logical design of the system. It is now proposed to summarise the levelled data flows.

The parent diagram, Fig. B8, shows sufficient details not to warrant levelling for each data flow therefore only a number of composite data flows have been levelled and these are contained in the following summary. Refer to Figs. B9 to B17.

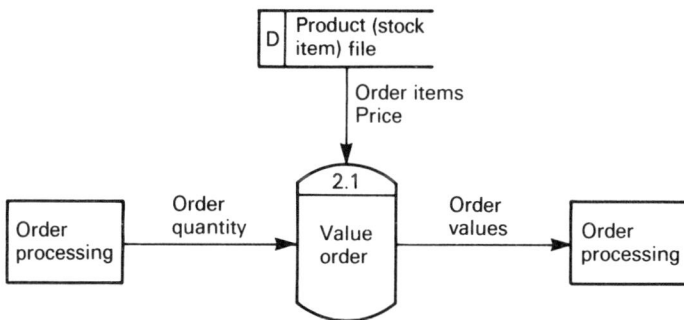

FIG. B9   *Data flow diagram: process 2, level 2*

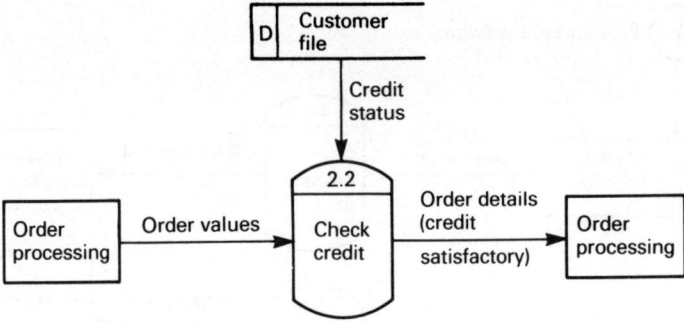

FIG. B10   *Data flow diagram: process 2, level 2*

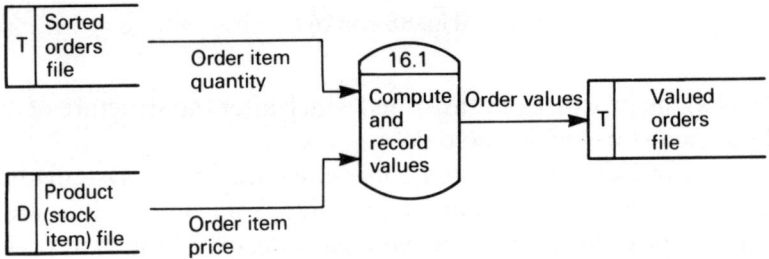

FIG. B11   *Data flow diagram: process 16, level 2*

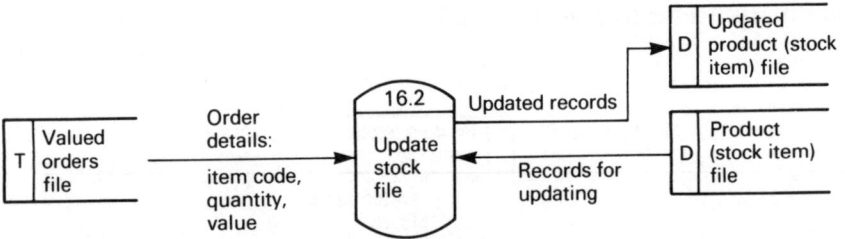

FIG. B12   *Data flow diagram: process 16, level 2*

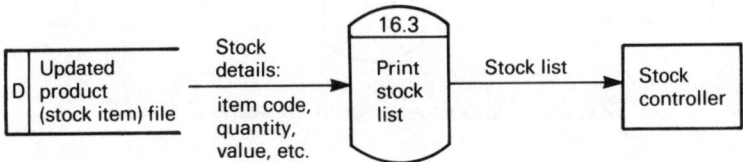

FIG. B13   *Data flow diagram: process 16, level 2*

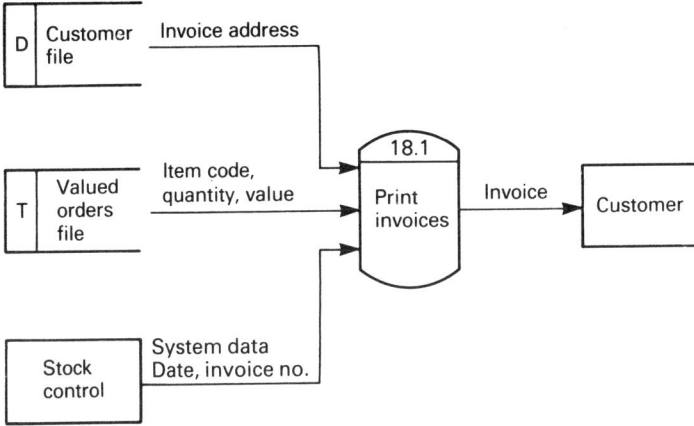

FIG. B14   *Data flow diagram: process 18, level 2*

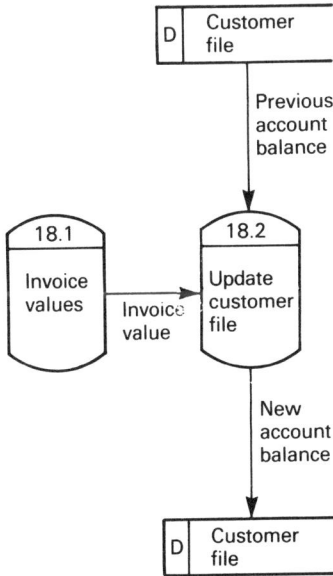

FIG. B15   *Data flow diagram: process 18, level 2*

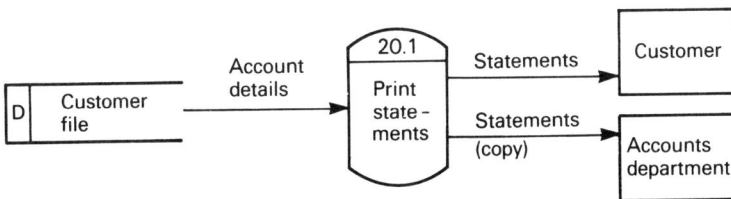

FIG. B16   *Data flow diagram: process 20, level 2*

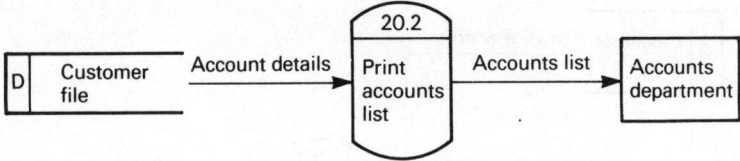

FIG. B17 *Data flow diagram: process 20, level 2*

Summary of levelled data flows

Process	Source	Data flow	Sink
Level 1 (see Fig. B8)			
1	Customer	Orders	Order processing
Level 2 (see Figs. B9 and B10)			
2.1	Order processing	Order values	Order processing
2.2	Order processing	Order details	Order processing
	Customer file	Credit status	Order processing
Level 1 (see Fig. B8)			
3	Process 2.2	Account details	Customer
4	Order processing	Quantities in stock	Order processing
	Product file		
5	Order processing	Order items for which stock is available	Orders file
6	Customer	Alternatives	Order processing
7	Order processing	Alternatives	Order file
8	Order processing	Stock shortages	Back-order file
9	Back-order file	Stock shortages list	Buying office
10	Orders file		
	Product file	Valid orders	Valid orders file
11	Order processing	Invalid orders	Customer
12	Customer	Corrected orders	Valid orders file

13	Order processing	Batch control slip	Order processing
14	Valid orders file	Sorted orders	Sorted orders file
15	Sorted orders file	Picking list	Warehouse

Level 2 (see Figs. B11 to B13)

16.1	Sorted orders file		
	Product file	Order values	Valued orders file
16.2	Valued orders file	Updated records	Product file
16.3	Product file	Stock list	Stock controller

Level 1

17	Valued orders file	Despatch note	Customer

Level 2 (see Figs. B14 and B15)

18.1	Valued orders file	Invoice	Customer
	Stock control Customer file		
18.2	Process 18.1	New account balance	Customer file

Level 1

19	Valued orders file	Despatch list	Internal audit

Level 2 (see Figs B16 and B17)

20.1	Customer file	Statements	Customer Accounts department
20.2	Customer file	Account list	Accounts department

Stage 9 Data modelling

The first stage of data modelling is to identify the data stores required by the order processing system which can be established by inspecting the data flow diagram which contains stores (files) relating to customers, order items, stock items, back-orders, despatches and valued orders. Incoming orders need to be separated into orders which can be despatched and those which are out of stock or in short supply. As the primary record in the system is the order, it is most appropriate to inspect the unnormalised order record before normalising it on the basis of 3NT, i.e. Third Normal Form analysis.

Unnormalised order record
The unnormalised order record contains a mixture of keys and attributes which combine to provide the details listed below (see Fig. B18):

> **Order number**
> Order date
> Delivery date
> Customer code
> Customer name
> Customer address
>   Item code
>   Item description
>   Quantity
>   Price

First normal form
Identify and remove any repeating groups.
Repeating groups indicate there are more specific aspects in the data which should stand-alone. Repeating groups occur for the different items ordered when an order consists of more than one item. This necessitates their separation into fixed data and variable data relating to each order.

It is also necessary to establish if there are any composite keys in the records. These do not occur in this system as each entity is uniquely identified by a single key except additional keys are added for cross reference purposes. Refer to Fig. B19.
1 Order record

> **Order number**
> Date of order
> Delivery date
> Customer code
> Customer name
> Customer address

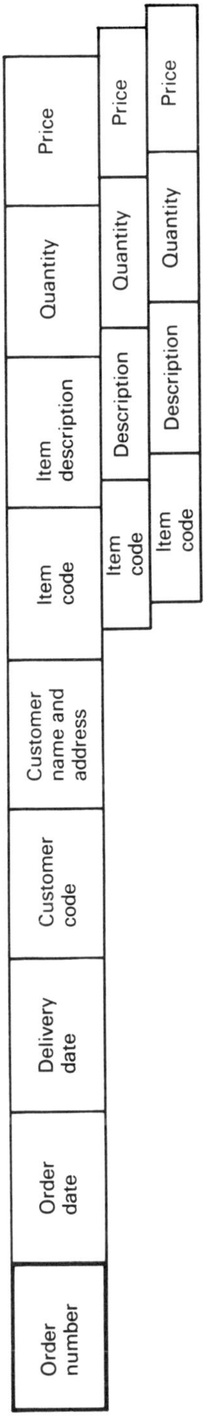

FIG. B18 *Unnormalised order record*

2 Order item

> **Order number**
> Item code
> Item description
> Quantity
> Price

The order number must be included with the repeating group for cross reference needs.

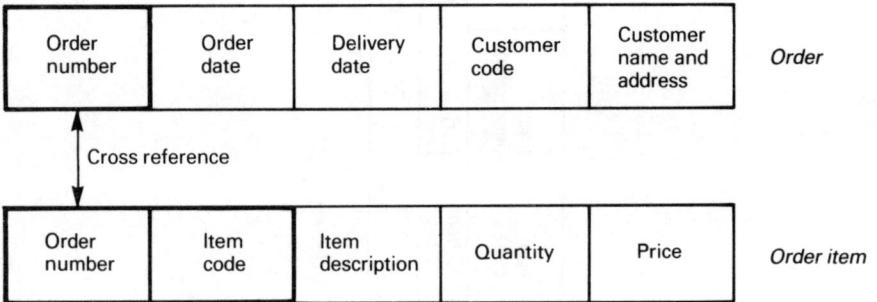

Order number	Order date	Delivery date	Customer code	Customer name and address	*Order*

Cross reference

Order number	Item code	Item description	Quantity	Price	*Order item*

FIG. B19   *First normal form: remove repeating group*

Second normal form
Remove attributes not dependent on the whole of a (concatenated) primary key.
Refer to Fig. B20.
1 Order record

> **Order number**
> Date of order
> Delivery date
> Customer code
> Customer name
> Customer address

2 Order item

> **Order number**
> Item code
> Quantity

The order item has two keys – the **Order number** refers to the relevant order and the **Item code** cross references to the stock item.

3 Stock item
> **Item code**
> Item description
> Price

This stage of normalisation separates details relating to the item held in stock (**stock item**) from the details of items ordered (**order item**).

Third normal form
Remove attributes dependent on other than the primary key. Refer to Fig. B21.

1 Order record
> **Order number**
> Date of order
> Delivery date
> Customer code

2 Customer record
> **Customer code**
> Customer name
> Customer address

A new record is introduced at this juncture as the order record at the second normal form stage included details relating to a customer

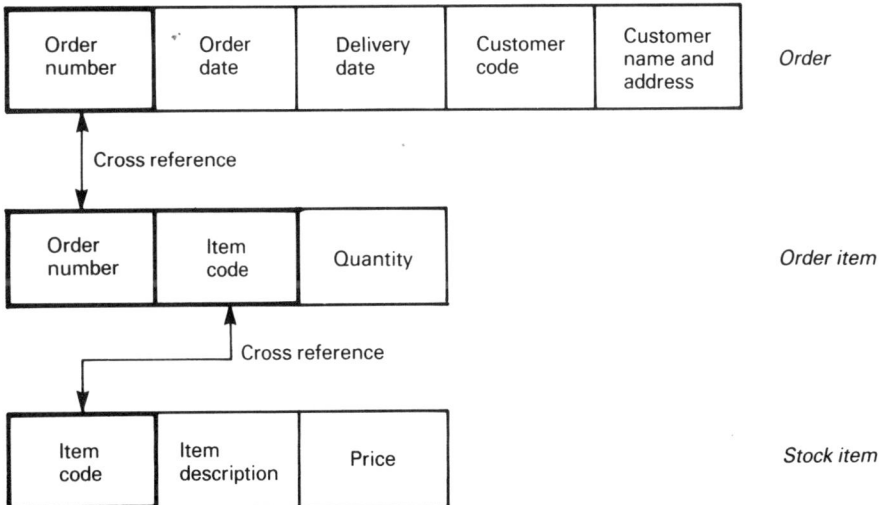

FIG. B20   *Second normal form: remove attributes note dependent on the Refer to p. 244 for continuation.*

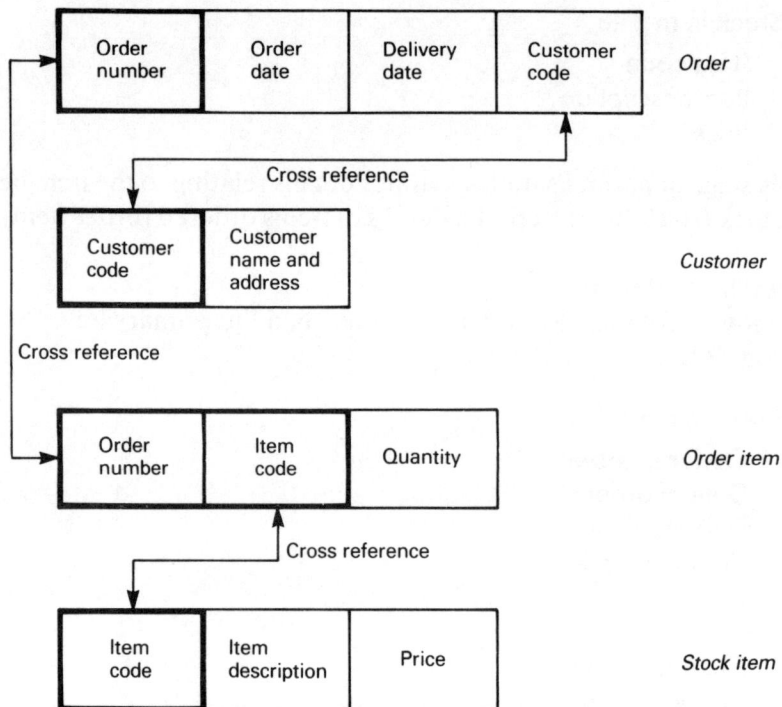

FIG. B21 *Third normal form: remove attributes dependent on other than the primary key*

record which contains attributes dependent upon other than the primary key, i.e. the order number. The customer record, as can be seen, contains name and address attributes which are dependent upon the customer code.

The customer record needs to contain additional attributes for credit control and accounting as shown in the full record below:

Customer Record
Customer code
Customer name
Invoice address   – line 1
                       – line 2
                       – line 3
                       – line 4
Delivery address   – line 1
                       – line 2
                       – line 3
Credit limit   – line 4
Account balance

Account balance age analysis-current
                        — 1 mnth
                        — 2 mnths
                        — 3 mnths
                        — 4 mnths and over
Area code
Turnover

3 Order item record

Order number
Item code
Quantity

4 Stock item record

Item code
Item description
Price

Files relating to back-orders, despatches and valued orders are normalised in a similar way.

5 Back-order item data-header
Back order data (stock shortages)

Order number
Date or order
Delivery date
Customer code

6 Back-order item data-item details

Order number
Item code
Quantity

7 Despatch order item data-header
Order number
Date of order
Delivery date
Customer code

The order number must be included in the repeating group for cross referencing

8 Despatch order item data-item details

Order number
Item code
Quantity despatched

The valued orders data is segregated to allow for repeating groups as shown below:

9 Valued orders data-header

Order number
Date of order
Delivery date
Customer code

It is necessary to include the order number with the valued order item data for cross reference to the order and for identifying the customer when necessary to do so.

10 Valued orders data-valued order item

Order number
Item code
Quantity despatched

The file also was formerly the orders for despatch file and accordingly contains the same attributes. In addition attributes transferred from the product (stock item) file includes:

Item description
Selling price
VAT rate %
Quantity discount rate %
Carriage charges data

Computed values includes:

Gross value
Quantity discount
Net invoice value
VAT
Total
Carriage charge
Invoice total

11 Product (stock item) data
Item code
Item description
Selling price
Cost price
VAT rate%
Quantity discount rate %
Carriage charges data

This file also contains attributes essential for stock management as shown below:

Quantity in stock
Value of stock @ selling price
Value of stock @ cost price
Reorder quantity
Reorder level
Minimum stock level
Maximum stock level

The details to be recorded on invoices when all items have been valued and printed are: Total VAT, Total including VAT, Carriage charges and invoice total.

COURTING

Nature and purpose
This process is for the purpose of identifying any data stores which describe the same entities and which could be combined to avoid unnecessary redundancy. Courting is also concerned with identifying relationships between data stores and brings together related data as indicated. The various diagrams illustrating the relationships between data stores use relational lines.

Order processing
The valued order data listed above needs sufficient details for printing on invoices and for recording the computed totals on the customer file for recording the current balance owing. The data for this requirement are obtained from both the despatch item data (order file) and the stock item data (product file). The valued orders data is derived from the original order despatch data and details relating to selling price, VAT, discount rate and carriage charges are obtained from the stock item (product) file. See Fig. B22. Normalisation is applied to individual data stores and it is quite possible that overlapping data exists. This has been taken into account in the data modelling illustrated here.

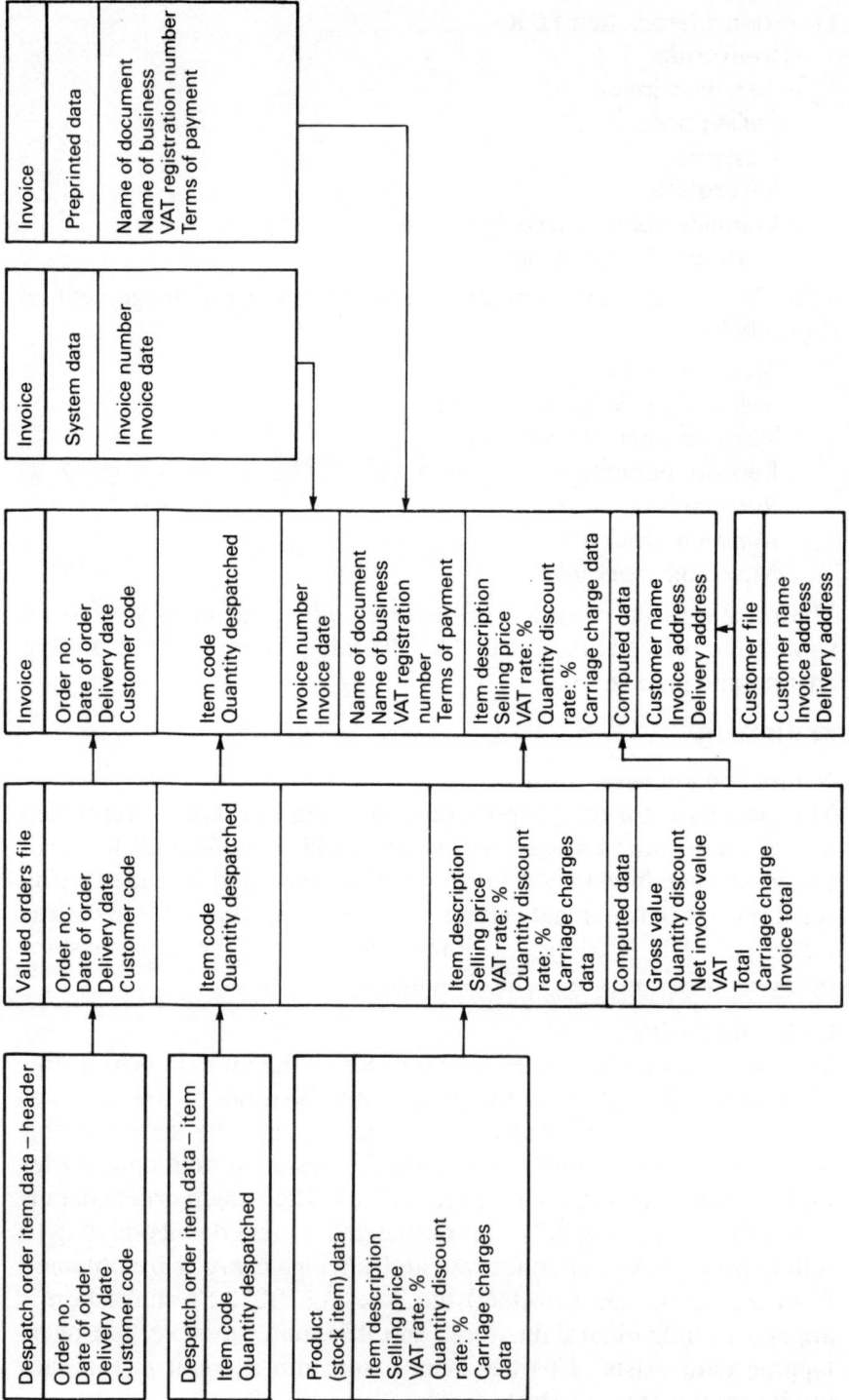

FIG. B22   Sources of information for preparing invoice

Back-order data

Referring to Fig. B23, outlining the relationships between files relating to back-order data, the single line from order item data to and from stock item data infers that it is a one-to-many relationship, i.e. one stock stores many order items. In this instance it is for checking stock availability. The line from stock item data to shortage item data indicates the recording of shortages, again a one-to-many relationship. The relational line from the order header data to the order item data indicates that one order can have many items – a one-to-many relationship.

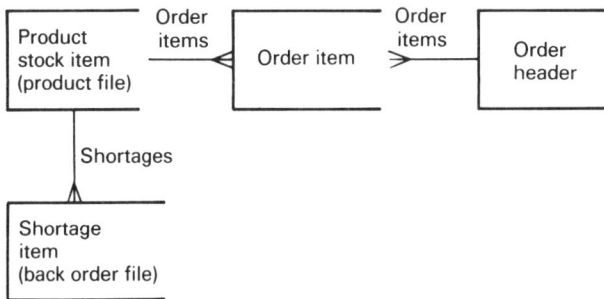

FIG. B24   *File relationships: order despatch data*

Order despatch data

The diagram outlining relationships with regard to order despatch data (Fig. B24) shows a line from stock item to order item data which is a one-to-many relationship. Some systems would produce two separate files at the stock checking stage in which case back-order data and despatch data stores would be prepared as separate files at the same time. In this instance however, the system must provide for discussing alternatives with the customer before preparing despatch item data. This means that the shortage item data can be processed but not the despatch item data until the customer indicates an alternative choice which is the 'trigger' for recording and checking order details for entry into the order/despatch file. It is important to be aware that, as shown on the diagram illustrating a composite logical model of the system, shortages are only recorded after the customer has decided that no substitutes are required and that the initial order requirements stand. Obviously if the customer did not wish to place an order for items in short supply then a shortage need not be recorded if the normal quantity was in stock. Available items are recorded as despatch item data on a one-to-many basis. The relationship between the order header data and the order item data shows a one-to-many relationship the same as the back-order situation.

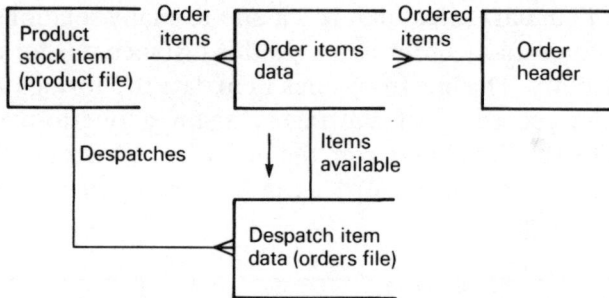

FIG. B23   *File relationships: back order data*

Despatch item valuation and stock updating

The diagram relating to stock item updating illustrates a relational line to stock item (product) data from valued despatch item orders file which signifies a one-to-one relationship, i.e. each stock record is updated by the relevant order item. It is interesting to note that the stock item file provided the price of items for computing the value of despatches. This subsequently enables the stock item data to be revised with the quantities and value of items despatched which records the new quantity and value of items remaining in stock. Refer to Fig. B25.

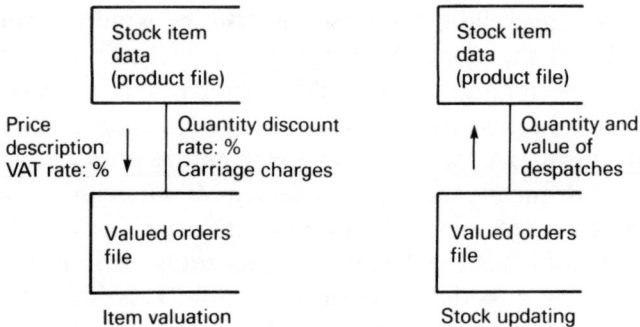

FIG. B25   *Despatch item valuation and stock updating*

Customer file updating

Similarly customer file updating shows that the value of customers' invoices are recorded on the respective customer record, i.e. the appropriate customer's account from the valued order file. This is a one-to-one relationship, i.e. one invoice with the total value of the order revises the customer's account balance to show the current status of the amount owing. Refer to Fig. B26.

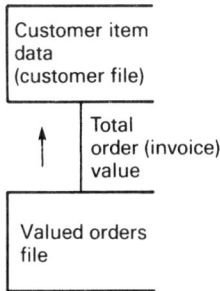

FIG. B26   *Customer file updating*

Stage 10: Functional decomposition of processes

A decomposition diagram is constructed to show the primary functions (activities and/or processes) concerned with the order processing system. It analyses high level definitions of a function into more detail for further analysis. The decomposition diagrams are shown in Fig. B27 and B28.

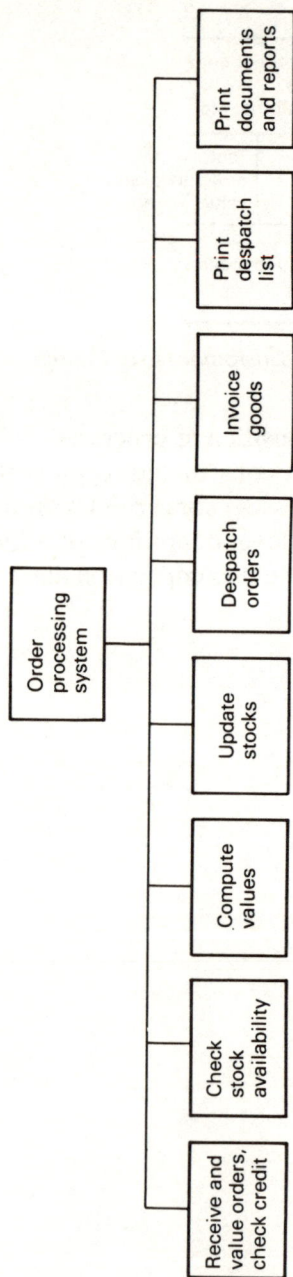

FIG. B27   *Integrated order processing: functional decomposition: level 1 outlining primary function*

```
                        ┌──────────────┐
                        │ Order        │
                        │ processing   │
                        │ system       │
                        └──────┬───────┘
      ┌────────────┬───────────┼────────────┬──────────────┐
┌─────────────┐┌────────────┐┌────────────┐┌──────────────┐┌──────────────────┐
│ Receive     ││ Check      ││ Check      ││ Prepare      ││ Sort order       │
│ value order,││ stock      ││ product    ││ batch control││ items to         │
│ check credit││ availability││ details   ││ slip         ││ product/         │
│             ││            ││            ││              ││ customer code    │
└──────┬──────┘└─────┬──────┘└─────┬──────┘└──────────────┘└──────────────────┘
┌─────────────┐┌────────────┐┌────────────┐
│ Inform      ││ Record     ││ Inform     │
│ customer if ││ items      ││ customer of│
│ credit      ││ available on││ errors    │
│ unsatisfactory││ orders file│└─────┬──────┘
└──────┬──────┘└─────┬──────┘
┌─────────────┐┌────────────┐┌────────────┐
│ Reject      ││ Discuss    ││ Record     │
│ order       ││ alternative││ corrected  │
│             ││ products   ││ items on   │
│             ││            ││ orders file│
└─────────────┘└─────┬──────┘└────────────┘
               ┌────────────┐
               │ Record     │
               │ alternative│
               │ items on   │
               │ orders file│
               └─────┬──────┘
               ┌────────────┐
               │ Record     │
               │ back       │
               │ orders     │
               └─────┬──────┘
               ┌────────────┐
               │ Prepare    │
               │ shortage   │
               │ list       │
               └────────────┘
```

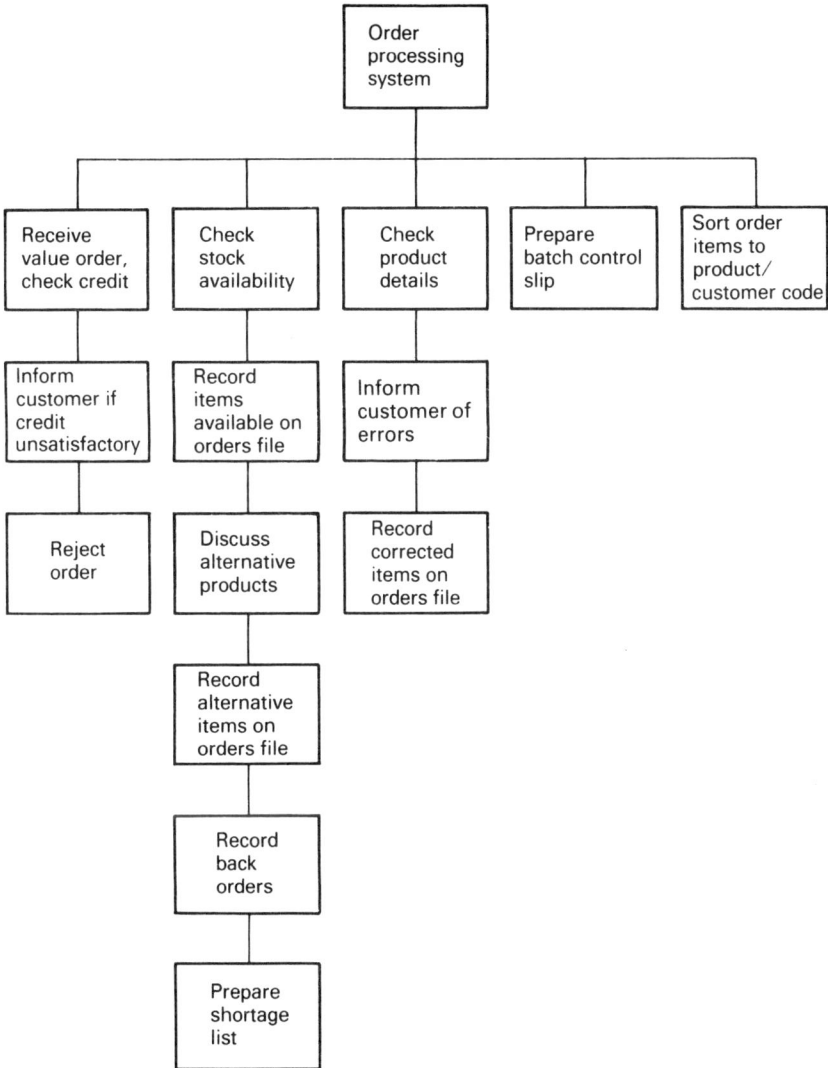

FIG. B28   *Integrated order processing: functional decomposition; level 2 expanding decomposing primary functions*

Refer to p. 244 for continuation.

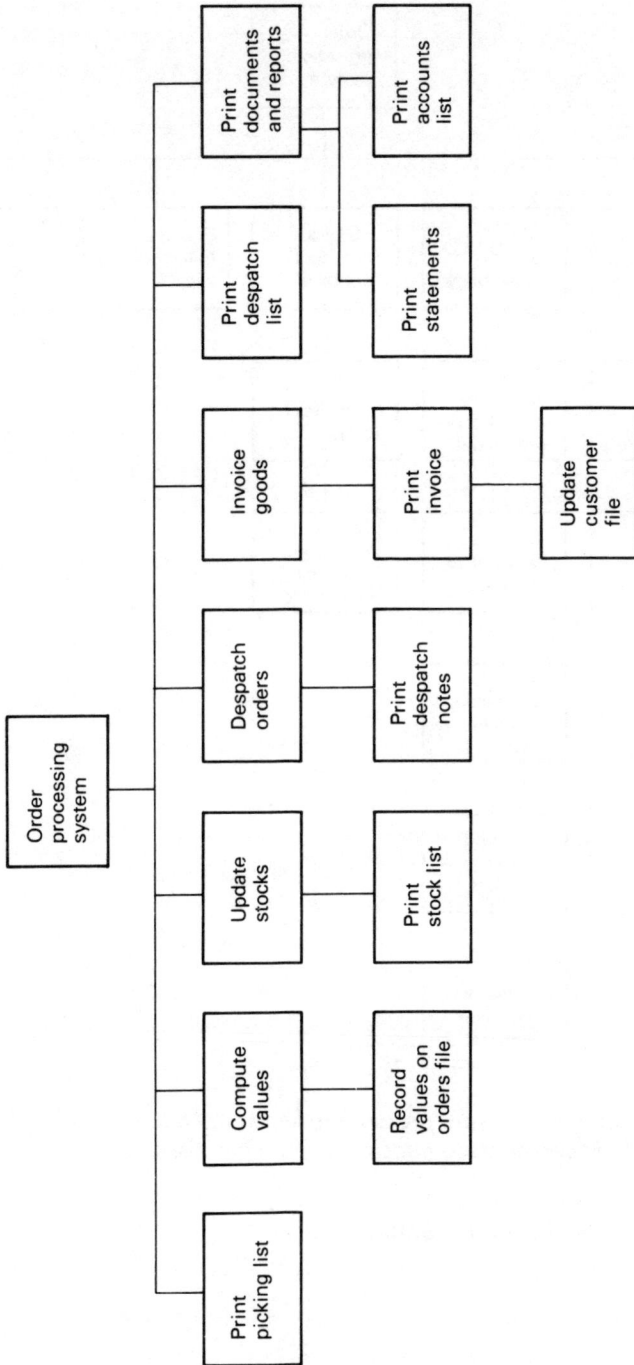

(Fig. B28 contd)

Summary of functional decomposition

Integrated order processing
    Level 1
          Order processing
          receive and value orders, check credit
          check stock availability
          compute values
          update stocks
          despatch orders
          invoice goods
          print despatch list
          print documents and reports
    Level 1
          Receive and value orders, check credit
          Level 2 Inform customer if credit unsatisfactory
                  Reject order
    Level 1
          Check stock availability
          Level 2 Record items available on orders file
                  Discuss alternative products when required
                    items are unavailable
                  Record alternative items on orders file
                  Record back orders
                  Prepare shortage list
    No level 1
             Level 2 Check product details
                    Inform customer of errors
                    Record corrected (valid) items on orders file
    No level 1
             Level 2 Prepare batch control slip
    No level 1
             Level 2 Sort orders items to product/customer code
    No level 1
             Level 2 Print picking list
    Level 1
          Compute values
          Level 2 Record values on orders file
    Level 1
          Update stock file

Level 2   Print stock list
Level 1

Despatch orders
Level 2   Print despatch note
Level 1

Invoice goods
Level 2   Print invoice
          Update customer file
Level 1

Print despatch list
Level 1

Print documents and reports
Level 2   Print statements
          Print accounts list

Stage 11 Construct flowchart portraying logical model of the system
This can be constructed either from the comprehensive data flow
diagram constructed in stage 7, or it may be constructed from diagrams of levelled data flows prepared in stage 8. The decomposition
diagrams may also be used for this purpose in order to consolidate
data flows and processes. Refer to Fig. B29 which portrays the logical
model of this system. Note it does not mention any matter relating to
hardware, only the logical sequence of processes and the data flows
between file and processes.

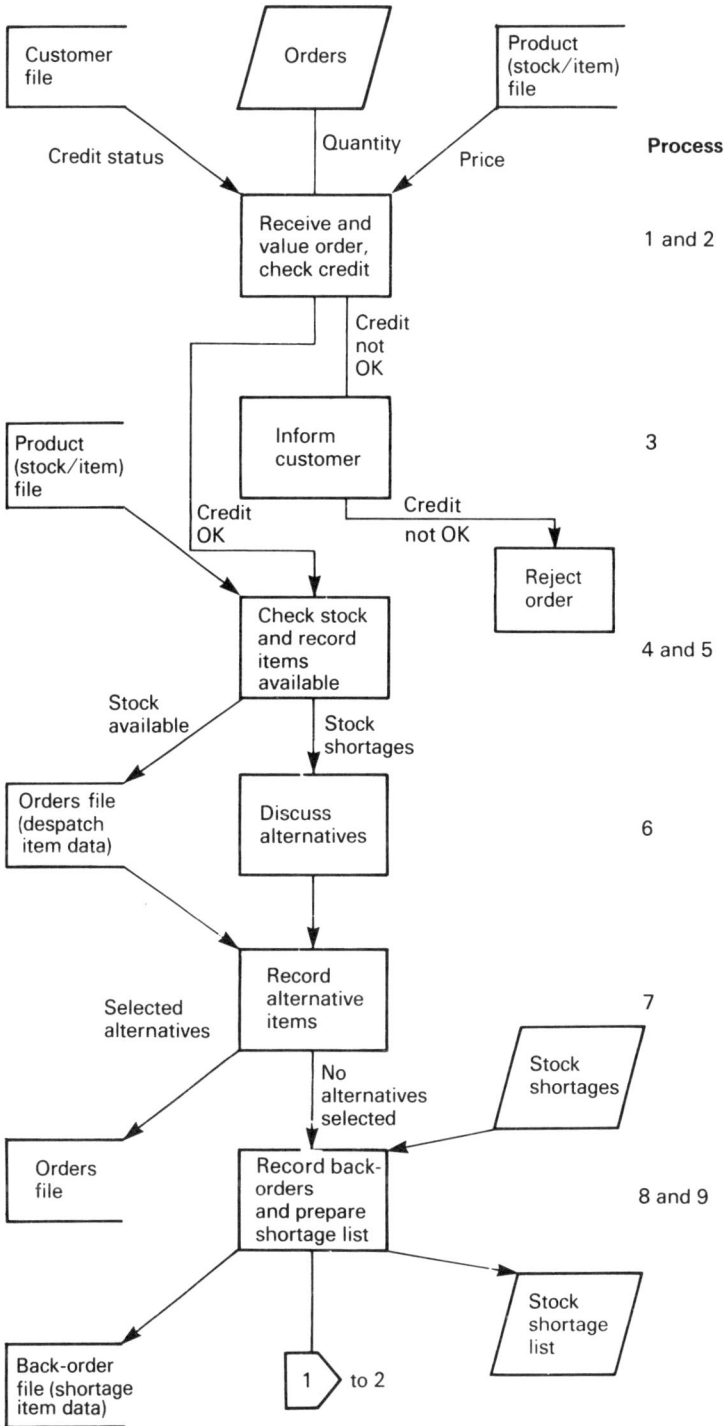

FIG. B29   *Composite logical model order processing system*

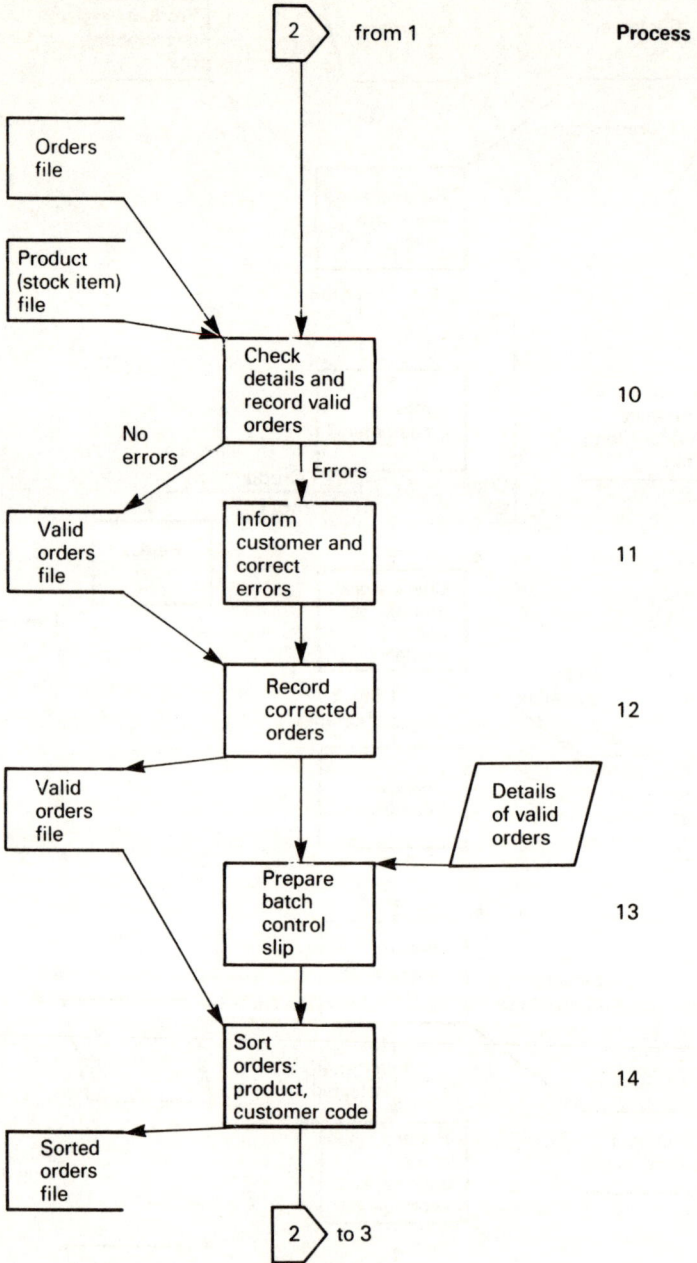

(Fig. B29 *contd*)

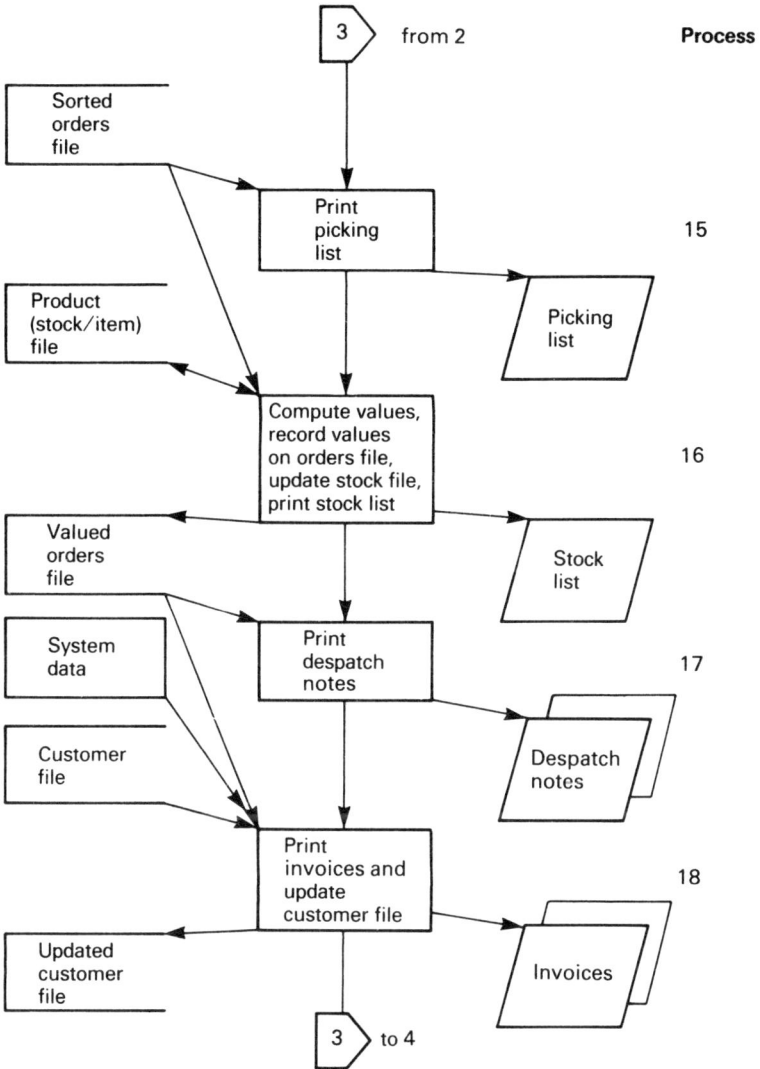

(Fig. B29 *contd*)

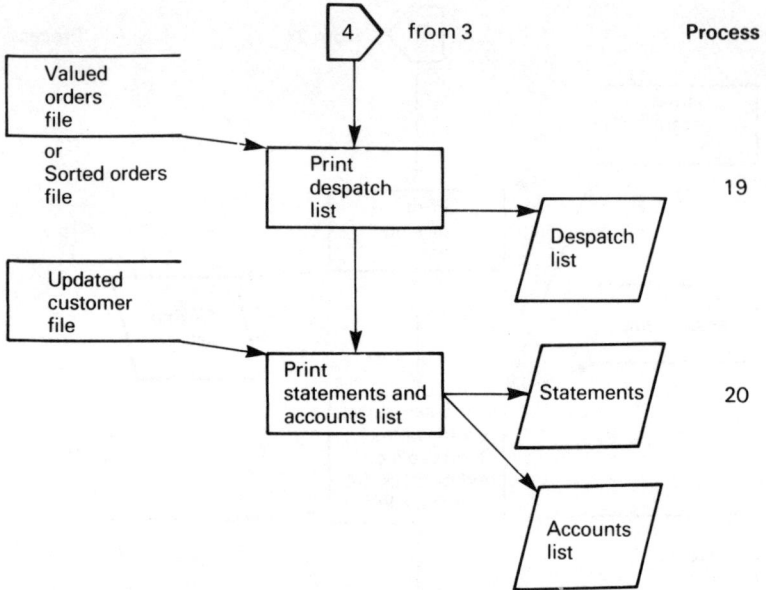

(Fig. B29 *contd*)

Stage 12 Initial design of physical system – first sketch

Having spent considerable time mapping data flows and establishing the logical requirements of users this stage of system development accords to the traditional approach, as it is now necessary to consider *how* the user requirements can be met by the use of physical methods, hardware and complementary software. The volumes of data to be processed and the number of stock records to be updated tends to imply the use of a small mainframe or minicomputer equipped with hard fixed discs – Winchesters – of a capacity of 20–40 Mb. The data is input by means of terminals in the order processing department.

A first sketch is produced of the proposed physical design of the system which is portrayed by means of a system flowchart. The flowchart introduces symbolically the hardware devices to be used for input, storage and output as well as providing the sequence of processing stages required to achieve the system requirements. It is considered that a mixed on-line/batch processing system is most appropriate for the operational needs of the business. Refer to Fig. B30.

Process 1, 2 and 3: Receive orders, check credit and inform customer: When orders are received by telephone or by post immediate access to a customer file is achieved by means of an on-line terminal connected to a minicomputer which provides instant access to the account of a customer for checking the credit status before accepting the order. The details are displayed on the video screen. This removes one of the problems of the present system of increasing bad debts, as the order is rejected immediately if necessary.

Process 4–7: Check stock availability, inform customer, discuss alternatives, print stock shortage list and record on back-order file: Delays and inaccuracies in stock recording which caused stock shortages will be eliminated by the operator gaining direct access to the product (stock item) file, by means of a terminal, to assess the availability of order items required while the customer is still on the telephone. Items for which stock is available are recorded on an order file. If specific items are unavailable or the full order quantity cannot be met from stock, then the customer is informed and alternative order items are discussed. Selected alternatives are added to the order file. This avoids the possible loss of an order and will boost profitability as well as increasing goodwill. Stock shortages are recorded on a shortages (back order) file and a shortage list is printed out which is sent to the buying office as a basis for placing replenishment orders.

Process 8 and 9 Record and validate orders: Order items details are input and validated by checking items with data stored on the product (stock item) file. Valid items are recorded on the orders file. Invalid order items are printed out and referred back to the customer, corrected, reinput and subjected to further validation. The correction of invalid items may be done while the customer is on the phone but is more likely to be carried out later requiring further contact with the customer.

Process 10 Sort orders file: The order items stored on the valid orders file are sorted into product/customer code sequence to facilitiate efficient sequential file processing. This avoids having to move the read/write heads to the specific track storing the record on the disc drive which would be necessary if the file remained unsorted.

Process 11 Print picking list: The sorted orders file is input and a picking list is printed which is used by the warehouse staff to make up the order requirements of customers ready for despatch. It is necessary to record the quantity available for despatch when the quantity in stock is less than the quantity ordered but this situation has, to some extent, been circumvented in the proposed system as shortages have been previously discussed with customers and alternatives negotiated. This has necessitated an amendment to the initial order quantity of an item to the quantity available in stock, but in cases where alternatives are unacceptable the stock shortage has been recorded on the back-order report in which case the quantity being made ready for despatch will be less than the quantity ordered. It is of course essential to ensure that the quantity invoiced is compatible with that despatched and not ordered in such cases.

Process 12 Compute values, update product file and print stock list: Data from the product file and the sorted orders file is required for this stage of processing. Details from the sorted orders file includes product code and quantity and details from the product (stock item) file includes item code, description, selling price, VAT rate and quantity discount rate. The computations are structured as follows:

Gross value   = Quantity despatched × item price
Quantity discount = Gross invoice value × discount rate
Net invoice value = Gross value − discount
VAT   = Net invoice value × VAT rate
Invoice value   = Net value + VAT + carriage charges

The cost of carriage may be a standard charge but may depend upon delivery distance and value of the order. The carriage charge may be reduced for higher order values. This would need to be provided for according to company policy. The product (stock item) file is then updated to record the latest stock status. The updating process is structured in the following way:

	Quantity	Cost	Value
Brought forward stock balances:	x	x	x
subtract-			
despatches	x	x	x
stock adjustments*	x	x	x
add	x	x	x
returns from customers*	x	x	x
receipts*	x	x	x
stock adjustments*	x	x	x
Carried forward stock balances:	x	x	x

*not provided for in this case study

A stock list is produced which is sent to the stock controller and the valued orders are recorded on the valued orders file.

Process 13 Print despatch notes and invoices, update customer file and print despatch list: Detailed of valued orders are input from the valued order file from which is produced despatch notes and invoices which are sent to customers. Despatch notes contain details of the order items despatched to customers but excludes prices. Multi-part sets may be prepared including despatch notes and invoices with special blanking of sections on despatch notes to exclude details of prices and values. Despatch details are spooled on disc for subsequent printing on a despatch list for the internal audit department. The customer file is updated, the primary action of which is to modify the brought forward amount outstanding by adding or deducting the value of transactions and adjusting the account balance by applying journal adjustments to the various customers' accounts. A carried forward balance is then computed which is recorded on the respective customer accounts in the customer file (sales ledger), viz.

Brought forward account balance	x		
Add:			
Invoice value	x		
Journal adjustment (+)*	x		
		x	
Deduct:			
Credit note value*	x		
Journal adjustment (−)*	x		
Remittance*	x		x
Carried forward account balance			x

*not provided for in this case study

Customer accounts can be either balance-forward, i.e. balance carried forward as indicated above which simply states the amount outstanding, or may be open-item which specifies the invoices still unpaid, i.e. the items still open which have not been cleared by remittances, credit notes or journal adjustments.

Process 14 Print statements and accounts list: The details of customer accounts are input and printed out on statements of account for posting to customers to inform them of the amount owing which may be analysed according to age. Details are spooled on disc ready for subsequent printing to produce an accounts listing for accounts department. The customer records.

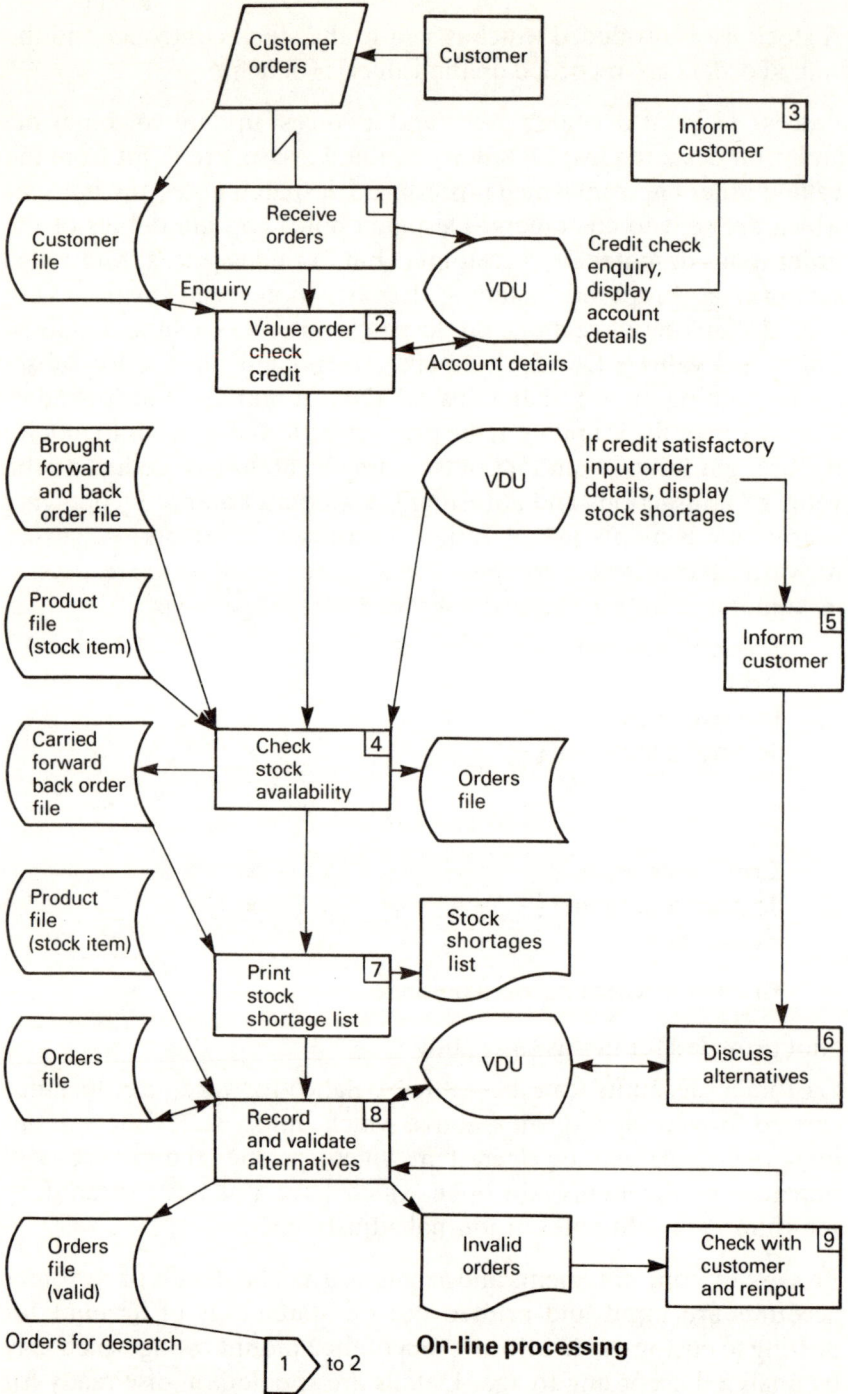

FIG. B30 *First sketch of physical system on line combined with batch processing*

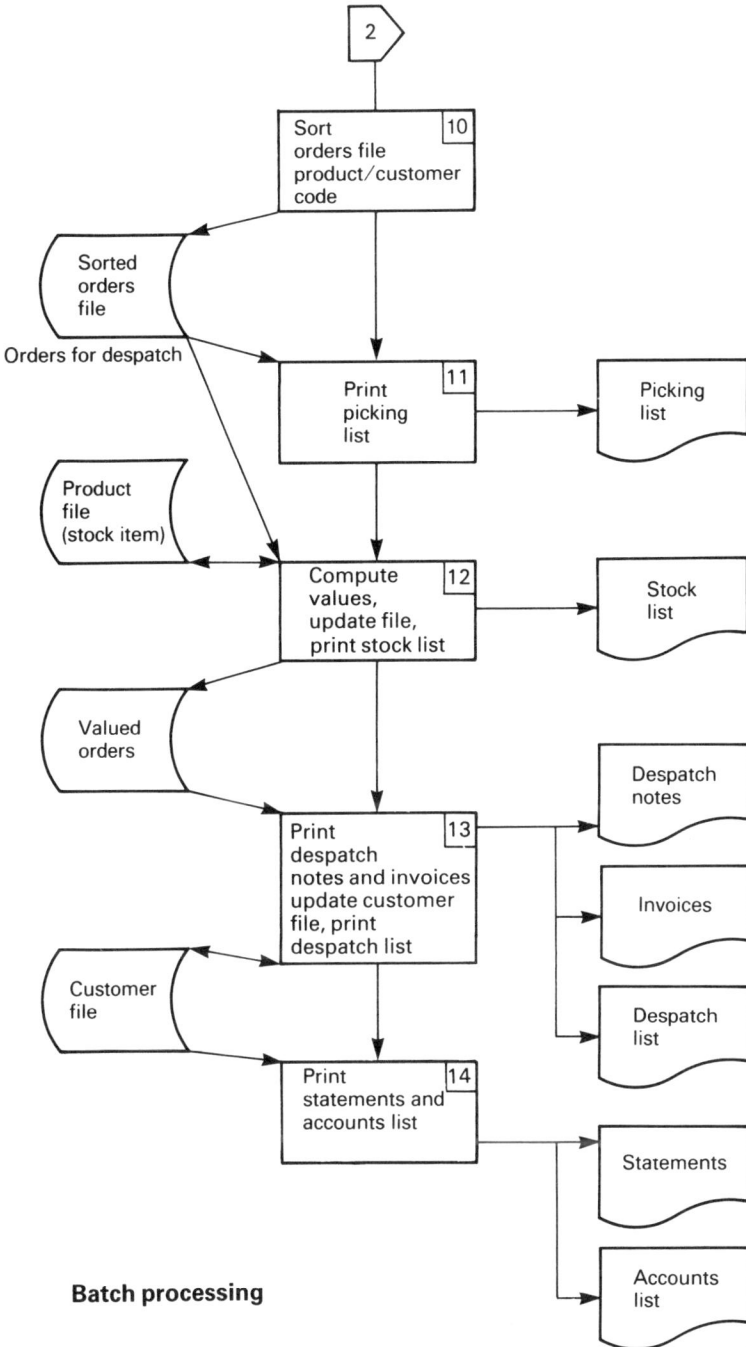

Batch processing

(Fig. B30 *contd*)

INDEX